Garlands, Conkers and Mother-Die

British and Irish plant-lore

ROY VICKERY

continuum

Continuum UK
The Tower Building
11 York Road
London SE1 7NX

Continuum US
80 Maiden Lane
Suite 704
New York, NY 10038

www.continuumbooks.com

First published 2010

British Library Cataloguing-in-Publication Data
A catalogue record for this book is available from the British Library.

ISBN 978-1-441-10195-2

Typeset by Pindar NZ, Auckland, New Zealand
Printed and bound in Great Britain by the MPG Books Group

Contents

Preface

Harvard University's Richard Evans Schultes (1915-2001) is generally
considered to have been the twentieth century's greatest ethnobotanist.
His work in tropical South America inspired generations of students to
visit these countries and continue his pioneering work. Schultes had a
habit of dropping into botanical institutions unannounced, asking if they
had received any new specimens of rubber (*Hevea* spp.) and expecting to
see the head of the organization. One day in the 1990s he dropped in on
the Department of Botany, at the Natural History Museum in London.
As the Head of Department was busy when he arrived, the great man
was brought along to me. We established that no new *Hevea* specimens
had been received, and I attempted to make conversation. I remarked
that I had an interest in the ethnobotany of the British Isles. His reply
was instant: 'The British Isles have no ethnobotany'. Admittedly, if one
defines ethnobotany as being the use that 'primitive' people, or people
in remote agricultural communities, make of plants, or the beliefs they
have concerning these plants, Great Britain and Ireland have little, if
any, ethnobotany. However, even if the majority of the population of
these islands is not concerned with the daily gathering or cultivation
of plants, they are as dependent on plants as inhabitants of other parts
of the world. Also, early in the twenty-first century it is still possible to
talk to people in the British Isles who have knowledge of wild plants
as food, traditional herbal remedies, and folk beliefs, or superstitions,
concerning plants.

This book seeks to explore some of this material, but I have rejected
the term 'ethnobotany', and have preferred to use the word 'plant-lore'
instead. All too often ethnobotany seems to involve outsiders visiting a
community, to collect and tabulate its traditional knowledge of plants.
Frequently the work of ethnobotanists provides us with a list of plants
and the ailments that they are supposed to treat, without giving us a great
deal of information about how this treatment is carried out. There has
been an urge to collect information about how plants were used (possibly
due to an unspoken but mistaken belief that such information is only
of any interest if it is collected from people living in exotic locations),
and less importance has been attached to folk beliefs, which might be
considered useless and hardly worthy of record.

The study of plant-lore involves the collection and study of the ways in
which people in one's own country or community view and use plants.

It places equal importance on use and belief.

Schultes was not alone when he stated that the British Isles has no ethnobotany; many people assume that they once had their own traditions, but these are now dead. Until quite recently it was thought that Geoffrey Grigson's *The Englishman's Flora*, first published in 1955, had gathered together all that was worthwhile; there was no need for further investigation. Alternatively, people recognized that interesting material could still be collected, but only from people living in the 'Celtic Fringe' – remote north Wales, the Highlands and Islands of Scotland, Ireland, and, possibly, bleak moorlands or quaint fishing villages in Cornwall and Devon. If these people spoke a minority language, then their lore was somehow more 'authentic' and more worthy of collection and study. England, particularly the south-east corner of England, was of no interest. This belief probably arose from the fact that while the Irish, Scots and Welsh have had to struggle to assert their national identity, and have used their folk traditions as a way of doing this, the English have not had to do this. Consequently, English folk traditions as a whole have been neglected.

However, there is abundant evidence to suggest that, even in England, plant-lore thrives in the twenty-first century.

People have an increasing interest in growing their own food; consequently, traditional ways of doing things are remembered, or taken from books, and passed over allotment fences. The growing interest in 'foraging' – seeking and gathering wild foods – leads to an increased knowledge of almost forgotten recipes and such beliefs that blackberries are contaminated by the Devil and should not be eaten after certain dates. Although it is extremely doubtful if many people still believe that the Devil is responsible for the poor quality of late fruit, they remember the dates, and either avoid blackberries, or comment if they find good ones, after those dates.

Other superstitions that continue to thrive are those that suggest that certain flowers are unlucky when taken indoors. Many people refuse to have flowering hawthorn or lilac in their homes; others feel uneasy when they see snowdrops or altar lilies. It only needs a coincidence to occur – a fall that breaks a leg, the death of an elderly uncle, or the breaking of a favourite vase – to reinforce the idea that it is unsafe to bring hawthorn flowers indoors. Many hospitals are reluctant to allow vases of red and white flowers in their wards due to a belief, apparently dating from no earlier than the late nineteenth century, that such flowers are a sign of death. Lucky white heather, which was first valued in the second half of the nineteenth century, continues to decorate greeting cards. Even more recent in origin, dating only from the 1970s, is the belief that the possession of a money tree, the succulent houseplant *Crassula ovata*, will ensure financial well-being.

People are re-evaluating natural resources in a way that they last did during World War II. We are rediscovering uses of native and commonly cultivated plants. Slices of potato are rubbed across car windscreens to prevent the formation of ice, orange skin is used to deter cats (and to kill pubic lice). More and more people seek what they consider to be natural cures. Twenty-five years ago when talking about British herbal remedies one could safely assume that most of the audience considered such remedies to be faintly amusing and would never attempt to use them. More recently it has become necessary to start each talk with a warning that most of the remedies are untested, and people are not advised to use them on their families. It has become widely accepted that cabbage leaves can help relieve sore breasts, and banana skins can be used to remove verrucas.

Children are shown how to make daisy chains and to make 'fish-bones' from horse chestnut leaves. Many people remember other children's pastimes that used plant materials: making banjos or guitars from greater plantain leaves, blowing dandelion seedheads to tell the time, and biting into the bases of honeysuckle flowers to extract the nectar.

Perhaps surprisingly in a country that has become increasingly urbanized, and where many wildflower books are available, local plant names continue to survive, and it is still possible to record names that seem to have been missed by earlier collectors. Occasionally, cow parsley is known as stepmother's blessing. According to a belief, not recorded until early in the twentieth century, if flowering cow parsley was taken indoors one's mother would die. Being applied to more than 30 plants, bachelor's buttons is a name that continues to cause confusion.

Legends about plants continue to be repeated in local guidebooks, and in more scholarly works such as Jennifer Westwood and Jacqueline Simpson's *Lore of the Land* (2005). Some of these legends, such as that of the Glastonbury, or Holy, Thorn, have histories that stretch back through many centuries. Others, such as those of St Newlina's fig tree in Cornwall, and the trees that grow from atheists' tombs in Hertfordshire, appear to have been invented in the first half of the twentieth century.

As is the nature of such events, some customs that involve plant materials are thriving, while others have declined. Thriving customs include the World Conker Championships at Ashton, Northamptonshire (first held in 1965) and the World Nettle Eating Championship, held in Marshwood on the Devon-Dorset border since 1997. Events that seem to be in decline are those which involve growing giant leeks or pumpkins. However, customs can be revived after decades of neglect. The Hastings Jack-in-the-Green was described as having 'long since died out locally' in 1913, but has thrived since its revival in 1983.

The people of the British Isles have strong surviving folk traditions concerning plants, but this book makes no claim to be more than an introduction to these traditions. It is hoped that others will go out, collect and make further studies.

About this book

In a book of this nature it is impossible to provide a comprehensive account of British and Irish plant-lore, giving details of when and where various customs and beliefs prevailed. Instead it tries to provide an impression of the ways in which people viewed and used plants.

While an attempt has been made to indicate the distribution of beliefs and customs, our knowledge is so incomplete that little can be said about where things were known, or unknown. It might be thought that the absence of a species as a wild plant in certain areas might suggest that beliefs relating to it would be unknown in such areas, but attractive species such as fritillary, globe-flower and moss campion were ruthlessly uprooted and taken to adorn distant gardens. When it is written that a belief was known in, say, Derbyshire in the late nineteenth century, in most cases we have no idea how many people knew of it; perhaps it was known only by one family, or held only by one eccentric individual. Sources of information include previously published material and material collected by the author since the mid 1970s; priority has been given to the latter.

It must be stressed that information about the uses of plants, including cures, are given as they are recorded. No attempt has been made to test their efficacy, value or safety. Readers who might be tempted to experiment do so at their own risk.

Acknowledgements

I thank the great many people who have contributed to information in this book, particularly Margaret Gale for the loan of her collections relating to the plant-lore of the Christian year, and people who have consistently supplied information and support over many years: David Allen (Winchester), Hilary Belcher (Cambridge), Mary Briggs (Pulborough, Sussex), Charles Nelson (Outwell, Cambridgeshire), John Smith (Bath), Jean Tsushima (Great Bedwyn, Wiltshire) and my parents, Bert and Elsie Vickery (Thorncombe, Dorset). Diana Galvin's comments on the final typescript, and John Hunnex's assistance with the preparation of the illustrations, are greatly appreciated.

1

A TIME FOR EVERY PURPOSE

Farmers and gardeners who started working the land before World War II inherited a wealth of local knowledge which provided guidance on what crops should be planted and when they should be harvested.

However, before anything was sown or planted, plants already growing wild on the site might be examined to indicate the fertility, or otherwise, of the soil.

In Shetland, arvi (common chickweed) was believed to grow wherever the soil was fertile, whereas a profusion of meldi (corn spurrey) was considered to indicate that the soil was infertile and manure was required.[1] Similarly, on the sandy soils of the Surrey/Sussex/Hampshire border, corn spurrey was known as hunger-weed, and its appearance in a garden implied that manuring was required.[2] In Ireland thistles were believed to indicate fertile soils:

A blind man went to buy a farm. 'Tie that horse to a thistle,' he said to his son. 'I don't see any thistles,' said the son. 'Oh,' said the old man, 'we'll go home son, I won't buy this land, it's too poor and bad.'[3]

In Lincolnshire it was said that there was a sixpence at the bottom of the root of a thistle.[4] Presumably this referred to the idea that thistles indicated good soil, or it might imply that each thistle plant removed a sixpence worth of goodness from the land.

Heather indicated poor soil. In Cumbria it was said, 'Where there's bracken there's gold, where there's gorse there's silver, where there's heather there's poverty.'[5] While in County Kerry it was recorded: 'Gold under furze, silver under rushes and famine under heath'.[6]

Sometimes the flowering or leaf production of one plant indicated the time for the sowing of another. Spring was said to have arrived when one could place one's foot on a number of daisies:

'It ain't spring' said an old cottager to me, 'until you can plant your foot upon twelve daisies.'[7]

In Cambridgeshire, spring had arrived 'when you could put your foot on seven, or, in some places nine daisies – the number could vary even between neighbours'.[8]

Herefordshire farmers would sow their spring barley when whitlow grass – an inconspicuous white-flowered herbaceous plant – flowered.[9]

The flowering of blackthorn was widely believed to coincide with a spell of cold weather, known as the 'blackthorn winter'.[10] However, this time was frequently held to be ideal for sowing barley. In Wiltshire it was said: 'When the blackthorn is white, sow barley both day and night'.[11] Alternatively, when soil felt 'warm to one's bare bottom' it was sufficiently warm to sow barley.[12]

The production of elm leaves could also provide guidance. In Warwickshire:

> When the elmen leaf is as big as a mouse's ear,
> Then to sow barley never fear;
> When the elmen leaf is as big as an ox's eye,
> Then says I, 'Hie, boys, Hie!'
> When the elm leaves are as big as a shilling,
> Plant kidney beans, if to plant 'em you're willing;
> When elm leaves are as big as a penny,
> You must plant kidney beans if you want any.[13]

Also in Warwickshire: 'do not plant your kidney beans until elm leaves are as big as sixpences, or they will be killed by frosts'.[14]

Similarly, in Guernsey:

> *Quánd tu veit la fieille d l'orme,*
> *Prends ta pouque et seme ton orge.*
> When you see the elm in leaf,
> Take your seed-bag and sow your barley.[15]

In Huntingdonshire it was thought that 'on Valentine's Day, beans should be in clay'.[16] Presumably the beans referred to are broad beans, which are cultivated on a field-scale for horse-food, rather than runner, or kidney, beans which are grown in domestic gardens. People in West Yorkshire were advised not to plant kidney beans until hawthorn buds had opened.[17]

Fishermen also watched such things. In Herefordshire:

> When the bud of the aul [alder] is as big as a trout's eye
> Then that fish is in season in the River Wye.[18]

Guernsey fishermen set to sea for mackerel when foxgloves bloomed.[19]

In the western counties of England it was believed that frosts cease when mulberry trees burst into leaf.[20] However, Devon gardeners were advised to keep tender plants indoors until St Frankin's Days were past. According to a legend recorded in 1894, the Devil made a pact with a local brewer, named Frankan. The Devil would ensure frosts on three nights from around 19 to 21 May to damage apple blossom and hence diminish the apple crop and limit production of Devonshire cider for as long as the brewer adulterated his beer. Thus when frosts occurred at this time it was a sign that brewers continued to fulfil their side of the contract.[21]

Farmers needed good dry spells for their hay and corn harvests. The opening of oak and ash buds was supposed to indicate what sort of summer might be expected. It was generally believed that if ash trees produce their leaves before oak trees, the summer will be wet. In County Antrim:

> If the oak before the ash,
> Then we'll only have a splash.
> If the ash before the oak,
> Then we'll surely have a soak.[22]

In Somerset:

> Oak before ash - splash;
> Ash before oak - soak.[23]

Christian festivals and local revels, many of which had forgotten associations with local saints' days, could provide guidance for the planting. In theory, but apparently rarely in practice, shallots were planted on the shortest day (21 December) and harvested on the longest (21 June).[24]

The weather at Easter might provide an indication of the success or failure of some crops. In the Ilmington district of Warwickshire it was said:

> Wet on Good Friday and Easter Day
> Much good grass but little good hay.[25]

Similarly, in Herefordshire:

> Rain on Good Friday, or Easter Day
> A good crop of hops, but a bad one of hay.[26]

In Derbyshire[27] and elsewhere it was believed that if the sun shone through the branches of apple trees on Christmas Day, an abundant crop was foretold. According to a north Dorset couplet:

> If wold Christmas Day be fair and bright
> Ye'd have apples to your heart's delight.[28]

Guernsey farmers believed that they should start digging the ground for their parsnip crop while they were still eating bread baked at Christmas.[29] This preparation of ground appears to have been accompanied by a form of communal celebration. Bob Copper has described similar celebrations in Sussex, where Tater Beer Night, an evening of drink and song, followed the Saturday afternoon on which farm labourers planted their potatoes.[30] At Shottery in Warwickshire, bean setting was traditionally started on St Valentine's Day (14 February) and should be completed before 21 March. On the completion of the work, farmers would provide a meal of butchers' meat and plum pudding. Elsewhere in the same county, cheese and cider were provided.[31]

In north Devon it was thought unwise to plant kidney beans until after George Nympton Revel,[32] which until about 1939 was held on the Wednesday after the last Sunday in April, and probably associated with the feast of St George (23 April). Similarly Hinton St George Fair, which was held on the third Thursday in April, was believed by some south Somerset gardeners to be the day for planting kidney beans;[33] others preferred to wait until early May:

> May 6 was known . . . as Kidney Bean Day, and it was believed that if you did not plant your beans then they would not flourish.[34]

A third option in the same area was Tintinhall Club Day, the first Monday in May.[35]

Many people recommended that four bean seeds should be planted for every one they hoped to germinate. During World War II in Gloucestershire it was said: 'One for the mouse, one for the crow, one to rot and one to grow'.[36]

St Patrick's Day (17 March) was an important day in Ireland for sowing or planting crops. Corn was sown as near as possible to this day,[37] and:

> Potatoes should be planted . . . about St Patrick's Day, when he 'turns up the warm side of the stone'.[38]

However, in much of Ireland, as in the rest of the British Isles, Good Friday was the most important day for planting and sowing. This day seems a peculiar choice as it is a moveable date that can fall at any time between 20 March and 23 April. Most work, including mining, household washing, work with horses, and fishing, were banned on Good Friday,[39] but it was a day for a great deal of activity in gardens. Presumably part of the reason for this activity was simply that people who were forbidden to do their day-to-day work had time to devote to their gardens. However, Good Friday commemorates Christ's crucifixion, making it possible that people thought that the soil on to which Christ's blood flowed on this day was in some way blessed.

In Breconshire (now Powys), 'seed potatoes were always planted on Good Friday . . . gardeners would not deviate from this date. They were always planted east to west, never north to south.'[40] Although the belief that potato rows should be aligned east to west appears to be unusual, the belief that they should be planted on Good Friday seems to have been standard, and is still known in places such as Merthyr Tydfil, Mid Glamorgan,[41] Sittingbourne, Kent,[42] Barrow-in-Furness, Cumbria,[43] and Newcastle-on-Clun, Shropshire.[44]

Dorset gardeners thought that if Brompton stocks were sown on Good Friday they would in some parts of the county flourish, or in other parts produce double flowers.[45] Similarly, on Exmoor, seeds should be sown at twelve noon on Good Friday if double flowers were desired.[46] Other seeds sown on this date included onions:

> My father, an Essex man, always sowed onions on Good Friday (whatever the date!)[47]

and, in Sussex, peas.[48]

Throughout much of the British Isles Good Friday was the day for planting parsley:

> Old gardeners told me that I would never succeed in growing parsley, which was the Devil's plant, unless planted on Good Friday.[49]

> We had to sow parsley seed on Good Friday because it had to go three times to the Devil before it germinated.[50]

> Sometimes it was thought that the germination of parsley seed would be speeded up by watering the drill with boiling water before the seed was covered.[51]

The idea that parsley seeds went to Hell, or visited the Devil, before they germinated was widespread. The number of visits varied in different parts of the British Isles, but does not appear to relate to climatic or soil conditions. In Shropshire they went down to the Devil three times before they came 'up to the sun'.[52] Six visits were made in south Wales,[53] and seven in Sussex.[54] However, nine visits appear to have been most usual, being recorded in Herefordshire,[55] Gwent,[56] and the North Riding of Yorkshire.[57]

Another widespread belief was that parsley should be sown by the head of the household: 'parsley will only grow for the one who wears the trousers in the house'.[58] Or parsley grew best where the wife was dominant:

> My late husband [was] an officer and later Merchant Navy master who found it difficult to settle ashore. On his allotment he planted parsley which came up in abundance and he was delighted, but a few days later a neighbour told him that if parsley flourished the wife was boss in the house. He dug it up.[59]

The idea that parsley grows best where a wife is dominant is shared with other culinary herbs, including sage[60] and rosemary.[61]

In 1969 it was recorded that in Cambridgeshire it was thought that parsley sown at the time of a new moon would rapidly germinate.[62] In Somerset it was believed that seeds should be sown when the moon is growing.[63] A Herefordshire couplet advised:

> Sow beans when the moon is round
> They'll pod down to the ground.[64]

An East Anglian saying, 'Sow when the moon is waxing; weed when it is waning',[65] extends this belief and demonstrates how great an influence the moon was believed to have on the growth of plants. The most widespread of such beliefs suggested that root crops should be sown when the moon was waning and top crops when the moon was waxing.[66]

After crops had been planted, local events continued to provide guidance as to when things should be done. In east Devon and west Dorset it was thought that swedes should be singled by Honiton Fair.[67] Now mainly a pleasure fair, this event held on the Tuesday and Wednesday after 19 July was formerly important for the sale of cattle and ponies.[68]

Also, by mid-July, or earlier, the first fruits of the summer were ripe and ready for harvesting. In south-west England the first gooseberries were welcomed by holding feasts and revels. At Stoke-sub-Hamdon, Somerset, villagers climbed the local hill and enjoyed a Gooseberry Feast, described as a 'curious old custom' in 1875,[69] but apparently not surviving until the end of the century.[70] At Drewsteignton, Devon, gooseberry pasties and cream were traditionally eaten at Teignton Fair, held at Trinity Tide – the first Sunday after Whit Sunday.[71] Helston, in Cornwall, held a Gooseberry Fair on the third Monday in July,[72] while a similar event

6

was formerly held at Hinton St George, Somerset, on the first Sunday after Old Midsummer's Day (5 July).[73]

In Lichfield, Staffordshire, in 1830:

Lamb and gooseberry, it is well-known, are customary dishes at Whitsuntide. In this city, the usage seems to be religiously kept up. The number of lambs killed here, on Friday and Saturday was 252; and many besides were sold by country butchers who attend the market.[74]

It was widely believed that people should make a wish when they ate the first fruit or vegetable of the season.[75]

Farmers who made hay had to make sure it was thoroughly dry before it was stacked, if it was not dry the rick would heat up and possibly ignite.

They used to sow rye-grass and clover and cut that for hay twice a year. It made a very black-looking hay, but it was good. Rye-grass was the worse thing there was for heating up the rick. I once heard an old man say for a joke, 'If you make a rick of rye-grass you should call the fire engine at the same time.'[76]

In parts of Brecknock and Radnor great burnet was known as hot-weed, as it was 'said to cause hay to heat up if present in large amounts'.[77] In the Cotswolds ribwort plantain caused problems:

When building a hay rick in rather showery unsettled weather, old Durrant would casually mention 'There's a fair bit of fire grass hereabouts Gaffer' and again the Manager knew that the rick was in danger of beginning to overheat. 'Better put a chimney in Durrant,' he would say. Fire-grass was the name given to the older men to the ribwort or narrow-leaved plantain, which holds quite a bit of moisture in its leaves.[78]

Farmers in Gloucestershire knew hoary plantain, and in Herefordshire knew devil's-bit scabious as fire-leaves:

We have seen a farmer in Gloucestershire with a plantain leaf and he of Herefordshire with a scabious leaf, select specimens, and violently twist them to ascertain if any water could be squeezed out of them. If so, this moisture is said to induce fermentation in newly carried hay sufficient to fire the rick.[79]

In west Dorset if passers-by saw an over-heated rick being dismantled they would sarcastically enquire if anyone had lost a pocket-watch.[80]

The most important country fruit was the apple. One widespread belief was that apples should not be gathered before St Swithin's Day (15 July), or, according to a Cornish report, St James's Day (25 July).[81] In west Dorset it was hoped that one year's apple crop would last sufficiently well for the last of it to be made into a pie eaten at the end of sheep-shearing time, in May, the following year.[82] Thus it seems that apples would be absent from country-dwellers' diets for only about two months each year.

In common with other folklore associated with St Swithin's Day, rain played an important role. Apples were said to be christened on this day and, in some parts of the country, including Berkshire, Oxfordshire and Surrey, the alternative name, 'Apple-Christening Day' was in common use.[83] The benefit that apples received from being christened varied in different parts of the English countryside. Around Banbury in Oxfordshire, apples were reputed to grow large and mature quickly after they had been rained upon.[84] In Huntingdonshire it was said that if no rain fell on St Swithin's Day, apples would not keep well during the winter,[85] while in south Nottinghamshire apples eaten before they had been christened were believed to make one ill.[86]

The pre-Reformation church blessed each year's apple crop on St James's Day;[87] thus the Cornish belief can be traced back to church ritual. In the mid-nineteenth century similar memories of this blessing were recorded in Somerset and Wiltshire, where it was believed that apples were christened on this day.[88] It is claimed that apple trees were venerated in pre-Christian Europe,[89] so the church's blessing, which may have involved sprinkling the trees with water, could have been an adaptation of earlier pagan ceremonies, and the christening of apples by rain was a half-remembered variation of the blessing.

A third date for the christening of apples was St Peter's Day (29 June), when orchard-owners in Herefordshire visited their trees; rain during this visit foretold a good crop.[90]

A fruit that was frequently combined with apples in tarts and jams was the blackberry, the gathering of which was the subject of a number of folk beliefs. A superstition that was apparently widespread in France was that Christ's crown-of-thorns was made of brambles, consequently their fruit – blackberries – should never be eaten.[91] Although this belief does not appear to have been recorded in the British Isles, it seems that in some places blackberries were not considered good to eat. According to E. M. Leather, writing of Herefordshire in 1912:

> An old gardener at Dadnor, near Ross, used to say that blackberries were not good to eat, 'the trail of the serpent is over them,' he said. My informant added that blackberries were not eaten in the district until comparatively recent times.[92]

In County Monaghan during World War I, blackberries were gathered by children, presumably for export to the UK, but very few local people ate them, and 'the one man who did we thought a bit touched on that account'.[93]

Although many people appreciated (and still appreciate) wild blackberries, there is a widely remembered belief that they should not be gathered after a certain date. This date varied around the country. According to a Middlesex correspondent, blackberries should be gathered before the end of August 'or witches will poison the fruit'.[94] Around Buxton in Derbyshire, early in the twentieth century, 'blackberries should not be picked after 30 September, because then "the witch got into them"'.[95]

In England Michaelmas Day (29 September) or Old Michaelmas Day (11 October) were probably the most usual days after which blackberries should not be eaten. Michaelmas celebrates the banishment of Lucifer from Heaven by St Michael the Archangel, Captain of the Heavenly Hosts, so perhaps it is not surprising that it was said that the Devil entered contaminated blackberries on this day.

Blackberries should not be eaten after Michaelmas Day as they have the Devil in them after that.[96]

In rural Somerset at Michaelmas the Devil 'peeps over the hedges and blasts' blackberries,[97] or witches pee on them.[98] In Norfolk the Devil spat on blackberries on Old Michaelmas Day.[99]

However, in north-east England, the autumn school half-term – usually about the second or third week in October – children gathered blackberries, and sometimes referred to the time as Blackberry Week.[100]

Irish blackberries should be left ungathered after Hallowe'en:

It is said that blackberries shouldn't be eaten after Hallowe'en (31 October) as Pooka (a kind of naughty fairy) spits upon them that night, or does worse, depending on who is telling the story.[101]

The Pooka is out at Halloween. It is supposed to crawl on blackberries and after that no one will eat a blackberry.[102]

Writing of the Lake District in 1976, Marjorie Rowling, recorded that it was still believed that after blackberries have been frosted they became Devil's fruit and unfit for human consumption.[103]

Farmers who had overwintering livestock would find it useful to get some idea of the severity and length of the winter, so that they could accordingly ration fodder and bedding. According to a Welsh miner, living in the United States, tall weeds indicated a harsh winter. Thus they remained above the snow, and their seedheads provided food for birds. Apparently, this belief was referred to by Welsh preachers as an instance of God's watchful care over his creation.[104] Similarly, it was widely thought that a good show of autumn berries, particularly haws, would be followed by a severe winter. Again God was providing food for birds.[105]

Less frequently, onions were examined to show what sort of winter was expected. In north Lincolnshire:

> Onion skin smooth and thin
> Mild winter coming in.
> Onion skin thick and tough
> Then the winter will be rough.[106]

Similarly, in Lancashire, the thicker the layers of onion skin, the harder the coming winter.[107]

Throughout the years crops were sown, tended and harvested, and older people living in rural areas still have knowledge of the traditions surrounding these crops. Some of these traditions were simple observations made by one family as they undertook their annual work, others were more widespread and may have been passed down through the generations for many years.

2

THE GOLDEN CORN

It has been convincingly argued that the development of cities and what we know as civilization depended on the growing of cereal crops – wheat, rye, barley and oats in Europe, rice in south-east Asia and maize in central America. In Europe bread, made from wheat, became an essential ingredient of the Christian eucharist, affirming wheat's importance as a staple food.

In the British Isles erosion of the traditional practices associated with the cultivation of cereals started with the introduction of binders early in the twentieth century. Thereafter, with the abandonment of scythes and sickles, the labour force needed on the harvest field rapidly declined, until by the end of the century one man working alone, using massive machines, could run a huge arable farm.

Some practices were devised to protect seed corn. In County Galway, where straw crosses were made on St Brigid's Day (1 February), grain from the sheath from which the cross was made was wrapped in cloth and hung beside the cross. At sowing time it was taken down and mixed with the seed grain.[1]

The actual sowing of corn seems to have attracted few traditional beliefs and customs. However, in the sixteenth century the completion of sowing was a time for celebration. Thomas Tusser recorded that East Anglian ploughmen enjoyed six feasts or holidays each year, the last on his list being 'Seed-cake, a festival kept at the end of wheat-sowing, when he is to be feasted with seed-cakes, pasties and furmenty pot'.[2]

Early in the twentieth century in Shetland ploughing did not start until Candlemas (2 February). Until about 1910 a tiny plot of ground was prepared, sown with corn and anxiously examined on Bogel Day (17 March). The prospects for the main crop depended on the success or otherwise of this plot. Some Shetlanders would not sow their corn until they put a hen's egg in the *kishie* (creel or basket), where it remained throughout the spring. Presumably, once hens started laying, warmer weather had arrived and sowing could safely commence. Only those people who were thought to have a 'growin' hand' were allowed to sow.[3]

Writing of the Hebrides in 1716, Martin Martin observed a custom closely related to Irish celebrations on the Feast of St Brigid, and which foretold the success of each year's harvest. At Candlemas the mistress and servants of each family would dress a sheaf of oats in women's clothing, place it in a large basket and lay a wooden club beside it. They would then cry, 'Briid is come, Briid is welcome' three times and retire for the night. In the morning they would examine the hearth. If an impression of the club was found in the ashes there would be a good harvest and a prosperous year; if no impression could be found, misfortune was foretold.[4]

There was a widespread belief that if an area of the corn field was accidentally left unsown, ill luck, or even death, would result.[5] (Similarly, in Ireland, if a ridge of potatoes was left unplanted the whole crop, or even the prosperity of the entire farm, was threatened).[6]

Until about 1890 a custom known as corn-showing took place around Dilwyn and Henwood in Herefordshire. On the afternoon of Easter Sunday the farm bailiff, farm labourers and their families would go out into the wheat fields and enjoy a meal of plum cake and cider, after which they joined hands and marched across the fields repeating:

> Every step a reap, every reap a sheaf,
> And God send the master a good harvest.

The custom was also practised in the Golden Valley, where a small piece of cake was buried in the field and cider poured on to it as the gathering wished the master a good crop. The importation of foreign wheat in the 1880s is said to have caused the custom's demise.

T. D. Fosbroke, writing in 1821, stated that the purpose of corn-showing was to rid the growing corn of the weed corncockle.

Although the use of weedkillers and improved seed-cleaning techniques have reduced the purple-flowered corncockle to near extinction, it was formerly a major weed of corn fields, its narrow leaves looking not unlike those of the corn itself. The removal of corncockle seedlings was a back-breaking occupation, so it is hardly surprising that the provision of cider, cake, and in Fosbroke's time, a yard of toasted cheese, were provided to encourage labourers to enlist the help of their families. The first person to pull a corncockle was rewarded with a kiss and the first slice of cake.[7]

In some Irish bibles the 'tares' sown by an enemy in a wheat field in the New Testament parable (Mt. 13.24-30) are equated to *cogal*, which probably means corncockle.[8]

On arable farms the corn harvest is the climax of each year's expectations. Today the use of machines has decimated the agricultural workforce. In slower, quieter, days when activities were regulated by the speed of the sickle and farm-horse, harvesting was a communal activity in which almost the whole village participated. It was a social occasion that brought everyone together, toiling towards a common goal. Before

1. Corncockle (Leonhardus Fuchsius, *Icones Plantarum*, Basle, 1545).

the actual cutting of corn started there were a number of traditional practices that required attention. Sometimes it was necessary to recruit casual workers. In Cambridgeshire such labourers were often Irishmen, locally known as Patsies. The men appointed a spokesman to negotiate on their behalf. On the day before the start of harvest the spokesman and the farmer would examine the fields to be harvested and bargain until a satisfactory price had been agreed upon for harvesting the crop. When agreement had been reached the farmer would give a largesse of beer money and often add a little extra to the final price. The spokesman acted as supervisor of the men until harvesting was completed and was, in some villages, known as the Lord of the Harvest.[9]

In some areas it was usual for new workers in the harvest field to undergo an initiation rite known as 'footing'. Hugh Barrett, who between the two World Wars spent a year working on a Suffolk farm, described how this was done to him:

I rode down in one of the wagons to the field where the traves were 'aisled' and waiting. Once through the gate the head day-man,

13

Fred, called out: 'Hey, George, we aren't working with this young chap, here, not till he've bin shod and paid his footing' – 'Tha's right,' answered George. 'Do you collar him and we'll see to that job now.' Whereupon the day-man collared me firmly, tripped me up and sat on my chest, while one of the others grabbed hold of my feet. George then came up with a hammer taken from the binder-box and smartly hammered the soles of my boats until I hollered for mercy. Then, when they let me go and I got to my feet wondering what on earth this was about, the men stood round in a ring and, at a word from George, all shouted at the top of their voices, 'He's shod! He's shod! The colt is shod!' 'And now,' said George, 'you've got to pay for your footing – a gallon of beer'll do.' Unhappily, I hadn't a penny on me, but George lent me two and eightpence and sent one of Walter's boys off to the pub with it . . . so I was formally initiated and given freedom of the harvest field.

Barrett suspected that he was possibly the last person to be shod in the whole of England, in most areas the custom died out during World War I.[10]

In 1952 an elderly inhabitant of Little Shelford, Cambridgeshire, remembered a very similar ceremony. Every new worker in the harvest field had the soles of his shoes knocked with a stone by the Lord of the Harvest, and ordered to pay a shilling towards the purchase of beer.[11]

Some villages in south Cambridgeshire appointed a horn-blower who would go around the village at dawn and rouse the men so that they met in the fields at the correct time. The last of these horn-blowers died at Melbourn in 1935, aged 84. He had started to blow the horn when he was aged seven.[12]

At Llansilin, on the borders of Denbighshire and Montgomeryshire, it was customary for the first sheaf of the harvest to be threshed with flails on the day it was cut and the grain made into a kind of dumpling which was eaten at the midday meal.[13]

As the reapers steadily progressed towards a field's centre any small animals which had been sheltered by the corn would retreat into an ever-decreasing island of standing corn. Village people, accompanied by their dogs and armed with assorted missiles (for safety reasons guns were prohibited), would gather round, and, when the animals lost their nerve and bolted towards the hedges, there was much shouting and frantic activity as everyone tried to bag the odd rabbit or hare. The prospect of such excitement ensured great efforts to get all the corn in a field cut within a day.[14]

In Ireland it was frequently said that there was a small animal in the last patch of corn to be cut. This animal was usually identified as a hare, thus 'putting the hare out of the corn' meant finishing the harvest. Just before the last piece of corn was cut the workers often raised a shout and made a noise to 'put the hare out'. The hare was said to move to a nearby farm which had failed to complete its harvesting.[15]

Throughout the corn-growing areas of the British Isles it was usual for the final small patch of corn to be cut with some form of ceremony, and for it to be twisted or plaited into an ornamental shape.

Iorweth Peate collected details of this custom from different parts of Wales:

> When the corn harvest was reaped one tuft was left uncut in the centre of the last field reaped. When all the reapers had gathered together, each with his sickle, the head-servant would kneel before the tuft, divide it into three parts and plait the parts skilfully together in the same way that he would plait a mare's tail securing the plaited tuft a few inches above ground level. The reapers, six, eight or more would then stand at a distance of at least ten yards from the plaited tuft and, in turn, would hurl their sickles at it, the sickles travelling horizontally just above ground level. The intention was, of course, to cut off the plaited tuft. If this were not accomplished by one of the reapers, the head servant would then himself cut the tuft.[16]

Until the enormous changes in rural life brought about by, or coinciding with World War I, similar scenes could be observed throughout the British Isles, in some areas, related practices continued for at least another two decades. The writer Naomi Mitchison described an odd experience that took place in 1937 while she was assisting reapers on the island of Vallay, off North Uist. Without realizing it she gathered and bound the last sheaf:

> The two old men came up to me and I became aware that something was happening though I did not see what . . . The two of them put a straw twist round my waist, knotting it as though I too had been a sheaf. They spoke slowly and seriously in Gaelic and I do not know what they said but at the end one of them spoke in English saying to me 'go back to the house and keep the binding and you will get your wish'. It seems to me now that I was clearly the *cailleach*, the old woman (or maiden), the sacrifice. At the time I felt rather shaken and I did not as a matter of fact get my wish. Perhaps I took the binding off too soon.[17]

The throwing of sickles as described by Peate seems to have been the most widespread method of cutting the final patch of corn. In different areas, or possibly on different farms in the same area, it was usual for a specific person to cut the final sheaf. In the Scottish Highlands[18] and in parts of Ireland[19] the youngest person in the field was usually chosen. In other parts of Ireland the field's owner cut the final sheaf,[20] while on the Isle of Man it was ceremoniously cut by one of the young women reapers.[21] In County Carlow each of the unmarried girls would have a stroke at the last sheaf with a reaping hook and the one who succeeded in cutting it down would marry within a year. Elsewhere in Ireland it was believed that whoever cut or bound the last sheaf would die unmarried.[22]

Farmers on Rousay in the Orkneys, who had to contend with some of the most difficult corn-growing conditions in the British Isles, would leave a small corner of the last field to be reaped uncut. It was said that this untouched corn was left for the birds.[23]

The names given to the final sheaf, or ornament made from it, varied. In the Orkneys a *bikko* (bitch) was made from the last corn to be reaped, and was, at one time, placed in a prominent position in the stack-yard, or on one of the farm buildings.[24] In England the names baby,[25] dolly,[26] or maiden[27] were most frequently used, while in Wales the names *caseg fedi*, harvest mare, or *caseg ben fedi*, end of harvest mare, were used.[28] Other names included *y wrach*, the hag, in Welsh-speaking parts of Pembrokeshire, neighbouring parts of Cardiganshire and west Carmarthenshire and parts of Caernarvonshire, and the neck in English-speaking south Pembrokeshire,[29] and parts of England, including Cornwall[30] and Wiltshire.[31] The *cailleach* (old woman or hag) was known is most parts of Ireland[32] and in Gaelic-speaking parts of Scotland, while the *carlin* (old woman) was found in some other parts of Scotland.[33]

It is, perhaps, noteworthy that the names given to corn ornaments or the last sheaf of the harvest in the British Isles are almost invariably feminine. In other parts of Europe this use of female names seems to have been less general. Although such names as the corn-cow do exist, the final sheaf could be spoken of as one of a variety of mostly domestic beasts, including bull, cat, goat, steer, pig and wolf.[34] In *The Golden Bough*, James Frazer devoted a great deal of space to what he termed 'the Corn Mother' and her representation as a human female or an animal.[35] Frazer thought he could trace the ancestry of late nineteenth-century corn ornaments back to ancient Greek gods, but although his theories were accepted for the best part of 50 years they have been rejected by more recent scholars.

After the ornament had been cut, there were several customs that were once commonly practised. In Cornwall, north Devon and some other areas it was usual to Cry the Neck. The reaper who cut the last tuft of corn would hold it aloft and shout, 'I have it! I have it! I have it!' to which his co-workers would shout 'What have 'ee?' 'What have 'ee?' What have 'ee?' and he would reply, 'A neck! A neck! A neck!' Then there would be cheers for the farmer, followed by cider and cake for the men.[36] A correspondent from north Devon in 1826 recorded:

> I have once or twice heard upwards of twenty men cry it, and sometimes joined by an equal number of female voices. About three years back, on some high grounds, where our people were harvesting, I heard six or seven 'necks' cried in one night, although I knew that some of them were four miles off.[37]

By the 1920s the custom had almost died out in Cornwall, and is believed to have been practised only on two farms near Gweek. However, late in the summer of 1928 the custom was revived by the St Ives Old Cornwall Society on a farm belonging to Hugh Dunstan, near the church at Towednack. Since then other Old Cornwall Societies have also revived the custom, so that in the 1970s it was held annually by the Societies of St Just, Madron, Penzance, Helston and Mullion. The ceremonies were usually followed by a short church service at which either a lesson is read, or the Lord's Prayer is recited, in the Cornish language. At Madron the service was held on alternate years in the parish church and the Methodist chapel. Refreshments, which varied from tea and biscuits or pasties to elaborate harvest suppers, were provided after the service.[38] In more recent years the number of annual celebrations has diminished so that in 2008 only the Societies of Madron, Redruth and St Ives cried the neck.[39]

Crying the neck has become emasculated. Members of the local Society supervise activities in the field and a church service followed by refreshments are considered essential. Formerly, the cutting of the last sheaf signalled a great deal of boisterous and unruly activity in many areas.

In the Highlands of Scotland and some other areas it was usual for a young man to seize the ornament – the *cailleach* – rush to a neighbouring farm that was still reaping, and throw it in front of the reapers. He would then run off at an even greater speed, for if he was caught his punishment would be rough, his beard and hair might be shaved off, or he might be stripped, beaten and sent home naked.[40]

It was considered to be a very bad omen for any farmer to receive a *cailleach*. As in other parts of the British Isles, it was believed in Ireland that a hag, or witch, could turn herself into a hare and steal cows' milk, thus the *cailleach* (hag) was driven from farm to farm until she reached the last field in the parish to be reaped. The owner of this field would have to support the *cailleach* until the following year.[41] Perhaps it was not unlikely that the farmer to be last to finish his harvest should also be inefficient during the rest of the year, and hence appear to have ill luck.

Similarly, in the western Highlands and the Hebrides the last sheaf was known as the *gobhar bhacach* (lame goat) and bloody battles might occur when a crofter threw his sheaf into the field of a more tardy neighbour. The last person to finish his harvest was considered extremely unfortunate for it was believed:

> Loss of cattle, loss on account of death and accident
> Will befall the luckless one of the *gobhar bhacach*.[42]

In parts of Wales it was the custom for the cutter of the mare to take it into the farmhouse living-room to show that all of the corn had been reaped. This process was usually enlivened by the servant girls who, being forewarned, would gather and try to drench the carrier with water or any other available liquid. If the dry mare was placed safely on the living-room table its bearer was rewarded with a place of honour at the harvest feast. If he was unsuccessful he was placed at the foot of the table, or forced to pay a forfeit to the women.[43]

In Wales it was usually considered to be lucky for the mare to remain dry, and, in some areas, a mare which had been soaked by the servant girls was not allowed into the house. In Ireland the bearer of the last sheaf, who was usually the person who cut it, was subjected to a variety of pranks, the most widespread of which was attempting to soak him and his burden with water. In County Leitrim it was believed that this would prevent drought during the next twelve months, and in County Clare holy water was sprinkled on the sheaf and its bearer.[44]

Some writers imply that the cutting of the last sheaf and its attendant rituals was the end of the harvest and led directly to the harvest supper. Indeed, in some parts of Wales it was common for the supper to be celebrated soon after the mare was brought home,[45] but the harvest was not completed until two or three weeks after the last field had been reaped. While the cutting of the corn was an important task, the conclusion of which merited celebration, the cut sheaves had to be left in the field until the grain was both dry and ripe. Around Northwich in Cheshire it was said that church bells should ring twice over wheat and three times over oats before the cut sheaves were stacked.[46] Similarly, in west Dorset:

> They always used to say about oats, three Sundays after it was cut. Whether it was cut on the Friday before the first Sunday or the Monday before the first Sunday, they always used to say it had to be left out for three Sundays.[47]

Around Woodstock, Oxfordshire, it was believed that if oats were not left out to have the 'church bells rung over them three times' there would be sickness in the village.[48]

The period while the sheaves stood in the field before they were stacked was crucial. If the weather was unsettled, grain that had been cut in excellent condition might begin to germinate and rapidly deteriorate so that it was, at the best, fit only for cattle feed by the time it was finally stacked. Any celebration that took place before the last load was safely stacked was premature.

The final load to be brought home to the rick-yard was often merely a token, a few sheaves placed on the bottom of the cart, which was decorated with leafy boughs, and full of joyful harvesters and children:

> Well ploughed!
> Well sowed!
> Well harrowed!
> Well mowed!
> And all safely carted to the barn wi narry a load throwed!
> Hip-hip-hip-hooray.[49]

Bob Copper has provided a vivid description of how the last load was brought home in the Sussex village of Rottingdean:

> The very last wagon would carry only a token load of just two layers of sheaves on the floor and would be decorated with flags and bunting slung between the corner poles. Jim would sit up forward . . . and the wagon would be drawn by a team harnessed up in tandem fashion with the best horse of each of the four gangs, with each carter leading his own horse and a boy riding on each of the three trace horses. All the rest of the company, sometimes as many as forty or more, would clamber into the wagon ready to make the last triumphant and ceremonial journey down into the village with the remainder of the wagons, carts and horses following on behind. Outside the White Horse inn Jim would shout:

> > We've ploughed, we've sowed,
> > We've ripped, we've mowed,
> > We've carr'd our last load
> > And aren't over-throwed.
> > Hip, hip, hip . . .

> The landlord and his staff would come out carrying beer; his health would be drunk, and various toasts such as 'God speed the plough' and 'May the ploughshare never rust' would follow. On hearing the noise the villagers would come out and join the tail of the procession as it moved onto other public houses and finally into the farmyard where it was greeted by the farmer and his family. After the horses had been stabled the company would continue

their celebrations, and dispose of the eighteen-gallon barrel of beer provided for the men and the crates of lemonade and ginger beer supplied for the boys.[50]

In some areas, including East Anglia,[51] and Hertfordshire,[52] water was thrown at the final, or horkey, load. Near Royston in Hertfordshire:

Through the village the light load rattled along at a great pace, while from Behind every wall, tree or gatepost along the route the men, women, and even children, armed with such utensils as came ready to hand, sent after the flying rustics a shower of water which continually increased in volume as the horkey load reached the farmyard, where capacious buckets and pails charged from the horse pond brought up a climax of indescribable fun and merriment![53]

In 1873 J. S. Udal described a harvest-home that he had recently attended in west Dorset. On the day of the celebration, labourers from several farms attended an afternoon service in the parish church, which was 'decorated in the usually seasonal manner'. The entrance gates to the larger farms were similarly decorated with arches of evergreens, flowers and corn, crowned with a sickle and scythe swathed in bands of wheat and barley, and surmounted by appropriate mottoes. In the evening the men, women, boys and girls employed on the farm assembled in the farmhouse kitchen. Long tables were laid out, and the master who carved a grand rump of roast beef, and members of his family sat at the head. When all had eaten as much beef and plum pudding as they could hold, everyone went out and gathered around a large tree, where they performed a custom said to be peculiar to west Dorset. This seems to have been a variant of crying the neck:

The men formed themselves into a circle, and each taking off his hat and holding it out in front of him, stooped to the ground: then, led by one standing in the centre, chanted the words: 'We have 'em' (or 'en). The first word 'We', is commenced in a very low tone, the men the while slowly and gradually raising themselves up, and so prolonged till they reached their full height. They close the sentence by saying 'have 'em' more quickly. This is done three times. They then shout 'Huzza!' once. Again they stoop down and go through the same performance; finishing up this time with two 'Huzzas'. This is repeated once more, and finally wound up by huzzaing three times. As soon as the men have finished the women come forward and go through the same ceremony. This, when well performed, has a not altogether unimpressive and unmusical effect . . .

The discharge of small cannon (the peculiar care of the boys) likewise gave considerable *éclat* to the whole proceeding.

Later the company returned to the kitchen and 'entered upon a course of singing and drinking, not unmixed with dancing'.[54]

It was usual for the first song at such celebrations to be in honour of the master; a humble farm-labourer might have difficulty in expressing appropriate thanks for the meal he had enjoyed, but a traditional song in praise of his employer would help rid him of his unease:

> Here's a health unto our Master,
> The founder of the Feast,
> And we do wish with all our hearts
> His soul in Heaven may rest,
> And that all things may prosper
> That here he takes in hand,
> For we are all his servants
> And all at his command.
> So drink, boys, drink, and mind you do not spill,
> For if you do you shall drink two, it is our master's will.[55]

The harvest feast was an important event at which traditional songs were sung, step dances performed, and tricks and tales repeated. Udal lamented that 'these congenial meetings are becoming scarcer year by year and ere long bid fair to rank amongst things that have been'. In many places sums of money were being given to workers instead of the traditional harvest feast.[56]

In most parts of the country harvest suppers had completely died out by the end of the nineteenth century, but they are frequently revived by parochial church councils, village-hall committees, Women's Institutes and similar organizations. On the whole the revived celebrations bear but slight resemblance to the traditional event. They are held more or less at harvest-time and usually consist of a good meal followed by some form of amateur entertainment, with the aim of producing a convivial evening and producing funds for the organizers. Revived harvest suppers rarely become annual events, and usual survive only for a few years. The organization and hard work required to produce a suitable meal may eventually exceed the committee's enthusiasm and resources.

While the harvest feast provided an event that fostered the survival of traditional entertainment among men, the women usually left soon after the meal, so that they could tend to their tired children. However, harvest-time provided village women with what was probably their main communal activity of the year, the time when they would meet together and glean – gather fallen ears of corn left among the stubble of the harvest field.

Although gleaning was a communal activity in that it brought women together, each woman and child worked towards an individual goal, trying to collect as much corn as possible for her family. If each family worked sufficiently hard it might be possible to gather enough corn to provide flour for a year, or, if sold, a year's rent. Gleaning was hard, back-breaking work, and the stiff, sharp stubble would soon scratch and redden any hands or ankles that were inadequately protected. In hot weather the sun would mercilessly scorch the back of the neck. The provincial bonnet, often displayed in provincial museums, was developed to provide protection during such work.

Because of the value of the gleaned corn it was essential that everyone had an opportunity to gather their fair share. Thus gleaning hours were often regulated by a special bell being rung, or horn being blown. In the early 1970s an elderly woman living in a remote Fenland village recalled that the hours for gleaning were regulated by the church bell, which would be rung at nine o'clock in the morning and at six o'clock at night. What she enjoyed about gleaning, an activity that she compared with summer holidays in later years, was listening to the stories that the older women exchanged as they sat waiting for the morning bell. Another woman, living in the same village, had less pleasant memories. Children trudged to the distant fields and were continually exhorted by their mothers to work harder. Once in the corn field all but the youngest children were expected to do their bit; babies were often given a small amount of laudanum on sugar to keep them asleep. Each gleaner would gather ears of corn into her apron, and in the evening would walk home with a large bundle balanced on her head. When her husband's employer was threshing, the gleaned corn would be threshed, and later taken to the mill to be ground.[57] Women were usually allowed to glean only in fields that belonged to their husband's or brother's employer.[58]

In Cambridgeshire it was usual for a respected older woman to be appointed Queen of the Gleaners. Her responsibilities included ensuring the good behaviour of the other women, and, more importantly, regulating the hours that they worked and when they took their meal breaks. At Little Shelford, in the south of the county, the Queen was also responsible for shoeing – knocking the soles of new gleaners' shoes with a stone.[59]

In Staffordshire it was usual for some of the gleaned corn to be made into miniature sheaves, which were hung from the rafters of the dwelling house. At Christmas or on Mothering Sunday the sheaves were taken down and their grain soaked and boiled for some hours to form the basis of furmety, a traditional dish consisting of boiled wheat grains, milk, dried fruit, nutmeg and spices, which was enjoyed on festive occasions.

Another custom in the same county was for the reaper who succeeded in cutting the last sheaf to be presented with it, and keep it for making Christmas furmety.[60]

For the farmer himself, or his bailiff, the final work of harvest was selling the grain, an operation which required skill and foresight if it was to be done when prices were at their best. Corn prices fluctuated according to weather conditions, and the international situation. A number of local omens have been recorded as means of predicting the price of grain. In west Suffolk the price at Bury St Edmunds market related to the level of water in Barton Mere, a stretch of water not far from the town. As the water rose and fell, so did the value of grain.[61] The Hungry Pool at Billingham, Staffordshire, was similarly prophetic, and several local farmers were said to have prospered as a result of watching its water.[62] In nineteenth-century Dorset the price of wheat was foretold by examining Madonna lilies: 'a . . . calculation is made from the number of blossoms shown on the majority of its spikes, each blossom representing one shilling per bushell'. An alternative form of divination, used in the same county, was to count the number of spots on a ladybird, each spot represented a shilling.[63]

The horkey load, harvest feast and almost all the other traditional activities associated with the harvest have gone, the last generation to remember them probably dying out in the 1970s. Gleaning was revived during World War II but became discontinued after the end of hostilities. The main reminder of the pre-mechanized harvest is the fluctuating popularity of corn dollies. In the late 1960s and the early 1970s, skilful men and women plaited elaborate designs, most of which were based on traditional, or at least nineteenth-century, patterns. Since then the craft has become less popular, but it is not unusual to come across corn ornaments, usually small 'harvest favours' which can be worn as jewellery rather than full-size dollies, at country shows and craft fairs. The accounts that makers give of their dollies are usually derived from James Frazer's *Golden Bough*, and the ornament is claimed to be an ancient symbol of fertility, or a representation of 'Mother Earth'. Coloured ribbons, without which no modern dolly would be complete, are said to represent various aspects of the corn field. Red and blue, the colours most frequently used, are said to represent the poppies and cornflowers that formerly infested the field, yellow ribbons are said to represent the ripe grain, and green the young growing corn.[64]

Taken as a whole such ideas are inaccurate, but the makers are, understandably, more interested in intricate and graceful designs than in tracing the dolly's origins. Some makers were fortunate and found elderly people who remembered making traditional dollies and were able to teach a new generation, others sought out dollies in local museums and were able to copy them, while others consulted books and pamphlets on the subject. Many of the dollies now found in museums are not ones that were made by people who had learnt to make them directly from earlier generations. In 1953 the Pitt Rivers Museum in Oxford received a 'corn dolly of ingeniously twisted corn stalks, made by Emmanuel Gibbs [of Castle Carey, Somerset], aged 86, and sold by him as a "token of harvest good luck"'. Subsequent enquiry revealed that the maker had copied his design from a 1937 issue of *Farmer and Stockbreeder*. When the craft was first revived, makers experienced difficulty in obtaining suitable long, hollow straw, but as interest increased several growers started growing traditional long-stemmed varieties solely for the use of corn-dolly makers. It was also possible to obtain special elongated drinking-straws, which were useful when the craft was being taught in schools, Women's Institutes and similar organizations.

In addition to being sold at country shows and fairs, corn dollies can also be found decorating 'olde worlde' country pubs. The elaborate designs are worthy of admiration, but have, without doubt, undergone great transformation since the days when corn ornaments were hurriedly produced at the harvest's end, or plaited to pass time when inclement weather prevented work in the field. The names given to modern dollies usually describe the dolly's shape, and the county from which it was said to have originated. Thus, a popular book provides illustrations of Herefordshire fans, Suffolk horseshoes, Cambridgeshire umbrellas and Northamptonshire horns.[65]

It has been suggested that the practical purpose of a corn ornament was to preserve seed corn for sowing the following spring. Although the final sheaf to be cut might be comparatively weed-free and therefore suitable for preservation as seed, there seems to be no British evidence to suggest that grain from it or corn ornaments was ever sown to any significant extent.

What eventually happened to the corn dolly varied throughout the country. Often it was hung in the farmhouse kitchen until it was replaced by a new one at the end of the following year's harvest.[66] The country kitchen, or hearth, which at one time was a favourite exhibit in many local, or folk, museums, often displayed such dollies. On some farms each dolly remained in place until it eventually disintegrated, so that dollies from many years' harvests might accumulate.[67]

In Scotland the *cailleach* was fed to horses at the start of ploughing,[68] or harvesting.[69] Similarly, in Ireland, corn ornaments were sometimes fed to horses to increase their strength, or poultry to ensure a good supply of eggs. In County Donegal some people made their St Brigid's crosses from the straw of the last sheaf. Elsewhere in Ireland the last sheaf was believed to have curative powers and was given to sick animals or fed to calving cows. When burnt to ashes its grain was used to make an ointment used to treat skin ailments. In County Laois the grain was thrown to the poultry and the first cock to reach it was selecting for killing on the eve of St Martin's Day (11 November). In Irish tradition it was usual to shed blood by killing a domestic animal on St Martin's Eve, and the wealthy were expected to present gifts of meat to their less fortunate neighbours. 'Burying the sheaf' was a sinister ritual sometimes attempted in north Leinster. A last sheaf was stolen and given the name of the intended victim. After it had been 'killed' by being stabbed or struck, it was buried, and as it died the victim would sicken and die. His life could be saved only if the sheaf was dug up and burned.[70]

Once again the final sheaf was thought to have human characteristics. An incident described in the first three Gospels, which forms the inspiration of the churches' celebration of the Lord's Supper, Holy Communion or Mass, tells how Jesus 'took bread, and having said the blessing he broke it and gave it to his disciples with the words "Take this and eat; this is my body".'[71] Man could think of no better way of elevating wheat, his staple food, to the glory of his God.

3

NECESSITY THE MOTHER OF INVENTION

By late in the twentieth century many of the skills and much of the knowledge that country people had accumulated over many centuries was rapidly diminishing. If they wanted heat, it was no longer necessary to chop down trees, leave them to dry, and then split them into logs which were carried indoors and placed on carefully tended hearths; people simply flicked a switch. They no longer knew most of the plants which were formerly collected to add variety to their diets.

Our ancestors not only appreciated wild plants for their beauty, they viewed them as resources. A fallen branch was noted and later collected to provide fuel.

Country people had practical knowledge of which trees provided good firewood:

> Beechwood fires are bright and clear,
> If the logs are kept a year;
> Chestnut only good they say,
> If for long it's laid away;
> Make a fire of elder tree,
> Death within your house shall be;
> But ash new or ash old
> Is fit for queen with crown of gold.
> Birch and fir logs burn too fast,
> Blaze up fast and do not last;
> Elmwood burns like churchyard mould –
> E'en the very flames are cold;
> But ash green or ash brown
> Is fit for queen with golden crown.
> Poplar gives a bitter smoke,
> Fills your eyes and makes you choke;
> Apple wood will scent your room
> With an incense-like perfume.
> Oaken logs, if dry and old,
> Keep away the winter's cold;

But ash wet or ash dry
A king shall dry his slippers by.[1]

One common wild plant that was valued as a fuel was gorse, also known as furze or whin. A man who spent his 1920s childhood in the fishing village of Cawsand, south-east Cornwall recalled:

> Gorse was most prolific on the cliff tops but was always named fuzz . . . The dry sticks of fuzz burnt with a bright, clear fierce flame and were prized for heating purposes and were crinnicks or crinnix, at least that's what it sounded like. Some of the old, clustered together cottages had a smallish deep hole running back in the wall in the kitchen usually, about a foot across and a couple of feet deep, with a cover. These were called fuzz ovens, where you burnt your crinnicks and then baked your pasty or whatever.[2]

Similarly, in Guernsey, the local delicacy bean-jar was cooked in the furze oven. This was a brick-lined bread oven in the kitchen. Furze was lighted on the oven to heat the bricks. When it was hot the food was put in.[3] Gorse roots, known as fuzz moots, were pulled up in Dorset and taken home for burning in the kitchen range, 'mother preferred them to coal as they burnt with a lovely hot clean flame'.[4]

If chimneys became blocked, they could be cleared using a branch of gorse, 'by the simple method of tying a piece of rope to each end of the branch, dropping it down the chimney, coming down from the low roof and entering the kitchen where he caught the rope and brought all the soot down and all with the branch'.[5]

Where gorse was not available, holly might be similarly used.

Wood of course had a huge range of other uses. Alder was valued as a building wood, but it had to be kept permanently wet or permanently dry. It was said to 'harden like stone' if kept constantly wet.[6] According to Dorset builders who used peeled alder poles for rafters:

> Thatch me well, keep me dry,
> Heart-of-oak I will defy.[7]

Complex constructions, such as watermills, required a variety of timbers. From Saxon times until the eighteenth century, when cast iron came into use, all watermill machinery was made from wood:

> The timberwork had to withstand the stresses and strains, and these were only as constant as the flow of the water. Accelerations caused major problems, not least to the teeth of the cog-wheels that had to take the increased forces. Thus watermills were made

of a variety of timbers. The paddles were of elm, the pit wheel and its cogs, down in the wet, were of oak, while beech could be used in the upper dry areas and cogs up there were of such timbers as beech, pear, apple, oak, and hornbeam.[8]

It is probable that some forgotten uses of trees are responsible for their present-day distribution. Alder buckthorn was so valued for the production of a 'very superior charcoal' which was used in the manufacture of gunpowder that it was cultivated in Kent and Sussex for this purpose.[9]

Equipment used by fishermen, or on farms, was made locally, using locally available plant materials. Fishermen in Beer, east Devon used traveller's joy, known locally as jewel guts, to make the bottoms of crab pots, it being both flexible and hard-wearing.[10] Along the coast in east Cornwall:

> Straight sticks of fuzz [gorse] bush about 10–12 inches long, pointed one end were called skivvers and were used to hold bait in the mouths of the old wicker-work crab pots. They were very resistant to salt water and had no pith.[11]

Apart from stinging nettles, wild plants did not contribute to clothing the population of the British Isles, although flax and hemp were both cultivated for their fibre, and straw was plaited to make hats. It is said that the Patent Office holds over 50 patents for different ways of preparing nettle fibres, which, depending on when in the plant's growth cycle they were prepared, could yield imitation silk fibres in the spring through to robust fibres suitable for making sacks in the autumn.[12] Nettle cloth is reputed to have been made in Britain until the 1920s, but, as it is difficult to distinguish between flax and nettle fibres, it is probable that some of the fabrics supposedly made from the latter were in fact made from the former. It appears that at one time 'nettle-cloth' was a general name for any fine fabric, regardless of which plant its fibres came from.

Alder wood was valued for making the soles of the clogs which were worn in mill towns and elsewhere.

> As a child in Herefordshire [before World War II] I saw, every few years, for a few weeks at a time, a small lorry passing thro' to the station with loads of roughly shaped clog soles. The wood was a rich red colour. Gangs of men cut down the trees and cut lengths to shape in a temporary camp.[13]

However, when it came to clothing, plants were most widely used as dyes or to tan leather. In 1942 County Herb Committees were asked to collect

100 tons of nettles. Ninety tons were collected, and from these a dark green dye was prepared, and chlorophyll, which was used as a tonic and in other medicines, was extracted.[14] Other plants that were used for dyeing included yellow iris, the rhizomes of which were used to produce a black dye on the Western Isles of Scotland,[15] alpine meadow-rue (known locally as redshank) which was used to produce a gold or olive dye in Shetland,[16] and bilberry, the fruits of which were collected in County Tipperary and exported to England where they were used 'to make dye or to mix with the cheaper kinds of jam'.[17]

But in the British Isles lichens, 'which have been brightening the clothes of the people of Scotland for hundreds if not thousands of years',[18] were the most valued source of plant dyes, and provided a much-needed source of income for people living in desolate upland areas. In north Wales the lichen *Parmelia omphalodes* was collected, steeped in urine, formed into a paste which was left to dry in the sun and had alum added to make a brown dye:

> This and the L[ichen] *tartarius* [now known as *Ochrolechia tartarea*] are so abundant, that the poor people employ themselves in gathering them for the use of the dry salters, at the low price of one penny per pound. They will, however, collect from twenty to thirty pounds a day. From these a beautiful dye called arcell, or archil, is prepared as follows:– The lichens, when dry, are placed under a large indented stone, with a circular motion, and bruised; they are then thrown into capacious vats, and mixed with lime and urine. Here they are permitted to remain six months, but stirred every day; and the materials thicken as the humid particles evaporate. In this part of the process the substance appears like mire; afterwards like the husks of grapes. When it has acquired the latter consistency, it is cut small, dried in a spacious room, sometimes reduced to powder, and packed in barrels for use; the most beautiful colours, such as purple, pink, greys and pompadour, are obtained from the composition.[19]

William Hooker, writing in 1807, recorded that in the neighbourhood of Fort Augustus in the Scottish Highlands a person could earn 14 shillings a week collecting *Ochrolechia tartarea*, 'selling the material at 3s 4d the stone of 22lb'.[20]

Harris tweed, the production of which was promoted by Lady Dunmore, wife of the owner of Harris, in 1844, was traditionally coloured with plant dyes, including a reddish brown from crottle (species of *Parmelia*, lichens), red from orchil (*Ochrolechia tartarea*), orange from ragwort, green from heather or yellow iris, and yellow from bracken roots or birch. However, by the mid 1970s only six weavers were reported as still using plant dyes, and in 1999 only one weaver (a woman originally from Hampshire) was weaving lichen-dyed tweed.[21]

Another way in which plants contributed to clothing was by being used to tan leather. The bark of oak was most usually used for tanning, but in areas where oak trees were scarce or absent other species were used. On Eigg, in the Hebrides, where there were few trees, the islanders dug up roots of tormentil, 'at no inconsiderable expense of time and trouble', to make an infusion for tanning shoe-leather.[22] Elsewhere on the Western Isles fishermen used tormentil for tanning their nets.[23]

Trees were scarce throughout much of Ireland, and in 1727 the Irish Parliament awarded £200 to William Maple, who discovered that leather could be tanned using tormentil roots. His pamphlet entitled *A Method of Tanning without Bark*, included an illustration of tormentil, and is considered to be the first illustrated botanical work to be published in Ireland.[24] In County Donegal bog myrtle was considered to be excellent for tanning leather.[25]

Bog myrtle was also used to make a candle-wax. In Scotland:

The shoots were washed in warm salted water, causing the wax to float to the surface like scum, and the candles made therefrom shed a rare perfume as they burned.[26]

Far more important as a source of illumination were rush-lights. In eighteenth-century Hampshire, for example, 'decayed labourers, women and children' collected soft rush during the summer. The outer skin would be peeled off to leave the inner pith and leaving 'one regular, narrow, even rib from top to bottom that may support the pith' and after drying for a few days they were dipped in scalding fat or grease to make the rush-light. However, when the government decided to tax candles, restrictions were placed on the production of untaxed rush-lights, so that they had almost gone out of use by early in the nineteenth century.[27]

Wild plants were collected to add variety to the diet. Although there has been a revival of foraging for wild foods in recent years, towards the end of the twentieth century only two wild foods – blackberries and mushrooms – were widely sought. Even in urban areas people ventured on to local commons and gathered blackberries, and in rural areas people remembered fields that were likely to yield worthwhile crops of mushrooms. However, as mushrooms thrive in pastures that are manured by horses, they have become increasingly scarce since tractors have replaced farm horses. In some areas it was believed that mushrooms grew where a stallion's semen had fallen.[28] Or:

There is a belief that a good crop of mushrooms will come from a pasture in which a male breeding animal is kept. The belief is that

31

the stallion, bull or ram crops the mushroom with his semen.[29]

A few plants were collected on a commercial scale and formed a valuable addition to the families' incomes.

Bilberries, also known as whortleberries, ripen slowly over several weeks during the summer. Early in the twentieth century, on Exmoor, the bilberry or 'hurt' picking season extended for five or six weeks. Although the fruits are abundant, they are small, and gathering them was a back-breaking activity. Children, sometimes accompanied by their mothers, would set off for the moors, with sandwiches and bottles of cold tea, and remain there all day:

> The whorts were sold to Mr Tom Webber and his sister, who had a horse and open cart . . . The price was 4d a quart at the beginning of the season, dropping to 3d or 2½d as they became more plentiful . . . Money earned was used to buy clothes for the winter.[30]

At about the same time, or possibly a few years later, in Munster, people would start gathering bilberries on the Galtee Mountains on 29 June and continue until the end of August:

> They often sing songs to lighten their work which was not always pleasant as in warm days flies are a torment and the pickers have their heads covered with a handkerchief soaked in Jeyes Fluid to hunt them away. Some people pick from three to seven gallons in the day and get nine pence to one shilling per gallon. The worts are sent across to England.[31]

The infestation of British woodlands by grey squirrels, deliberately introduced from North America in the late nineteenth and early twentieth centuries, has led to the decimation of the hazelnut harvest, but until about 1945 wild nuts provided a useful source of income in some areas. On Cranborne Chase, in Dorset:

> Annual nutting expeditions were great events. The women and girls made themselves special canvas dresses and the great part of the population went off to the woods . . . The nuts were sold to dealers for desert and also (chiefly) for use in the dyeing industry. Often not less than £200 a year was made by the village [of Ashmore] during this season, and most families reckoned to pay their whole year's rent, if nothing more, with the proceeds.[32]

It seems that the economic value of the nut harvest created various taboos to discourage the greedy from nutting at unreasonable times and thus getting more than their fair share of the crop. In the north of England unripe nuts were protected by the goblins Churnmilk Peg and Melsh Dick.[33] More common was the belief that people who gathered nuts on a Sunday would attract the Devil's attention.[34]

Even after their mothers had stopped collecting wild foods, knowledge of them survived among children, who would nibble various wild plants as they wandered along country lanes.

Until recently, young hawthorn leaves were frequently eaten by children, who knew them as bread-and-cheese,[35] but in earlier centuries adults gathered the leaves in times of hardship. In May 1753, following a poor harvest and cattle plague, enraged colliers who had heard a rumour that wheat was being exported from Bristol, marched on the town. 'Ravaged by hunger, they attempted to fill their empty bellies with sprigs of green hawthorn which grew along the way. This, with bitter irony, they called bread-and-cheese.'[36]

Although young hawthorn leaves were commonly known as bread-and-cheese, they taste nothing like the countryman's staple food, and it appears that bread-and-cheese was a name that was applied to almost any plant that was nibbled by children as food. During World War II in Elgin, Morayshire, children used to chew common bent grass, which they knew as bread-and-cheese.[37] At about the same time in the Basingstoke district of Hampshire, children ate wood sorrel leaves and called them bread-and-cheese,[38] while about ten years later west Dorset children knew wood sorrel as bread-and-cheese plant, and ate its flowers.[39]

Another plant known as bread-and-cheese, in Somerset,[40] was silverweed. According to John Ray, in his *Catalogus Plantarum Angliae* (1670), children in the West Riding of Yorkshire dug up silverweed roots and ate them. Anne Pratt, who was born at Strood, Kent, in 1806, noted that children in rural parts of England would place silverweed roots over a brisk fire and then eat them: 'They are very small, but to some of us in childhood they seemed quite as pleasant as the fruit of the chestnut.'[41]

Particularly during times of scarcity, silverweed roots were eaten throughout the Highlands and Islands of Scotland. Writing of Colonsay in 1910, Murdoch McNeill recorded that the roots of silverweed were gathered and eaten raw, or boiled like potatoes, and their value was recognized by the Gaelic name *am seachdamh aran* (the seventh bread).[42] It appears that before the introduction of potatoes, silverweed was cultivated on some Hebridean islands. At Lag nan Tanchasg in Paible, North Uist, it was said that a 'man could sustain himself [by cultivating silverweed] on a square of his own length'.[43] In May 2006 a woman recalled digging up and eating silverweed roots in Scotland during World War II.[44] One recent writer on wild foods describes silverweed roots as tasting like parsnips,[45] while another states:

I have no joy eating this plant. The roots are generally too small to be worthwhile, so how whole populations of Scottish islanders lived on them I cannot imagine.[46]

Minor plant foods that children collected incuded Japanese knotweed, which was eaten by Bristol boys who knew it as wild rhubarb[47] (in Cornwall it was known as donkey rhubarb);[48] young fruits of lime, known by Invernessian children as hen's eggs[49] and beech leaves in Kent[50] and Hampshire.[51] Possibly the most widely gathered of these plants were wild sorrel and pignut. Sorrel leaves, known as sour docks,[52] sour sabs,[53] or sour leeks,[54] were gathered in early summer and eaten for their 'vinegar flavour'.[55] Root tubers of pignut, also known as earthnut, were dug up and eaten at about the same time of year.[56] In parts of Scotland they were known as lucy arnots,[57] and in Cumbria yowky yowlings.[58]

Cramped, and often poorly ventilated, dwelling conditions led to a variety of vermin being present in homes. The *Royal Cornwall Gazette* reported in September 1805 that hound's-tongue, 'gathered full of sap and bruised with a hammer', would make mice and rats immediately quit barns and granaries.[59] In nineteenth-century Yorkshire, dried bunches of quaking grass, which was known as trimmling jockies or doddering dickies, were 'commonly stuck on the mantel-shelf' as they were believed to deter mice:

> A trimmling jock i' t' house
> And you weeant hev a mouse.[60]

Fleas were deterred using bog myrtle and eelgrass. In Northumberland bog myrtle, known as flea-wood, was placed among bedclothes to deter fleas,[61] while on Islay it was hung in kitchens to deter flies.[62] On Shetland eelgrass collected, dried and used for stuffing mattresses was 'believed to be proof against fleas'.[63] Conkers, the seeds of horse chestnut, were widely used to keep clothes moths away, particularly from stored furs.[64]

According to Theophrastus (b. 370 BC) spindle 'is hurtfull of all things . . . the fruits heerof killeth'.[65] More specifically, in the seventeenth century, John Evelyn recorded that spindle fruits were baked, powdered, and sprinkled on the heads of small boys to kill nits and lice.[66] In Gloucestershire and Warwickshire spindle fruits were known as louse-berries,[67] while in Somerset early in the twentieth century villagers 'scattered their houses with the powdered leaves of spindle-berry, a natural insecticide'.[68] More recently rubbing the infested area with orange peel has been recommended to kill head lice.[69]

Elder twigs were attached to the harnesses of horses,[70] and elder trees were planted outside slaughterhouses,[71] dairies,[72] and toilets[73] to deter flies. Bees are said to find elder obnoxious, so bee-keepers use sprigs of

2. Elder (Petrus Andreas Matthiolus, *Commentarii, in libros sex Pedacil Dioscoridis Anazarbei de medica materia*, Venice, 1554).

the tree when driving swarms into receptacles so that they can be taken.[74] Other plants that deterred flies included fennel, which in Jersey was attached to horses' harnesses;[75] stinging nettle,[76] and mint, which also was believed to purify the air:[77]

> I used to know this isolated place in Glen Luce, Wigtownshire/ Galloway, where the outside toilet was known as 'Mint Cottage', as there was a bunch of mint – which was replaced every week – placed above the door. Only ladies used it; the men had to go over the hills. I never discovered where they went.[78]

There was also a wide range of miscellaneous uses of common plants. According to a herbalist writing in the 1940s, elder had 'the unusual distinction of being useful in every part'.[79] Late in the nineteenth century, in Ireland, an elder stem would have its pith removed and molten lead was poured in to 'make a good weapon for protection on a journey or out walking at night'.[80]

Sliced potatoes were rubbed across the windscreens of cars to prevent them icing up.[81] Raw potatoes rubbed on tight shoes would make them 'give a little'.[82]

During World War II:

When stationed with the RAF at Tain in Scotland . . . we could build a bicycle from a pile of bits and pieces kept in a large shed. One problem was a shortage of tyre valve tubing. As a stop gap some bright spark discovered that a three-quarters of an inch length of dandelion stem would keep us going for a few miles, and the rest of the stem was kept as spare.[83]

Thus people turned to local wild, or commonly cultivated, plants and found uses, many of which we have forgotten.

4

HEALING HEDGEROWS

Before the introduction of the National Health Service in 1948 people often turned to local hedgerows, fields and gardens to find remedies for many ailments. Although it is sometimes supposed that this involved searching out rare species, it was, in fact, common widespread plants, rather than rarities which were usually used. The organization Ethnomedica, based at the Royal Botanic Gardens, Kew, which has collected traditional herbal remedies in England and other parts of the British Isles, has found that of the top ten plants remembered as being used, only one is exotic.[1] Gathering herbs and making simple preparations provided those who were caring for the sick with an activity, rather than leaving them to hopelessly watch at the bedside.

The most widely recorded cure in the British Isles is the use of dock leaves to relieve the pain of nettle stings.[2] Suffolk children were told that 'God planted the docks to soothe us if we got stung by the nettles'.[3] Although it is sometimes claimed that a substance in the dock leaf is responsible for the reduction of pain, it is more likely that the cure works on a psychological level – searching for a dock leaf provides a distraction from the pain. Other plants that have been recorded as being efficacious in the treatment of nettle stings include horseradish, the leaves of which somewhat resemble those of dock; dandelion and garlic mustard.[4]

In recent years, onion has probably been the plant most frequently used to alleviate the pain of insect stings:[5]

Mary's father used to do this in Ireland, and when Mary goes on a play-scheme outing she always takes an onion and a knife in the bottom of her bag, so that she can treat anyone who gets stung.[6]

Being readily available throughout most of the year, onions had many uses in folk medicine. Around Horseheath in Cambridgeshire it was said: 'If an onion is eaten every morning before breakfast, all the doctors might ride on one horse'.[7] A very widespread belief was that a cut onion attracted germs, but while some people used onions to absorb and remove germs, others threw out cut onions in the belief that they would draw germs into the house. A Worcestershire woman, who died in 1987 aged 94, believed that half an onion should be hung up in the house each winter as it would 'take the germs'.[8] Similarly:

> When I was living in Orkney in the early 1950s, I had no refrigerator or anything like that, just cold marble in the pantry. I used to put half an onion in the pantry to keep away the germs. I used to have to tell the children not to use it as it 'collected all the bugs'.[9]

In the Norwich area in the 1930s raw onions were put in a saucer beside a coffin while the corpse stayed in the house before burial.[10]

According to legend, the inhabitants of God's Providence House, in Chester, were spared from the plague after having placed onions around the entrances to their home. However, the last outbreak of plague in Chester occurred in 1647–8, three years before the house was built.[11] Elsewhere, including Warwickshire[12] and Surrey,[13] cut onions were considered to be particularly efficacious in preventing the spread of scarlet fever. More recently it has been claimed that cattle were protected from foot-and-mouth disease by placing onions around their sheds.[14]

An alternative viewpoint was:

> A cut piece of onion should never be kept as it will attract all the bad from the air into it.[15]

It is said that during World War I 'nasty people would rub their bullets on onions in the belief that wounds inflicted by such bullets would become infested with germs'.[16]

The most widely known use of onions in folk medicine was to treat earache:[17]

> Earache was cured by boiling an onion and taking out the central pip and inserting it into the offending ear.[18]

Almost as well known was the use of onions to treat colds, or prevent or cure, baldness. In Bedfordshire:

> If we had colds mother would boil an onion in milk. We had to eat the onion with plenty of pepper and drink the milk.[19]

Similar cures have been recorded from the Isle of Wight,[20] and Shetland.[21] Alternatively coughs and colds would be treated by taking syrup produced from (usually brown) sugar and onions:[22]

> My grandmother used to make her own cough medicine by placing a Spanish onion with the root end cut off on two tablespoons

of demerara sugar in a saucer. She then left it in her larder for a week and collected the resulting syrup which was administered to anyone with a cough up to four times a day.[23]

The idea that rubbing the scalp with raw onion delays baldness is widespread both in the British Isles[24] and beyond:

> My father was a well-known hairdresser in North Yorkshire, having served his time with a German expert named Walther in the 1890s. His cure for alopecia was to massage half an onion on to the bare patches. He told his customers to do this regularly . . . the treatment was most successful in some cases.[25]

Other cures that involved onions included rubbing raw onions on severe bruises[26] and chilblains.[27] More rarely it was recommended that carrying a small onion in the pocket would ward off rheumatism.[28]

The idea that carrying various objects in a pocket would prevent rheumatism is widespread. As far as plant materials go, the use of potato was probably most well known.[29] Occasionally it was said that the potato so used should have been stolen.[30] It is generally said that as the potato shrank the pain diminished, alternatively the potato was thought to 'draw the iron out of the blood', as too much iron, leading to stiffness was thought to be responsible for rheumatism.[31] Presumably, by extension of this belief, potatoes were thought to prevent cramp, cure toothache and bestow general good luck:

> A potato in the bed helps do away with cramp.[32]

> A peeled potato carried around in the pocket until it hardens will cure toothache. But you must carry it around on the same side of the body as the affected tooth.[33]

> In May 1978, when discussing the football pools with a group of middle-aged women working in South Kensington, they mentioned some of the 'lucky charms' that they hoped would bring them luck. These included short lengths of string, pressed four-leaved clovers, and tiny withered potatoes, all of which they carried around in their purses.[34]

Other plant materials carried in pockets to prevent rheumatism include conkers,[35] nutmegs,[36] pieces of the alder tree,[37] and acorns.[38]

Rural workers often considered rheumatism to be inevitable, but a large number of plants were used in an attempt alleviate it. In Tunstall, Staffordshire, in the late 1920s, a herbalist:

Used to collect sprigs of broom from the local countryside, which he then cut up into short pieces, placed in packets and sold as a cure for rheumatism, instructing the customer to make tea from the sprigs by pouring boiling water over them.[39]

In County Galway, where it was known as bog onion, royal fern root

is converted into a juicy substance and used as a rub for rheumatism and sciatica; it is often found to be a complete cure. First the root is cut into slices and then pounded up into a mash. It is then put into a bottle or some corked vessel and water supplied in proportion to the size of the root. It is then left to set for about two days until it forms a thick white juicy substance.[40]

Gypsies valued burdock as a remedy for rheumatism:

Infusion of leaves or flowers, or better still of crushed seeds, relieves rheumatism . . . Some gypsies carry the seeds in a little bag slung round the neck as a preventative of rheumatism.[41]

But in recent times, the stinging nettle was probably the plant most frequently used to treat or prevent rheumatism and arthritis. Often people would beat the affected part with nettles:

In the late 1930s I was a nurse-midwife in the Lake District. In the village where I lived a farmer was noted for his laziness. He would lie in bed in the morning saying his lumbago was so bad that he couldn't get up to do the milking. This chore fell to his wife and after a time she got fed up with it, so she went to the village 'know-all' for advice. The old woman told her to gather a bunch of nettles, a bunch of thyme, a few dock leaves, mix them together and tie them in a bundle. With this she was to lash the area of pain for at least 10 minutes (not too hard). After some persuading her husband made himself comfortable on his tummy and the treatment commenced, however the wife got a bit over enthusiastic and the nettles fell on to private parts. The husband leapt out of bed and dancing around the room swore he would kill the 'old hag' who had told her to do this. The story in the village was that he was never heard to complain of lumbago again and his wife was never again asked to do early morning milking. A sure cure.[42]

Alternatively, one could simply walk through nettles:

I was brought up in the north Pennines. The woman who ran the village shop in the late 1950s used to walk through stands of nettles on her ground to relieve arthritis.[43]

Less frequently, an infusion of nettles was believed to be good for rheumatism. Such a cure was considered successful in Moretonhampstead, Devon, in the 1960s.[44]

Other ailments for which people commonly sought local cures included chilblains, leg ulcers, piles, whooping cough and warts.

Perhaps the most widespread cure for chilblains was simply to soak the affected area in urine, but a number of plant remedies were also used. In County Antrim rotten apples were 'threaded' onto chilblained toes to ease the itching.[45] In Devon chilblains were rubbed with the leaves of navelwort, locally known as penny-pies.[46] Elsewhere, it was recommended that chilblains should be thrashed with holly until they bled.[47] Alternatively, in Wiltshire powdered holly berries mixed with lard were rubbed on.[48] In Worcestershire Madonna lily leaves – presumably preserved in some way from the preceding summer – were wrapped around cracked chilblains for about a week.[49] In Scotland in the 1930s:

As a young girl I used to suffer from chilblains on my little toes . . . My mother's remedy was to grate carrots into lard, and put this on as a poultice. The remedy worked, but it did ruin one's slippers.[50]

Late in the nineteenth century marigold was known as measle-flower, and had 'some local reputation as a remedy'. However, children believed that handling the plant would lead to catching measles.[51] In Suffolk a tea made by pouring a pint of boiling water over a dozen marigold flowers was given to children 'in a wineglass three times a day' to cure measles.[52] In 1975 in Somerset, a vile-tasting tea made from mistletoe growing on hawthorn was remembered as being used.[53]

Leg ulcers were extremely difficult to treat, but there were a number of herbal remedies that apparently achieved success.

My cousin had an ulcer on her leg from her ankle to knee. Ointment from the doctor did her no good. Someone told her to bathe the leg with comfrey – boiling the leaves – bathe two or three times a day. In just over a week it had gone down to [the size of] a postage stamp.[54]

I have been assured by an elderly neighbour, a lady, that a certain cure for leg ulcers and other hard-to-heal lesions is obtained by simply grating a portion of raw potato over the sore. She has used the treatment herself in the past with complete success.[55]

Early in the twentieth century it was remembered in Cornwall that water figwort was 'formerly held in high repute as an applications for ulcers'.[56]

The best-known herbal remedy for piles involved lesser celandine, which had the alternative name of pilewort, and was known to William Turner, in his *Names of Herbes* (1548) as fygwurt – 'fig' being a former name for piles. In Guernsey a remedy for piles was made by boiling fresh lard and straining it through celandine flowers,[57] but it appears that elsewhere the root tubers were more frequently used.[58]

Root tubers of celandines are said to resemble piles, and thus their use to cure piles is claimed to be an example of the Doctrine of Signatures. This theory, elaborated in the sixteenth and seventeenth centuries, claimed that plants displayed characters or 'signatures' that provided guidance on which diseases they were capable of curing. Although the Doctrine is frequently mentioned in books on plant folklore, it seems likely that it was most avidly accepted by the educated elite who could afford books, and was not a genuine folk belief.[59] It has been suggested that people discovered that a plant was effective against an illness and then sought a character of the plant to act as a reminder of this. The cure came before the signature, not vice versa.[60]

Like rheumatism, piles could be prevented by carrying a conker in a pocket,[61] while gypsies believed that a silk bag containing chestnuts worn around the neck would do the same.[62]

In Sussex an infusion of elder flowers in boiling water was considered to cure piles.[63] In County Antrim:

> Wild buttercups were used to treat piles for many generations. The ground-up roots were boiled with lard to make an ointment for external use, and two handfuls of leaves boiled in a pint of water made a decoction that was reputed to be of great benefit. A wine-glass full of the strained liquid was taken three times a day.[64]

Lincolnshire people swallowed the berries of mezereon, locally known as mazeerie, like pills as a cure for piles.[65]

Whooping cough was one of the dreaded diseases of childhood. In the Isle of Axholme, Lincolnshire, a moss gall (also known as bedeguar) from a dog rose 'gathered and hung up in the house will prevent whooping cough'.[66] In West Sussex in the 1860s a moss gall, known as Robin Redbreast's Cushion, hung around a patient's neck, was considered to be 'the finest thing known for whooping cough'.[67]

Another whooping cough cure appears to depend entirely on psychology or magic. The sufferer should be taken to a place where there is an arching bramble stem that rooted where it reached the ground, and be made to crawl through, or pass under, the arch.

The bramble-bush was supposed to be quite effectual in a recent case [of whooping cough] at Weobley, but the child was passed under nine times on one morning only, and an offering of bread and butter was placed beneath the bramble arch. 'She left her cough there with the bread and butter,' said my informant.[68]

Similar cures were attempted in Monmouthshire in the 1930s,[69] and in Staffordshire, where the child was passed over and under a bramble arch 'nine times on three mornings before sunrise, while repeating:

> Under the briar, and over the briar,
> I wish to leave the chin cough here'.[70]

Although whooping cough was the illness most frequently cured by crawling under a bramble arch, there were a variety of other ailments that received similar treatment. In Wales, children with rickets, or infants that were slow to walk, were put to creep or crawl under 'blackberry brambles three times a week'.[71] In Dorset, 'to creep under a bramble three mornings following against the sun, just as it rises, is said to afford a complete cure for boils'.[72] Around Zennor in north Cornwall crawling around a bramble bush nine times was considered a certain cure for blackheads,[73] while in Somerset passing the patient under a bramble arch was thought to cure hernias.[74] According to reports from County Kerry in the late 1930s and early 1940s, crawling under a bramble arch would ensure good luck when playing cards.[75]

The traditional herbal remedies that were used to treat warts is large. Some appear to depend on a substance in the plant destroying the wart; others seem to be more dependent on magic. Possibly the most widespread herbal remedy for warts is to rub them with the milky latex of a spurge,[76] dandelion,[77] fig,[78] or sow thistle.[79] Sometimes these cures worked, other times they did not. The use of the yellow latex of greater celandine, which had local names such as kill-wart in north Devon,[80] wart-plant in west Somerset,[81] and wart-wort in Gloucestershire,[82] was probably more efficacious:

> Lore of which I know from personal experience to work . . . the greater celandine. Its juice is a wart curer. I always make sure to leave a few seedlings growing in my garden every year.[83]

Styes and similar eye conditions could also be treated by rubbing them with greater celandine juice.[84] A local name in Cornwall was kenning-herb, from kenning or kennel, dialect words for an 'ulcer on the eye'.[85]

Wart cures, which contained an element of magic, involved burying objects or transferring the warts to twigs. Data collected as part of the

3. Greater celandine (R. G. Hatton, *The Craftman's Plant-book*, London, 1909).

English Folklore Survey conducted in the 1960s demonstrates that at that time the plant most often known as a wart cure was the broad bean.[86] The white, furry inside of bean pods was frequently rubbed on warts. Sometimes it was simply rubbed on and the warts disappeared.[87] More usually, some sort of ritual was involved.

> To cure warts – break open a broadbean pod – eat the beans and then rub the warts with the inside of the skin. Finally bury the skin, by the time it has rotted your warts will have disappeared. This is more effective when done by moonlight.[88]

> Rub the inside of a broadbean pod onto warts and put the pod in the middle of a crossroads; as the pod withers so the warts disappeared. I did this when I was young and the warts cleared.[89]

Francis Bacon (1561–1626) recorded: 'They say' warts can be cured by rubbing them 'with a Green Elder Sticke and then burying the Sticke to rot in Mucke.'[90] Similarly:

A 15-year-old girl, writing in 1954, says that her grandfather told her to pick a small twig of elderberry, touch her warts with it, chant the words,

> Wart, wart, on my knee.
> Please go, one, two, three.
> And put it 'down the toilet'.[91]

Alternatively, a notch for each wart might be cut on a small stick, usually of ash or elder,[92] and the stick presumably thrown away or buried.

In addition to illnesses, people also suffered from a variety of cuts, burns and bruises. If a labourer accidentally cut himself while mowing he would reach for a ribwort plantain leaf, chew it and place it on his wound.[93] Greater plantain was also valued to treat cuts. In County Longford, a leaf, 'the rough side to draw and the smooth side to heal' was bandaged on a cut or bruise.[94] Similarly, in Shetland, where it was known as wavverin leaf, greater plantain was used to treat cuts, burns and sores,[95] while in southern England:

> As instructed by my grandmother in the 1920s, my family always used the plantain leaf (*Plantago major*) for cuts and abrasions – the back or veined side of the leaf to draw out impurities and then the smooth side for healing – always worked. Granny always called it planty leaf (Hampshire colloq.)[96]

Solomon's seal has long been used to treat bruises. According to John Gerard (1545–1607), an application of the fresh root

> taketh away in one night or two at the utmost, any bruse, blacke or blew spots gotten by fals, or womens wilfulnes, in stumbling upon their hastie husbands fists, or such like.[97]

Gypsies made an ointment from the leaves, which when applied to bruised or black eyes would rapidly get rid of any discolouration.[98] However, knowledge of the cure seems to be poorly remembered:

> My mother, who was born in the second half of the nineteenth century, told me when I was a little boy of the wonderful efficacy of Solomon's seal (*Polygonatum*) in drawing out the blackness of a bruise . . . As I remember it, the washed rhizome was grated and the pulp was bandaged on the bruise as a cold poultice.[99]

Two wild plants – comfrey, a coarse herb of waste places, and houseleek, a succulent that grows on old roofs and walls – had such valuable healing properties that they were sometimes cultivated.

The only local plant-name I knew in Lancashire was heartsease; it's comfrey – the plant they grow in back gardens for herbal cures.[100]

Always grow comfrey – root and leaves have all kinds of medicinal uses.[101]

Comfrey, known sometimes as knitbone[102] or more rarely boneset,[103] was widely valued to treat sprains and bruises, and even broken limbs.

My primary school headmistress in the 1940s collected wild comfrey to make an infusion for bruises and sprains.[104]

My husband . . . when he was a Casualty Officer in the Royal Hospital, Sheffield in the 1950s, [found] it was not uncommon for patients suffering from suspected breakages and sprains to arrive at hospital with the affected bones swathed in comfrey leaves, held in place by bandages.[105]

Although such cures were most widespread, comfrey also had many other medicinal uses.

At the time [comfrey] flowers we killed the family pig . . . as the pig was cut up and fat rendered down, the fresh lard was boiled with the leaves of comfrey plant. The result was a great ointment in a pot. It cured all cuts, spots [and] septic wounds.[106]

Comfrey was always abundant in old cottage gardens and used in a strong infusion to cure diarrhoea (scour) both in animals and humans.[107]

In County Tyrone comfrey leaves were spread on arthritis to soothe the pain,[108] in County Limerick the roots were used to make plasters for broken limbs of poultry,[109] in the Scottish borders a compress of brewed leaves was used to treat goats with 'any leg injury',[110] and in Kent the plant was used 'to cure pigs of various diseases'.[111]

Although houseleek is widespread and included in many British wildflower books, its status as a wild plant is weak. It has been grown in British gardens since at least 1200 and known in the wild since 1629.[112] As it is believed not to set seed in the British Isles it is dependent on vegetative reproduction, and is only rarely found away from man-built habitats. In addition to being cultivated, or encouraged, for its medicinal properties, houseleek was also believed to protect the buildings on which it grew.[113]

4. Houseleek (Petrus Andreas Matthiolus, *Commentarii, in libros sex Pedacii Dioscoridis Anazarbei de medica materia*, Venice, 1554).

David Allen and Gabrielle Hatfield in their survey of British and Irish traditional herbal remedies consider houseleek and navelwort to be largely interchangeable in folk medicine.[114] Houseleek also seems to share many of the medicinal properties claimed for the exotic *Aloe vera* which attained great repute as a herbal remedy towards the end of the twentieth century. At present houseleek is probably used to treat a wider range of ailments than any other British plant.

In Cornwall a poultice of houseleek leaves was used to extract corns.[115] In County Mayo, when

> a young girl got in 'trouble' (unwanted pregnancy), her mother would take some of these plants, boil them, and give the water to her daughter to drink. Later on, she would tell the girl to climb up on a high wall and jump down. That would make the girl all right.[116]

Ailments for which houseleek has been considered efficacious in recent years include cold sores in Dumfriess-shire,[117] ringworm and warts in Cumbria,[118] impetigo[119] and staunching blood[120] in Norfolk, earache in Glamorgan[121] and West Yorkshire,[122] relief of shingles in Shropshire,[123] and insect bites and styes in Gloucestershire.[124]

It appears that these remedies have all been passed on by word of mouth, or perhaps people experimented using a species known to treat one ailment to treat another. However, there has been a continual flow of remedies from oral tradition to the written page or 'official' medicine and vice versa. Examples include various remedies that became well known and widespread towards the end of the twentieth century but apparently lack lengthy histories. Bananas feature in several such cures.

> Banana skins heal eczema miraculously. The inside of the banana skin is rubbed on the eczema. Although it does sting/itch the results are startling and achieved without scarring.[125]

> My late husband . . . cured his awful cramp in three weeks. Eat a good sized banana a day.[126]

The pain of a mosquito bite could be alleviated by rubbing the inside of a frozen banana peel over it.[127]

> Cyclists and marathon runners put bananas in their pants to stop them getting sore bums.[128]

Likewise some cures which use cabbage seem to be of recent origin and drift between print and oral tradition. Possibly the most widespread medicinal use of cabbage at the present time is to place a leaf on the breast to relieve breasts that are sore as a result of breastfeeding,[129] mastitis[130] or cancer[131] A second widespread use is to reduce the pain of arthritis:

> An orthopaedic surgeon at Bristol's Southmead Hospital was rather taken aback when a 72-year-old woman with severe arthritis of the knee lifted her skirt to reveal a large cabbage leaf firmly strapped in place – which, she claimed, was 'the only thing' that relieved her pain.[132]

At the start of a new millennium there appears to be a revival of interest in the use of native and common food-plants to treat minor ailments. Fear of catching infections when in hospital, a distrust of synthetic drugs, and a general desire for more 'natural' medicine all ensure that more people seek out and use herbal remedies. In the past people who preferred such treatments usually resorted to exotic imported dried herbs, now there is an increasing tendency for people to seek out wild plants, or grow their own herbs, to treat their ailments.

5

MOTHER-DIE AND FRIENDSHIP BUSHES

In addition to regarding hedgerows and field margins as sources of food and medicine, people saw plants as being able to influence human life, provide luck and protection, or bring about misfortune. Perhaps due to the uncertainty of life in earlier times the number of folk beliefs associated with bad luck seem to greatly exceed those associated with good fortune.

Many plants were, if gathered and taken indoors, believed to induce misfortune. Between March 1982 and October 1984 members of the London-based Folklore Society conducted a survey of plants which were believed to produce misfortune when picked or brought indoors.[1] It was found that flowering hawthorn – also known as may, and, in Ireland, whitethorn – was the most widely feared plant, responsible for 23.5 per cent of the items collected. Although the survey has not been repeated recently, information accumulated as part of the more general collection of plant-lore suggests that this statistic seems constant. Throughout the British Isles people banned hawthorn flowers from their homes, believing that if it was brought in death or some other misfortune would follow. Typically:

> My grandmother, who was born in 1898, always said that bringing hawthorn (which she called may) into the house meant a death within a year.[2]

In Wiltshire picking hawthorn blossom indoors 'would result in a dead child',[3] in rural Cheshire it was believed that if hawthorn blossom was gathered 'you would not get an apple crop as you would be depriving the bees of a supply of pollen',[4] and in Essex hawthorn brought indoors would result in illness.[5] Anecdotes about what happened when people were foolhardy enough to bring hawthorn indoors include:

> When I was at school, I regret over 40 years ago, a very unpopular teacher fell downstairs. It was said that this was because she had vases of hawthorn in her classroom.[6]

5. Hawthorn (R. G. Hatton, *The Craftman's Plant-book*, London, 1909).

My parents, originally from Oxfordshire, would never allow may flowers in the house. A certain great aunt had broken her entire tea service following may flowers in the drawing room.[7]

Various theories have been put forward to explain why hawthorn flowers should be considered inauspicious. Some people explain that Christ's crown of thorns was made of hawthorn, hence the tree brings misfortune.[8] Some writers claim that fear of hawthorn flowers derives from memories of pre-Christian May Day celebrations in which a May Queen was crowned with hawthorn blossoms before being ritually slaughtered.[9] There is no evidence to suggest that such rites ever took place. A theory that has received greater acceptance is that hawthorn blossoms were associated with pre-Reformation devotions to the Virgin Mary.

Superstition about May dates from the times when Catholics were persecuted for their faith.
During the month of May – which was dedicated to the Blessed Virgin Mary – May blossoms were used to decorate the little shrines which Catholics made in their homes in her honour. If anti-Catholic officials saw May blossom being carried into a house, they recognised the household as a Catholic one and acted accordingly. Hence, to bring these flowers into a house brought 'bad luck' to the owners.[10]

However, the association of the Virgin Mary with the month of May and may blossom originated after the Reformation, starting in Naples in the eighteenth century and spreading throughout the Catholic world to reach the British Isles in the mid-nineteenth century.[11]

In 1866 a correspondent to the *Gentleman's Magazine* noted:

> I have found it a popular notion among . . . country cottagers that
> the peculiar scent of the hawthorn is 'exactly like the smell of the
> Great Plague of London'. This belief may have been traditionally
> held during the last two centuries, and have arisen from circum-
> stances noted at the period of the Great Plague.[12]

More recently, the poet Sylvia Plath (1932–63) wrote of the 'death-stench
of a hawthorn'.[13]

Two species of hawthorn, which frequently hybridize, are native to the
British Isles. The common hawthorn, *Crataegus monogyna*, is widespread
and abundant throughout most of the British Isles: Midland hawthorn,
C. laevigata, formerly known as *C. oxyacanthoides*, was restricted to central
and south-east England, but both species have been extensively planted
as hedges. In May 1900 the amateur botanist R. P. Murray recorded:

> In Switzerland we had plenty both of *C. monogyna* and *C. oxyacan-
> thoides*; the latter flowering a week or two earlier than *C. monogyna*.
> But I often gathered a lot of *C. oxyacanthoides* for decorative pur-
> poses: and tho' in smell quite like the other when gathered, it
> used to absolutely *stink* of putrid flesh soon after: sometimes
> within half an hour. I do not remember this ever occurred with
> *C. monogyna*.[14]

Chemists have pointed out that trimethylamine, one of the first products
formed when animal tissues decay, is present in hawthorn flowers.[15]

> I heard that you didn't bring may blossom (hawthorn) into the
> house because the smell reminded people of dead bodies – First
> World War veterans couldn't stand it.[16]

When corpses were usually kept in the house awaiting burial, and refrig-
erators were unknown, our ancestors were familiar with the odour of
death and decay, and it is easy to understand that they would dislike
having hawthorn flowers indoors.

In Ireland isolated trees, known as lone bushes or fairy trees, were
sometimes considered to be associated with, and protected by, fairies.
Hawthorn was the tree that was most often considered to be a lone bush,
but other species sometimes considered as such included:

> The hazel, the blackthorn, the bourtree – which is the English elder
> – the sally [sallow], the alder, the holly, the birch, the oak – espe-
> cially the twisted mountain oak – the broom, the Scots fir; also,

to my personal knowledge, in at least two instances, the rowan or mountain ash.[17]

Tales of hawthorns which are considered to be fairy trees are frequent.

A lone bush was growing on the [Ulster] Canal bank and when the company was making the canal, a man was sent to cut the tree. He began cutting, but the chips would fly out and immediately fly back again. The man gave up the job. This bush is a great inconvenience to the company. When the horses came to it with the pull boats the men had to loose the cable and put it inside the bush, causing a great loss of time. The company offered £10 to anyone who would cut the bush, but no one accepted it, and the bush remains standing to this day.[18]

In Ireland, Donegal, where my husband comes from, they had to divert a road because they wouldn't cut down a hawthorn tree. I didn't believe it, but I've seen it.[19]

A County Meath man who attempted to cut down a lone bush died within a week,[20] while in County Wicklow a man found his horse dead in its stable when he returned from cutting down a thorn tree.[21] In County Sligo:

The house of Irish cousins of mine in Roscommon/Ballynote . . . was bought by a man, he wanted to cut one or more thorn trees down. No one would. He threatened to import Protestant labour from Derry, 70 miles north, so the locals cut them under protest. This annoyed the fairies, and they got into his bank balance and turned all the figures from black to red, so he went bust and left for Australia.[22]

An example of the survival of this belief comes from Belfast:

At the Ulster Folk and Transport Museum [founded 1961] they have these fields they try to make look like traditional fields, so they planted a hawthorn tree in the middle of one of them to look like a fairy thorn. A few years later they decided they didn't want a thorn tree there, so they asked the men to cut it down, but they wouldn't do so, because it was a fairy thorn. It was a different lot of men from the ones who planted it, but it does show how soon these things develop.[23]

The second most feared plant in the Folklore Society's survey was lilac.

Although people are happy to have lilac bushes in their gardens, many people are wary of bringing it indoors.

> My mother wouldn't allow lilac flowers indoors. I don't know why. That was in Enfield. We used to have a lovely tree, but she wouldn't allow any indoors.[24]

It appears that the flowers of lilac with their strong scent were used to line coffins, and, presumably, mask the odour of decaying flesh.[25] Hence they were not considered to be suitable for use on other occasions. White lilac seems to be more frequently feared than purple.[26]

Occasionally it was believed that the bringing of hawthorn blossom into a house would result in the death of one's mother.

> Only this week I have been told that if one brings may into the house one's mother will die within a year.[27]

Hence the blossoms were sometimes called mother-die,[28] or mother-will-die.[29]

For the same reason, the name mother-die has been given to a number of other species. James Britten and Robert Holland in their A Dictionary of English Plant-names (1878-86) list mother-dee as a west Cumberland name for red campion:

> There is a superstition amongst Cumberland children that if they pluck the flower some misfortune will happen to their parents. The same is said in Yorkshire of Veronica chamaedrys [germander speedwell] . . . but the name does not seem, as far as we know, to be extended to that plant.[30]

They also record mother-dee or mother-die as a Cheshire name for upright hedge-parsley.[31]

Thus it appears that in the nineteenth century the belief that picking certain flowers would lead to the death of one's mother, was restricted to three species – germander speedwell, red campion and upright hedge-parsley – and known only in northern England. During the twentieth century the belief seems to have become more widespread. There is one record, from south-east Norfolk, of alexanders being known as mother-die,[32] but more usually the name is applied to white-flowered members of the carrot family (Apiaceae, formerly known as Umbelliferae):

> I was always warned by my mother as a child (I am now 71) not to touch white umbellifers as they are poisonous. She did not differentiate at all and called them mother-die.[33]

Yarrow, which superficially resembles some umbellifers, was also some-times known as mother-die:

> Yarrow – known as mother-die or fever-plant – unlucky to pick or bring into house – it is thought to cause sickness.[34]

However, cow parsley was the plant most frequently and most widely known as mother-die,[35] and it is probable that when the name is given to the other white-flowered umbellifers, including upright hedge-parsley, they have been misidentified and cow parsley is intended. Cow parsley has a second name given to it, which relates to the belief that it should not be picked:

> As a child in Yorkshire, we would never pick the tallish, very small white flowers that grew by the wayside. They were very pretty, tall, graceful plants, and many times I was tempted to pick them, but was told not to as it was called stepmother's blessing, or mother-die. Needless to say, as I was very fond of my mother, I did not wish to acquire a stepmother, which was what would happen I was informed if I picked them.[36]

Another Yorkshire name for cow parsley was stepmother blossom.[37]

Possibly the mother-die belief was invented by adults to discourage youngsters from handling any white-flowered umbellifers, thus keeping them away from the poisonous hemlock, which can be mistaken for other species. Cow parsley and related species are initially attractive as cut flowers, but they soon shed masses of tiny petals, so it is probable that house-proud mothers would not welcome them indoors.

Although it appears that mother-die is a comparatively recent name, cow parsley has other names that suggest it is unpleasant or inaus-picious. Such names include: badman-oatmeal, de'il's meal, devil's oatmeal, devil's parsley and naughty-man's oatmeal,[38] adder's meat in Cornwall,[39] bad-man's baccy in Northumberland,[40] black-man's oatmeal in Yorkshire,[41] dead-man's flesh in Suffolk,[42] devil's porridge in Dublin,[43] dog's flourish – because it grows on the verges where the dogs have been – in Dunbartonshire,[44] shit-parsley in Cambridgeshire,[45] and snake-plant in Monmouthshire.[46]

There is only one record of a plant being associated with the death of one's father. In Cumbria in 1997 red campion was known as mother-and-father-die,[47] thus demonstrating the survival of the belief recorded by Britten and Holland 111 years earlier.

Another belief which seems to have developed at about the same time as mother-die was the idea that placing red and white flowers together would cause death. This first known record of this belief occurs in 'Sunlight' Almanac in 1896, under 'Dreams and their Significations': 'Flowers. If only red and white they are omens of death.'[48] Many, if not most, hospitals banned arrangements of red and white flowers from their wards.

> Red and white flowers must never be mixed in a vase in a sick room – as it is a sign of impending death. In hospitals where I have worked (London, York, Boston and Alford, Lincs) nurses always separated red and white flowers if they arrived together in a bunch and placed them in separate vases – and if this was not possible adding at least one flower of a different colour – usually yellow – to the vase. I have seen ward sisters remove a vase of red and white flowers from a bedside and make necessary adjustments – sometimes to the great surprise of the patient or visitors.[49]

A Kirkcaldy, Fife, woman recalled in 1992 how during World War II this belief caused consternation when Polish servicemen gave bunches of red and white – their national colours – flowers to their British girlfriends.[50]

It is usually explained that the red and white represent blood and bandages.[51] Perhaps there is also a connection with the red and white stripes of a barber's pole, which is said to represent 'the wand used in venesection, the two bandages and the barber's blood-letting dish'.[52]

However, arrangements of red and white flowers, which symbolize 'the fire and the wind of the Holy Spirit', are frequently used to decorate Anglican churches at Whitsun.[53] Red and white are the colours of the City of London, so when there are events at the Guildhall there are 'always masses of red and white flowers'.[54]

Snowdrops were widely associated with death or misfortune.[55] In 1982 a district nursing sister working in Lancashire recalled a story that an elderly patient had told her:

> For many years her mother had refused to have snowdrops in the house, even though they grew profusely in the orchard . . . After the old lady's death there was an occasion when a wedding party announced their intention, at short notice, of arriving to pay respects to an ailing relative. Snowdrops were brought in to decorate the tables, it being early in the year and no other flowers available so easily. Within three months the bridegroom was dead, and, needless to say, snowdrops have never since been brought into the house.[56]

Elder is probably the most enigmatic plant in the folk tradition of the British Isles. On the one hand it was considered to be a witch-tree and was generally feared, on the other it was considered to provide protection. In Oxfordshire in the 1950s:

> It was said at Beckley that if you burn elder wood you will become bewitched. You never cut it down. In Wootton they say elder is a witch tree. You should never mend a wattle hedge with it, as it will give the witches power. If you cut it, it will bleed.[57]

In County Cork it was thought that 'the family name dies out on the property where the elder grows in the kitchen garden'.[58] In Shropshire burning elder wood 'caused the devil to sit on the chimney'.[59]

In Counties Leitrim and Waterford and the south of Ireland:

> The elder or 'bore' tree is believed to have been the tree from which Judas Iscariot hanged himself. The proof of which is the fact that its leaves have an 'ugly smell', and, moreover, that its fruit has since degenerated from its original size and excellent flavour to become worthless both as to size and taste.[60]

Alternatively, but less frequently, it is said that elder provided the wood for Christ's cross. According to a verse current in the early 1940s:

> Elder growing near the gate
> Never crooked, never straight,
> Never a bush, never a tree
> Since our Lord was hung on thee.[61]

Sometimes it was thought that elder could be safely brought indoors only if the tree's permission was sought. Typically:

> If you take flowers or berries from the elder tree you must always ask the lady (tree) for permission. I still do. I am in my 60s.[62]

Despite some people considering elder to be a plant that was dangerous, or had to be treated with respect, others believed it to be beneficial or protective. In Northumberland:

> An old man told me that his aunt used to keep a piece of bour tree, or elder, in her kist (chest) to prevent her clothes from malign influence.[63]

More usually elder trees were planted near the homestead to provide protection (and deter flies).[64] In Wales an elder was planted by the doors of cow-sheds and stables to protect livestock from witchcraft and

sorcery.[65] Similarly in Scotland[66] and Guernsey[67] an elder planted near
the door would guard a building from witchcraft. In Ireland, it was
considered lucky to have an elder tree, particularly if it was self-sown,
near the house.[68]

On the Isle of Man, and occasionally other places, elder trees were
believed to harbour friendly fairies. In 1926 it was recorded:

> Each [Manx] cottage has a trammon, or elderberry tree, outside
> the door. This is used by the Phynodderree to swing in. He is a
> kind of faun who can bring much luck, and even helps materially
> in outside work.[69]

Seventy years later:

> My cousin in Port St Mary, Isle of Man, wished to have some elder
> bushes cut down which were shading her kitchen windows. There
> was a long argument with the men sent to do the work – 'They'
> wouldn't like it ('they' being fairies) and misfortune would follow
> within a year. The pruning was eventually done, with our neigh-
> bour shrieking from next door. The belief was obviously sincere
> and deeply held. What impressed me when I have been staying
> there is the strong belief even now.[70]

Regardless of whether elder is considered malevolent or protective, most
of the folk beliefs associated with it seem to encourage the tree's protection and preservation. According to herbalists who re-examined Britain's
herbal heritage in the 1940s, elder had 'the unusual distinction of being
useful in every part'[71] and was 'the healingest tree that on earth do
grow',[72] so perhaps the beliefs evolved to protect a valuable resource.

More widely appreciated as a protective tree is the rowan, also known
as mountain ash.

John Aubrey, remembering his boyhood in the 1630s, when rowan
was known as whitty-tree, wrote:

> In Herefordshire they are not uncommon; they are used . . . to
> make pinnes for the yoakes of their oxen of them, believing it had
> the vertue to preserve them from being forespoken as they call it,
> and they used to plant one by their dwelling-house, believing it to
> preserve from witches and evil eyes.[73]

Especially in the Highlands and Islands of Scotland, rowan's protective powers were valued to the extent that an exasperated writer in *The
Phytologist* of 1858 bemoaned 'this tree is seldom described by any author
unaccompanied by a more or less uninteresting account of superstitious

usages respecting it'.[74] Presumably he would have rapidly dismissed John Lightfoot's 1777 passage:

> [Scots] believe that any small part of this tree carried with them will be a sovereign charm against all the dire effects of witchcraft. Their cattle also, as well as themselves, are supposed to be preserved by it from evil; for the dairy-maid will not forget to drive them to the shealings or summer pastures with a rod of roan-tree, which she carefully lays up over the door of the sheal boothy, or summer-house, and drives them home again with the same. In Strathspey they make, for the same purpose, on the first day of May, a hoop of the wood of this tree, and in the evening and morning cause all the sheep and lambs to pass through it.[75]

In 1945 the new owner of a croft in north-west Scotland horrified her neighbours when she wanted to cut down a clump of rowans which obscured the view from her kitchen window: 'a rowan tree near the house keeps evil spirits away . . . and if you hang a wee sprigie of it over the byre door, your beasts will be well too, and bad luck willna come to themselves'.[76] About 40 years later, in County Limerick:

> The rowan or mountain ash is said to be the home of good fairies. I have one growing in my garden, given to me by my mother after I got married.[77]

More usually, however, rowan was valued to provide protection against witches.[78]

Another use of rowan was to protect people who attempted to rescue others from the fairy realms. In a Highland folk-tale recorded in 1823, a man successfully rescued his brother from a *shian* or fairy hill, after being advised: 'Return to the *shian* in a year and a day from the time you lost him, fasten a rowan cross to your clothing and enter boldly, and in the name of the Highest claim your brother'.[79] In his *Celtic Folklore*, published in 1901, John Rhys described how a captive dancing in a fairy ring could be rescued. Two or more strong men should hold a long rowan pole so that one end of it rested in the middle of the circle. When the invisible captive is felt to grasp the pole the men should pull with all their strength; the fairies will not be able to intervene because of their aversion to rowan.[80]

However, rowan was not always welcome in gardens. Two records, both from Accrington, Lancashire, make it clear that rowan was considered inauspicious. In about 1940 a woman refused to buy a house, which she liked in every other way, because two rowans grew in its garden.[81] In 1983 an Accrington schoolchild claimed that it was 'unlucky to transplant mountain ash, or bring cuttings into the house'.[82]

It is often assumed that the protective qualities of rowan are due to its 'red berries – there is no better colour against evil'.[83] However, it seems that some Accrington people noticed the white, scented, messy flowers – similar to those of hawthorn and other species that are considered unlucky – rather than the berries.

Other plants that provide protection include bay, which in the New Forest area of Hampshire afforded protection against 'all things evil'.[84]

> My brother and sister-in-law moved to a house in south Devon . . .
> 30 years ago, they were told that the bay trees which grew at the
> entrance would protect the house, but my sister-in-law said they
> didn't, because she always said the house had a ghost.[85]

Houseleek, known in parts of Ireland as *Buachaill a'tighe*, 'the warden of the house',[86] was said to be planted on buildings to protect them from thunder. It was, of course, also valued for its medical properties.[87]

> Ireland shared fully in the very common European belief that
> the houseleek (*Sempervivum*) protected the house from conflagra-
> tion and lightning, and the growing of this plant on the roofs of
> thatched houses, or in specially made niches or nooks in or about
> the roofs or porches covered with other materials, was known in
> every Irish county.[88]

Similarly, houseleek was thought to protect against thunder in Nottinghamshire[89] and Norfolk.[90]

Many writers on plant folklore state that oak provided protection against lightning. They claim that the bobbins on old-fashioned window-blinds were acorn-shaped to provide such protection. Possibly bobbins were this shape simply because it was easy to produce, but a writer who was born in 1926 records:

> In the Sussex cottage, where the writer stayed as a child, oak twigs
> and oak apples and acorns stood in a spill jar on the mantelpiece,
> summer and winter, against lightning.[91]

Furthermore, according to the *Weekly Telegraph* of 5 February 1938:

> Quite a number of airmen carry with them when flying an acorn.
> Ever since the day of the Druids, the acorn has been the accepted
> charm against lightning. And it is not only airmen who have this
> belief . . . At an inquest on the body of a farm labourer killed by
> lightning, a witness testified that it was the worst storm he had

ever been out in. 'But I was not frightened' he added. 'I had an acorn in my pocket.' Not only airmen but others carry this charm; among them steeplejacks. Many steeplejacks would not dream of going aloft without carrying an acorn.

Picking some flowers could cause thunder and lightning. A north Staffordshire name for wood anemone was thunderbolt, and the 'natives' explained that if it was gathered there would be a thunderstorm, during which the gatherer would undoubtedly be struck.[92] Around Macclesfield in Cheshire in the 1940s the picking of rosebay willowherb would provoke a thunderstorm, or cause the death of one's mother.[93] In Wiltshire, where it was known as thunder-flower,[94] and in Ireland,[95] picking ragged robin would cause thunder. In Shropshire bindweed, a common weed of arable land, was known as thunder-flower, 'because if we picked them it would be sure to thunder before the day was out'.[96]

Early in the nineteenth century, around Wooler in Northumberland, children knew the scarlet poppy, another arable weed, as thunder-flower or lightnings, and believed that if they picked one, and its petals fell off, they would be struck by lightning.[97]

More usually it was said that poppies caused headaches:

Red poppies that grow in cornfields in Ireland are in the counties of Carlow, Wexford, Wicklow and Waterford called headaches, and are particularly obnoxious to females, the more so to young unmarried women, who have a horror of touching or being touched by them.[98]

In England:

Poppy – called heead-vahhk (headache) – because it gives you one.[99]

As a boy I was told not to sniff poppies as to do so would give you a headache.[100]

Around Workshop in Nottinghamshire both wild and cultivated poppies were known as earaches: 'if they are gathered and put to the ear a violent attack of earache will be the result.'[101] In Yorkshire poppies were known as blind-eyes, because if they were placed too near they would cause blindness.[102] Cornish people often knew poppies as wart-flowers and believed that handling them would produce warts,[103] while in Cambridgeshire children were taught that they should avoid smelling poppy flowers as to do so would cause nosebleeds.[104]

It seems probable that these beliefs were propagated by adults in the hope that they would discourage children from venturing into corn fields and trample down growing crops to pick poppy flowers.

Other beliefs seem to have been brought into being to discourage children from venturing into potentially dangerous places.

> From an elderly friend in Porthmockie, about 30 miles from Burghead [Moray]: Deadman's bells = sea campion . . . it was untouchable, never picked and brought into the house; she thinks the reason for this ban was that in that area of steep cliffs it grew on rock ledges, highly dangerous for children. A friend who used to live in Buckie knew sea campion as devil's hatties; it grew in a dangerous area called 'The Back o' the Head', i.e. the headland of Burghead'.[105]

In east Dorset, yellow waterlilies, known locally as dillflowers, and marsh marigolds, also known as kingcups, were among the flowers that were not allowed indoors.[106] In Derbyshire,[107] Hampshire[108] and Staffordshire[109] bulrushes, which grow at the margins of ponds and rivers, were considered to bring bad luck when brought indoors. In the 1950s Birmingham children were told that bringing bulrushes indoors would bring a death to the family.[110] As they dry, the seedheads of bulrushes release masses of tiny fluffy seeds that drift around and attach themselves to furnishings, thus providing another reason for banning them from the homes of the house-proud.

Duckweed, one of the world's smallest plants, often forms dense mats on the surface of still water, making it appear solid. In parts of north-west England, the bogey Jenny Greenteeth was associated with duckweed-covered pools:

> As a child about 50 years ago in the Liverpool area, I was frightened by Jenny Greenteeth, a sort of fairy, who would drag people down into deep pools. Jenny was particularly associated with pools covered with duckweed.[111]

Alternatively Jenny (or Jinny) Greenteeth was simply a name given to duckweed:

> I was brought up in the Upton/Cronton area of the west side of Widnes in Lancashire (now Cheshire) about 12 miles inland from Liverpool. It was, and still is, largely a farming area, and many of the fields contain pits – never ponds – which, I believe, are old marl pits. Some of them have quite steep sides. Jinny was well known to me and my contemporaries and was simply the green weed, duckweed, which covered the surface of stagnant water. Children who strayed too close to the edge of these pits would be warned

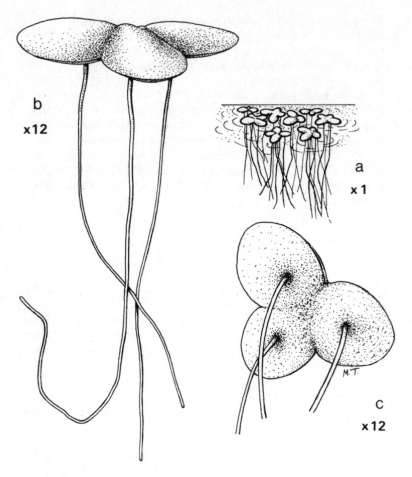

6. Duckweed, drawing by Margaret Tebbs, 1983.

to watch out for Jinny Greenteeth, but it was the weed itself which was believed to hold children under the water. There was never any suggestion that there was a witch of any kind there.[112]

Plants that stimulate good fortune are comparatively few. Four-leaved clovers, which are supposed to produce good luck, have a history going back to early in the sixteenth century. The idea that white heather is lucky seems to date back only to Victorian times.

In the *Gospelles of Dystaues*, published in 1507, it is stated:

He that fyndeth the trayfle [trefoil] with foure leues, and kepe it in reuerence knowe for also true as gospell yt he shall be ryche all his lyfe.[113]

John Melton in his *Astrologaster, or the Figurecaster* of 1620 recorded that if anyone found a four-leaved clover, 'he shall in a small while after finde some good thing'.[114]

In Ireland it was said that four-leaved clovers were found only where a mare drops her first foal.[115] According to the summary of part of a recording made in 1976 on the Hebridean island of Barra:

When a foal is born, it sneezes before trying to get to its feet so as to dislodge *dubhliath* [looks like cormorant or rabbit's liver, about the size of a crown coin] from its nostril. [The informant] kept one to prove its existence to young people. If it is kept for seven years, a four-leaved clover will grow from it.[116]

Four-leaved clovers are usually odd white clovers, which can be difficult to find, but once one leaf is found it is often possible to find several as some plants have a tendency to produce such leaves. In recent times four-leaved clovers have been considered to simply be lucky,[117] and as such they are frequently shown on greeting cards throughout the world. It is probable that a rhyme collected in 1965 from a factory-worker in Kingston, Jamaica, originated in such a card:

Luck is a question of pluck,
Doing things over and over;
Patience and skill,
Perseverance and will,
Are the four lucky leaves of a clover.[118]

In Cheshire the four leaves were said to represent health, wealth, success and a lover.[119]

In earlier times it was believed that the possession, or carrying, of a four-leaved clover would enable one to see fairies and break their powers of enchantment. Michael Aislabie Denham, in an article published in the 1840s, told of a Northumberland dairymaid, who returning from milking in the fields saw many fairies gambolling, but they were invisible to her companions:

the cause at length [was] discovered in her weise [pad of grass placed under a pail when carried on the head], which was found to be of four-leaved clover persons having about them a bunch or even a single blade of four-leaved clover being supposed to possess the power of seeing fairies.[120]

A similar story is given in Robert Hunt's collection of Cornish folklore, first published in 1865. A cow that had an udder containing at least three gallons of milk would never yield more than a gallon. One evening her milker accidentally placed a four-leaved clover in the pad on her head, whereupon she saw 'hundreds and thousands of Small People' swarming towards the cow and taking its milk.[121]

A widespread Irish folktale, which is also known throughout Europe from Scandinavia to Romania and can be traced back to the thirteenth century, tells of the showman and the cock.[122] This tale tells of a travelling showman who creates astonishment by displaying a cock that drags a heavy beam tied to one of its legs. Crowds gather to see this marvel, but an old man carrying a bundle of rushes on his back wonders what they are looking at. All he can see is a wisp of straw being pulled by a cock. He is unable to see the great wonder, and concludes everyone is mad. The showman, noting his disbelief, offers to buy the rushes, and the old man names his price. Once his rushes have been taken from him, the old man, like the rest of the crowd, sees a cock pulling a beam. Unknown to him, the old man had a four-leaved clover in his bundle, and this made him see through the showman's magic. The showman would have paid three times the value of the rushes.[123]

Years ago it was necessary to be either lucky or diligent to find a four-leaved clover. Nowadays plants that produce four leaflets are grown commercially.

> There are clover farms in the USA that specialize in producing four-leaved clovers. One of these clover farms covers 1.5 acres, with two large greenhouses and innumerable clover plants. A secret ingredient (biogenetically treated) is added to the feed to produce many four-leaved clovers on the plants. About 10,000 leaves are harvested daily and each is enclosed in plastic and sold as 'Good Luck' charms. Plants from the farm are not for sale, only the leaves, and the secret ingredient is jealously guarded![124]

Plants of four-leaved clovers are sometimes sold, but they are often of species of wood-sorrel (*Oxalis*), rather than a true clover.

The idea that white-flowered heather is lucky appears to be a Highland belief that was widely popularized by Queen Victoria. Charles Nelson, of the Heather Society, notes the lack of any reference to white heather being lucky in, for example, Ann Pratt's *Flowering Plants of Great Britain* (1855). Pratt observes that heather occasionally produces white flowers, and lists various uses made of heather in Scotland, but makes no mention of the white-flowered forms being lucky.[125] On 29 September 1855 the Queen recorded:

Our dear Victoria was this day engaged to Prince Frederick William of Prussia . . . during our ride up Craig-na-Ban this afternoon he picked a piece of white heather (the emblem of 'good luck'), which he gave her; this enabled him to make an allusion to his hopes.[126]

In 1862, when Queen Victoria met Princess Alexandra of Denmark, future wife of the Prince of Wales, she presented the Princess with 'a sprig of white heather picked by the Prince at Balmoral, saying she hoped it would bring her luck'.[127]

The reasons why white heather should be considered lucky are vague and unconvincing. One suggestion is that it is lucky because, unlike plants that produce normal coloured flowers, it escaped from being stained by blood that was spilt in ancient battles.[128] An alternative explanation links white heather with the Ossian epic cycle, which were supposedly discovered (or possibly forged) by James MacPherson in 1761. However, white heather does not feature in MacPherson's original work.

The story . . . is about Ossian's daughter, Malvinia, and her lover Oscar . . . a handsome, gallant hero, a warrior. One day a 'ragged' messenger brought Malvinia a bunch of purple heather, Oscar's last token of love before he was slain. Malvinia burst into tears and her tears fell on some heather turning the flowers from purple to white. Ever afterwards, as she wandered the moors, crying for her dead lover, the tears that dripped on to the heather instantly transformed the purple flowers. 'Although this is a symbol of my sorrow,' she declared, 'may white heather bring good fortune to all who find it'.[129]

White heather features as the clan badge of the MacPhersons, one of whose ancestors in post-Culloden times attributed his escape from searchers to the fact that he was sleeping on a clump of white heather.[130]

Since at least early in the twentieth century white heather has featured on greeting cards, Scottish postcards, wedding stationery and items of sale in Scottish gift shops.

An interesting example of a plant that has become 'lucky' within the last few decades is the money tree. This is the easily grown succulent houseplant *Crassula ovata* (formerly known as *C. argentea* and *C. portulacea*); English names include dollar plant,[131] jade plant, tree-of-happiness[132] and tree-of-heaven.

It appears that the name money tree was known as far back as the early 1970s,[132] but it was not until January 1978 that the name became widespread. In January that year a woman interviewed on the BBC television programme *Nationwide* explained how her luck had dramatically improved since she had acquired a 'money tree', which she exhibited for viewers to see. The 'tree' created a minor sensation and was eventually identified as *Crassula ovata*. By August many London florists were stocking small plants priced between 50p and £1.50 each.[134] Television, often stated to be the destroyer of folklore, can function as a super-efficient propagator of folk beliefs, particularly when it is reinforced by the popular press.

On 23 August 1982 *The Sun* reported:

Joyce Brown proved that money DOES grow on trees when she won £20,000 on The Sun's bumper bingo competition. Three weeks ago her sister Maureen gave her a money plant – told her if she talked nicely to it she would have a win. Last week Mrs Brown, 60, of Norwich, Norfolk, won £70 at a local bingo club. 'I said thank you very much to my plant, went to bed and the next morning my husband Neville woke me up shouting "You've won on The Sun."'

Similarly, on 24 January 1983 it was reported that 'green-fingered granny Clarice Cowell celebrated a £40,000 Sun Bingo win in champagne style yesterday – and said a big thank you to her lucky money plant'.

Occasionally it is said that if a money tree is given away its owner's luck goes with it.[135] Apparently, more widespread is the belief luck could be encouraged by placing a coin, or several coins in, or under, a money tree's pot. In January 1996 an author reported that the day after she had placed three one-pound coins under her money tree's pot, a cheque for £100 arrived from the US as payment for a magazine article.[136] In August 1997 the owner of a fish-and-chip shop in Balham, London was advised by a customer to put 10p in her money tree's pot:

I put 10p in the bottom of mine, and the next week I won £10 on the Lottery; I'd never won anything on the Lottery before. I read about it in a book. A woman had a cousin staying from Mexico, who told her that she should put a 10p piece at the bottom of her money-tree's pot – just 10p would be enough, it needn't be more. So I did that, and next week I won £10 on the Lottery.

Culinary herbs attracted their own folk beliefs. Parsley should be sown by the head of the household, or thrived where the 'wife wears the trousers',[137] and should not be given away or transplanted.

Someone gave me a root of parsley and a neighbour said it was unlucky. Anyway, I tossed my head and thought 'so what'. Not long after my husband died. So that's the last I will grow.[138]

In west Dorset in the late 1950s it was said: 'Transplant parsley, transplant death'.[139]

When offered parsley seedlings a friend recoiled in alarm: Transplant parsley, transplant sorrow.[140]

Another herb that was said to thrive best where the wife is dominant was sage.[141] At Bishops Nympton in Devon:

After a wedding the bride and bridegroom must each plant a small sage bush brandise-wise. The size to which the sage bushes grow will show which will be the ruler in the house; it will of course be the planter of the larger of the two bushes.[142]

Early in the 1880s a Buckinghamshire farmer informed Hilderic Friend that the health of sage plants in their garden indicated a family's prosperity, 'at one time when he was doing badly, the sage began to wither; but as soon as the tide turned the plant began to thrive again'.[143]

Occasionally rosemary was said to flourish best where the wife was dominant.[144] In the 1920s, a Mrs Taylor of Norwich recalled:

A woman came to ask me with many apologies whether I would plant some rosemary cuttings, she did not wish to be rude, and Mrs Wist had said it was a very delicate thing to ask anyone to strike rosemary cuttings, but she did want a bush so badly. I said I did not mind doing it for her, why should it be such a delicate thing to ask anyone. She replied 'don't you know it will only strike in the house where the mistress is master, and if it won't strike here, it won't strike anywhere'. So I got 14 shoots off the branch. Eleven grew, three didn't. My husband was so interested that he went to look at the cuttings every day, and said the three that did not grow were evidently where he got a look in.[145]

More widespread was the belief that a bush in the garden provided protection. On Guernsey, where it was grown for good luck, 'the luck was stronger if the plant was received as a gift'.[146] In east Dorset a rosemary bush should be grown beside the doorway, to keep the witches away,[147] while in Essex rosemary in the garden would deter 'witches, goblins or even the Devil'.[148] In Dorset and Hampshire, rosemary was known as the friendship bush:[149]

You always had to plant rosemary in your garden, so that you wouldn't be short of friends.[150]

Thus people viewed plants as liable to bring misfortune, or less usually good luck, and many of these superstitions continue to survive. As is the case with horoscopes, it only needs one coincidence for a half-forgotten saying to emerge as a deeply held belief. People who have been told that having lilac indoors causes death are unlikely to take the belief seriously, until they fill vases with lilac blossom and an elderly relative dies. Even if the death was not unexpected, they will think twice before bringing in lilac in the future, and, whereas in the past superstitions were slowly spread from neighbour to neighbour by word of mouth, now they can be transmitted around the world in less than a few minutes.

6

SIMPLE PASTIMES

Children who found a summer afternoon seemingly endless, or who were banished to distant fields to scare birds, turned to surrounding plants to provide amusement.

The first simple pastimes they learnt came from adults.

> Daisy chains were made by children to hang round their necks. The end of each stalk was split a little way with the finger nail to make an opening big enough to poke the next daisy's head through and so on until the chain was long enough to go round one's neck.[1]

Some folklorists have rather unconvincingly suggested that daisy chains prevented children from being carried off by fairies: 'daisies are a sun symbol and therefore protective magic'.[2]

Another pastime used by adults to amuse small children was the squeezing of the calyx of a hedge, or large, bindweed flower causing its white corolla (petals) to be ejected.

> As a child my granny taught me to 'pop' the open flowers out of their sepals chanting 'Granny, granny, pop out of bed' – as children my brother and I would see how far we could make them fly.[3]

In north Kent people said 'Granny jump into bed, Granny jump out of bed',[4] while 'Granny jump out of the rocking chair' has been recorded from the Isles of Scilly.[5] No doubt children living on the Weald of Kent found a local name for bindweed – pisspots[6] – to be another source of amusement.

Adults would remove the leaf-tissue of sweet chestnut,[7] and horse chestnut leaves, leaving the veins, thus creating 'fishbones'.[8]

Children blew dandelion 'clocks' – ripe seedheads – to tell the time: 'if it took three puffs to blow [the seeds on] the head away, it was three o'clock'.[9] Local names that refer to this pastime include: old-man's clock in Devon,[10] one-o'clock-two-o'clock,[11] and shepherd's clock in Somerset,[12] time-tables in Hampshire,[13] and doon-head clock in Scotland.[14]

Alternatively:

We used to blow dandelion seeds and count – 'This year, next year, sometime, never' (to get married)[15]

Or:

Dandelion seed-heads when perfect were used to find out whether someone loved you or not by blowing short breaths at the plant and with each breath reciting 'He loves me, he loves me not', until all the seeds had blown away and the last blow decided the result![16]

The floating seeds of dandelions and similar seeds were known as fairies and it was thought lucky to catch one.[17] In the 1940s, in Elgin, Moray:

We believed that the flying seeds were fairies, and blowing them released them from capture! If you could catch a passing fairy, you would make a wish before releasing it, then let it fly away in the wind.[18]

However, youngsters must have been wary of doing such things as there was a widespread belief, both in the British Isles,[19] and in Europe,[20] that the handling of dandelion flowers would lead to bed-wetting. Thus dandelions were known as pee-beds in Cumbria,[21] pee-in-bed in Lancashire,[22] piss-in-the-beds in County Offaly,[23] and wet-the-bed in Stockport, Greater Manchester.[24]

If buttercup flowers held under a child's chin produced a yellow reflection it indicated that the child liked butter.[25] Sometimes, by extension, a yellow reflection indicated a wealthy life ahead,[26] a life in which one would eat butter, rather than dripping or margarine. In the nineteenth century 'rustics in the Midland Counties' knew buttercups by the name of crazy:

'Throw those nasty flowers away,' said a countrywoman to some children who had gathered their handfuls of buttercups, 'for the smell of them will make you crazy.'[27]

Although this belief seems to have died out many years ago, the name crazy was remembered in Gloucestershire in the 1990s.[28]

A widespread activity was blow a blade of grass,[29] or a privet leaf,[30] placed between the thumbs to produce a 'whistle', or, perhaps more accurately, 'strange noises'. On the Isles of Scilly children made similar use of leaves of the naturalized eastern gladiolus, which they knew as whistling jacks,[31] or, in 1940 on St Martin's, as squeakers.[32] In County Antrim leaves of montbretia, another naturalized member of the iris family, were similarly used; 'different tones are produced depending on the breadth of the leaf'.[33]

I was taught by other children in my Dorset village 70-odd years ago to produce an ear-splitting whistle from a leaf of common lime. Leaves were at their best for this purpose in June, when fully developed but flexible. I recently demonstrated to impressed grandchildren that I have not lost this art. The leaf is held taut against the lips.[34]

Toy musical instruments could be made from the leaves of greater plantain, known in Somerset as banjo leaves.[35] In Helston, Middlesex, in the 1930s, greater plantain leaf

was picked and the stalk partly severed to expose the tough veins, these then made a violin (my grandchildren now make guitars!).[36]

In Hampshire:

Broad-leaved plantain: after making a cut across the stem with the thumb nail, the lower part of the stem could be gently pulled down leaving the veins exposed – a 'banjo'.[37]

Devon children made 'music' using biting stonecrop, known as crowdy-kit-o'-the-wall, stems, 'stripped of their leaves and scrapped across each other fiddle-fashion'.[38] In the same county, water figwort was known as crowdy-kit:

An interesting word, coming from the Welsh for fiddle . . . this plant is known as 'fiddles', and fiddle-wood' in some places, 'so called because the stems are by children stripped of their leaves and scraped across each other . . . when they produce a squeaking noise.[39]

Girls in the Cambridgeshire village of Horseheath:

made whistles . . . [using] the stems of white dead-nettle which were soft to cut. It was easy to make the mouthpiece by cutting off a stem slantwise and shaving a flat on top and it was not hard to make the vent. Never the less, many attempts had to be made before an instrument was produced that would whistle.[40]

Boys made whistles from twigs, usually of sycamore. In the Pembrokeshire village of St Nicholas in the late 1920s:

Spring arrived to the music of hedgerow whistles. First efforts began at the end of March when buds of hedge sycamore were pushing out pale green spikes, tinged with pink, covered with pale silky hairs, though best results came later when the tinted veined leaves as well as flowers were fully formed. Then the shoots, thick as walking sticks, were cut off and trimmed into six-inch lengths, scored round with a penknife an inch from the end. The sugary wand was soaked with spittle, and then, holding it rigid in a handkerchief, first attempts were made to loosen the bark. It had to come off – snickingly – in one piece or one had to begin again. Then with a little channel to let in air, and the bark replaced and pulled over the tapering mouthpiece, the whistle was ready to join the birds – though unlike those music-makers, sycamore whistles became gurgley with spit.[41]

In the Furness district of Lancashire, whistles were made from willow twigs:

> After the small branches are cut to proper form the bark is notched round with a knife, it is then beat on the knee with the knife haft, and the following lines are repeated:
>
> Sip sap, sip sap,
> Willie, Willie, Whitecap.[42]

Elsewhere children removed the central pith from elder stems to make whistles. Or, in County Donegal, boys made whistles from the stems of water horsetail, known locally as *feadoge* or pipes.[43]

Another pastime that required similar skills was the production of peashooters. In Wales:

> Japanese knotweed was increasingly being used for making peashooters from the 1920s onwards . . . In some parts of north Wales this plant had no name and it was referred to generally as a form of wild rhubarb. However, by the 1930s it was being referred to generally as *cegid* or *cecs* (i.e. a plant with a hollow stem) which might indicate its acceptance into Welsh plant folklore – or at least children's folklore! As a child in north Wales in the 1950s this plant featured in our efforts at making peashooters – we called the plant peashooter, a name which persists as in 'there are peashooters growing down by the river'. However, fieldwork among schoolchildren in the 1980s in north Wales failed to elicit one example of such use.[44]

Shetland children made their peashooters from stems of hogweed (spootitrump) and wild angelica (swittik).[45] Similarly, in Middlesex:

We used cow parsley stems as peashooters, using hawthorn berries – agars – as peas.[46]

The *Belfast Newsletter* of 10 February 1992 carried a short article about 'missile launchers' in Ulster. In Sion Mills, County Londonderry, blowpipe guns were made from elderberry, locally known as boothery. A native of Ardstraw, County Tyrone, recalled how '70 years back . . . he took the pith out of a branch of the [elder] bush and used it as a rustic rocket launcher for such missiles as peas and chewed up paper', while in Mallusk, on the outskirts of Belfast:

Bob Anderson and his mates used the hollow stem of wild parsley or myrr [sic], as it was commonly called . . . this was perfect for propelling haws. 'A well directed haw to the ear sure made the target yelp, The flesh was eaten off the haw and the stone was the ammunition.'

Children seem to have got great amusement from throwing cleavers, or goosegrass, at playmates, so that it stuck to their clothing.

During my childhood in Sussex/Kent in the 1920s and 1930s: if goosegrass was thrown at a girl's back and stuck there without her being aware of it, she had a sweetheart. If she took it off and dropped it, it would form the initial of her sweetheart-to-be.[47]

The sticky burs of goosegrass, which stick on one's clothes when walking in long grass are known as sweethearts, and are considered certain proof that one has been with one's sweetheart.[48]

In Shropshire, rough balls of goosegrass were thrown at a playmate's clothing, and the number of burs which remained on the clothing indicated the numbers of suitors its wearer might expect.[49]

Local names that seem to relate to such practices include: hug-me-close in Dorset,[50] kisses in Shropshire[51] and Suffolk,[52] lovers' knots in Wiltshire[53] and sticky backs in Dublin.[54] Another widespread name for the plant, sticky willy (or willies),[55] no doubt also added to the general amusement.

A Guernsey name for goosegrass was *la coue* (the tail). On April Fools Day country children would 'slyly stick wisps of this clinging plant on each other's backs, and then start the cry "*La coue! La coue!*"'[56]

In Essex:

As children . . . we threw burs of burdock on to the backs of unsuspecting friends. If they stuck they had a sweetheart; if they fell off after a short while their affection was not reciprocated. I lived in the then countryside of the Chigwell/Hainault area, but my children played the same game 20 years later at Witham, Essex.[57]

More frequently burdock burs were thrown by rather vicious children, who perhaps wanted to settle old scores. In the Market Drayton area of Shropshire in the 1930s and 1940s:

> Burdock heads were thrown into the hair or woolly clothing of others. You sometimes had to cut them out of hair, so tangled did they become.[58]

A pastime that must have occupied many summer afternoons used the flowers of ribwort plantain, In County Longford:

> As children we played a game called 'Fighting Cocks' with the long-stemmed seed-heads of ribwort plantain. Two children each took a 'cock' and they kept hitting them against each other until the head was knocked off one. Then 'My cock won.'[59]

According to Iona and Peter Opie:

> In the historical poem *Histoire de Guillaume le Maréchal*, written soon after 1219, the story is told of how the boy William Marshall, later to become Earl Pembroke and Regent of England, but then not ten years old, was detained as a hostage in the king's camp, while Stephen was besieging Newbury. One day the boy picked out the plantains (*les chevaliers*) from the cut grass strewn on the floor of the tent, and challenged the king, '*Beau sire chiers, volez joer as chevaliers?*' The challenge being accepted, William laid half the 'knights' on the king's lap, and asked who was to have the first stroke. 'You' said the king. Holding out his knight, which the small boy promptly beheaded, greatly to his own delight. King Stephen (strictly in accordance with the rules of the game) then held out another plantain, but the game was interrupted. It matters not whether the story is apocryphal; as early as the thirteenth century a poet has shown himself to be familiar with the game.[60]

This game had a variety of names, including Blackmen, Cocks and Hens, Hard Heads, Knights,[61] and Soldiers,[62] and, in Scotland and northern England, kemps (cf. the Old English *cempa*, a warrior, and Middle Englsh *kempen*, to fight or contend with).[63] In Aberdeen in the 1930s the game was known as carl doddies, a name that extended to the plant itself:

During the 45 rebellion supporters of Charles, the Young Pretender, were known as Carls, the supporters of King George were known as Doddies – Doddie being the local name for George. Children emulated their parents and took sides, hence the game's name.[64]

Unfortunately for this theory, the name carl doddy and variations thereof have been given to a variety of other species, none of which appear to be associated with similar games. In Angus melancholy thistle was known as carl doddie,[65] and in south-west Scotland daisies were known as curl-doddies.[66] Both names have been interpreted as 'curly heads'. An Orkney name for white clover was curl-doddy,[67] in County Donegal devil's-bit scabious was known as carl doddie: 'the idea is a long-stalked flower. Doddie = bald.'[68] Even more confusingly, in Shetland curlie-doddie was a name for early purple orchid,[69] or curly doddies was 'a general name for all Shetland orchises'.[70]

In northern Ireland, children would twist the stalk of a devil's-bit scabious flower, and 'as it slowly untwists in the hand, say to it, "Curl doddy on the midden, Turn around an' tak' my bidden".'[71]

In another game involving ribwort plantain:

The stem and flowering heads of plantain were used as a missile, by somehow knotting and flicking the ripe seed-head.[72]

Competitions would be held to see who could fire their seedheads the furthest.[73] In Monmouthshire in the 1950s:

Cameras – plantains which grow in grass – flexible stems bent around to pop the seed-head at someone, which was called 'taking their photo'.[74]

In Kent:

I have no idea what the plant is called, but I believe it is some kind of plantain . . . They were used as weapons; if you wind the stem around itself, then fire off the head. The correct thing to say when firing these weapons is 'Grandmother said' (pause) 'Jump out of bed'. The first phrase should correspond to the command 'Ready'. The pause would be 'Aim'. 'Jump out of bed' is 'Fire'. They can go quite a long way if you do it right.[75]

In the late nineteenth century boys in Norwich area called the horse-chestnut leaf-stalks knuckle-bleeders:

Boys try to get one another to allow them to hit them over the knuckles with the end which grows nearest the branch.[76]

Similarly, in Somerset hands-in-pockets was a local name for Virginia creeper. In the autumn its leaf-stalks were 'used by children to whip the knuckles of others with the admonition "Hands-in-pockets."'[77]

Another game that used horse-chestnut leaf-stalks was played in Chesterfield, Derbyshire, in the 1950s:

> A stalk was held at each end by one person and another person would place a similarly held stalk between it at right angles. Each would pull in an attempt to break the other's stalk. The winner would then be challenged with another fresh stalk.[78]

Girls used to spend a great deal of time trying to work out who, or when, they would marry. Petals were plucked off a daisy, or an ox-eye daisy (also known as dog daisy).

> In Wales the daisy is generally selected by the doubting maiden who is wishful to test the fidelity of her lover. Gathering a daisy, she commences plucking the petals off, saying with each one, 'Does he love me? – much – a little – devotedly – not at all,' and the last petal decides the question.[79]

> The flower [of dog daisy] was used in a game where one would pluck a petal each time as he/she recited: he/she loves me, she/he loves me not, until all the petals were gone.[80]

Another simple method of divination involved rye-grass. In Sussex:

> Children still play with the flowers and grasses as they did in days of yore, and every year they sit on the grass and pull off the seeds of what's-your-sweetheart grass (rye-grass) to find out the profession of their future husbands: 'Tinker, tailor, soldier, sailor, pot-boy, plough-boy, gentleman, thief.[81]

Local names for rye-grass provide widespread evidence for similar activities: aye-no-bent in Gloucestershire,[82] love-me-love-me-not,[83] tinker-tailor-grass and yes-or-no in Somerset,[84] and tinker-tyler grass in East Lothian.[85]

A slightly less easy method of divination involved an even-ash leaf, which could be difficult to find. Most ash leaves have a terminal leaflet, thus having an odd number of leaflets; even-ash leaves lack a terminal leaflet and thus have an even number. In the late nineteenth-century County Donegal:

> A girl carries a leaf with an even number of leaflets. The first man

she meets she asks the name of. His Christian name will be that of her future husband.[86]

In Dorset, at about the same period:

The girl who wishes to divine who her future lover or husband is to be plucks an even ash, and holding it in her hand, says:

> 'The even ash in my hand,
> The first I meet shall be my man.'
> Then putting it into her glove, adds:
> 'The even ash leaf in my glove,
> The first I meet shall be my love.'
> And lastly, into her bosom, saying:
> 'The even ash leaf in my bosom,
> The first I meet shall be my husband.'

Soon after which the future lover or husband will be sure to make his appearance.[87]

According to a 52-year-old west Dorset woman, in 1976:

Start at the bottom leaflet on the left-hand side and say:

> An even ash is in my hand
> The first I meet will be my man.
> If he don't speak and I don't speak,
> This even ash I will not keep.

As each word is said, count a leaflet around the leaf until the rhyme is completed (this probably entails going round the leaf several times). When the rhyme is finished, continue by reciting the alphabet until the bottom right-hand leaflet is reached. The letter given to this leaflet gives the initial of your boyfriend. Two or three leaves may be used so that you get a greater range of letters.[88]

The same woman also recalled making cowslip balls to find out who she would marry:

You would go out, pick bunches of cowslips, and bring them back home. You'd have two chairs and tie a piece of string, about 12 inches long, between them (like when you're making a cord). Then you would pick off the flower-heads and hang them on the string with about half the flowers on either side – the more flower-heads the better. Twist the string and tie the ends together to form a ball. Toss the ball backwards and forwards continually saying:

> Tissty-tossty tell me true,
> Who am I going to be married to?
> Tinker, tailor, soldier, sailor,
> Rich man, poor man, beggar man, thief.

You would eventually marry a man with the same occupation as the one named when the last flower fell out.[89]

In Wales children would toss cowslip balls and catch them using only their right hands while reciting:

> Pistey, postey, four-and-forty,
> How many years shall I live?
> One, two, three, four
> and so on until the ball falls at the fatal number.[90]

A Gloucestershire woman recalled in 1992 how an aunt took the children out into the fields, where she made cowslip balls:

We tossed them in the air and she would recite:

> Tisty Tosty cowslip ball
> Tell me where you're going to fall?
> Dursley, Uley, Coaley, Cam,
> Frampton, Fretherne, Arlingham?

. . . all the places mentioned are in the Severn Valley.[91]

Elsewhere children made cowslip balls as toys, or fragrant decorations. In County Laois, where they were known as dodge-balls: 'children have great sport dodging with their hands in the air seeing how long they are able to keep doing so'.[92] In the 1940s Cambridgeshire children made cowslip, or to use the local name, paigle, balls and placed them in a saucer of water.[93] A man who spent his childhood in Cradley, Herefordshire in the early 1930s recalled:

In those days the visitor's room was devoid of running water, but had a beautiful marble-topped washstand on which stood a very large and pretty porcelain bowl, with an equally large matching water jug standing in it . . . The cowslip ball was placed carefully in the visitor's water jug, and the strings tied round the handle to suspend it there. We were told that this would 'make the water smell nice'. I don't think it actually imparted any delectable odour, but at least it was a nice welcoming gesture.[94]

Small corn-dolly-like ornaments were made from the grass-crested dog's-tail. In Yorkshire:

> During the summer children were fond of making 'trees' or 'dollies' out of dog-tail grass (*Cynosurus cristatus*). Gathering a handful, they twist other individual heads of grass round the stalks of the former, binding some bunches of more heads at intervals down the stems, so that they stick out from the sides in a fancied resemblance to branches of trees. In Lincolnshire, the men used to amuse themselves by making similar devices on Sunday afternoons. Beyond passing the time, it did not appear to be done for any definite purpose, though the 'tree' was often presented to the lady-love when completed.[95]

In the twentieth century similar ornaments were made in Dorset, where they were known as cat's-tails,[96] Surrey, where they were known as trees or rat's-tails,[97] and Cornwall.[98]

Other pastimes that involved grasses were less pleasant. Meadow foxtail was avoided by children evacuated to Elgin during World War II, because it was believed to be infested with fleas,[99] but elsewhere:

> In north Derbyshire in the 1950s, the flowers would be stripped off the stalk of meadow foxtail grass, leaving the stem with the floret stalks. This would be quietly twiddled into the hair of the child sitting in the desk in front, A swift yank would speedily remove all the hair attached.[100]

> Talking of Chinese haircuts brought back painful memories of my Warwickshire preparatory school in the early forties. In my experience it was invariably meadow foxtail that was used. It produces flower-heads in time to function as an instrument of torture at the start of summer term, deployed on heads intently watching cricket.[101]

A flowering stem of a grass such as bent was said to represent a 'summer tree'. When its flowers were removed by pulling it between the thumb and forefinger it became a 'winter tree' (i.e. it was leafless). The removed flowers were a 'bunch of flowers', until thrown in the air, when they became 'April showers'.[102] In Aberdeen, during World War II:

Another trick we used to play on each other used feathery-seeded grasses of various kinds (e.g. *Agrostis*). The person performing the trick would pick two long stems with seeded heads and grip the middles of the two stems in his mouth so that the respective heads were on each side of his mouth. He would then use his lips to waggle the heads and stems backwards and forwards. 'Bet you can't do that!' he would challenge his stooge. As soon as the latter placed the grasses in his teeth to try to perform this feat, the trickster would quickly pull the two ends so that he was left spitting out a mouthful of grass seeds, He was never caught that way again![103]

A woman born in Enniskellen, County Fermanagh in 1921 remembered this pastime as the 'whisker game'.[104]

Wall barley, also known as barley-grass, appears to have been used in more pastimes than any other wild grass. In Shropshire in the 1940s:

Barley-grass was believed to have almost magical properties. If a complete head was placed stalk first inside the cuff of one's jacket, as one walked and swung one's arms it would ride up the sleeve and come out at the top.[105]

Presumably, the name caterpillars given to wall barley on Bermondsey, London, referred to this pastime.[106]

In Leicestershire in the 1940s, wall barley was known as grandmother grass. Children would surreptitiously break the flower-stalk in half and then reassemble it. They would then say 'Grandmother, grandmother, jump out of bed' and flick the top half off.[107]

North London children in the late 1950s and early 1960s would 'pick a flower-spike of barley-grass . . . and break it into quite effective darts which could easily get lodged in the hair or clothing of whoever we threw them at – dislodging them was, of course, another matter!'[108] It was sometimes believed that such darts dispersed fleas. Children in the Southampton area, Hampshire, in about 1950:

used to bombard each other with grass darts which we said were flea-ridden. They stuck on very well to woollen clothes when thrown, and as children we used to get very ratty if we got one on our jumper without realising it for sometime, as everyone said they were full of fleas![109]

Sometimes these darts were known as 'flea darts', their 'irritating hairs would presumably have been the fleas'.[110] In the Whitstable area of Kent, wall barley was 'put down the neck to annoy people'.[111]

Children (and rural workers) chewed or sucked young grass stalks for refreshment:

When we were down on the moors (now known as the Levels . . .) working at hay-making, etc., if we ran out of something to drink and the ditches were nearly empty or full of water-weeds, we would gently pull out the middle part of a big grass shoot and suck and nibble the lovely pale yellow part which had been hidden down in the bottom of the plant.[112]

Although there was a widespread belief that the picking or handling of poppy flowers could cause thunder, headache, earache, or blindness,[113] girls collected them to make poppy dolls:

We made Chinese-men poppy dollys. The petals were turned back, Two pieces of stalk were used, one as a cross-piece for the arms, and another to add to the still attached stalk to make a second leg. A piece of wool gave a waist to the poppy petal dress, and a Chinese face drawn on the exposed seed-box.[114]

When my children were at school in Craigavan, Northern Ireland, c. 1969, they used to say to me 'Do you want to see the fairies dance?' They would pull a flower – either a field poppy or lesser [i.e. field] bindweed – and pull the petals back over the stem to make a 'skirt', and holding the stem between thumb and forefinger just behind the flowerhead (within the skirt) move the finger to and fro to cause the flower-head to partially rotate and return – this caused the 'fairy' to dance.[115]

Giving pretend tea parties, or playing shops were two ways in which an afternoon might be filled:

Daisy petals could be rice or coconut, and sorrel seeds packed tightly in a glass jar with a little water added looked very much like jam, while the heads of pineapple-weed made dainty cup-cakes for a doll's tea-party. Probably the plant which contributed most to the pretend house was dock. The seeds, varying in plumpness, could become several things, e.g. sugar, pulses, grains, or even rough salt, but the stalks were almost always rhubarb. Dock leaves were very versatile too, but perhaps topped the list as kippers, followed fast by other fillets of fish and bacon rashers.[116]

Although many of the wild plants that were nibbled by children were probably also eaten by adults in earlier times, or in times of famine, some of these plants were probably only eaten by children. Although most parts of yew are poisonous, the red flesh (aril) that surrounds its seeds, can be eaten.

> When I was yoong and went to schoole, divers of my schoole fellowes and likewise myselfe did eat our fils of the berries of this tree . . . without any hurt at all, and that not one time, but many times.[117]

No doubt part of the attraction of these rather tasteless morsels lay in the names given to them: red-snot in Wye, Kent in the 1940s,[118] snat-berries in Northamptonshire,[119] snodgoggle in Essex,[120] snot-berry in Lincolnshire,[121] snot-gobbles in Bedfordshire in about 1915,[122] snots in Somerset,[123] snotter-berries on Staffordshire,[124] snotter-galls in Wiltshire,[125] snottle-berries in Yorkshire,[126] and snotty-gogs in Sussex.[127] Children sucked various flowers to extract the small amount of nectar they contained. The best known of these flowers, was, as its name suggests, honeysuckle:

> As children (I was born in 1943) we used to pick honeysuckle, remove the tip at the base of the flowers and suck the juice (nectar).[128]

Other plants known as honeysuckle for the same reason include fuchsia in Ireland,[129] red clover,[130] and white clover,[131] which was known as milkies in Moray,[132] and white dead-nettle.[133] Lousewort was known as honeysuckle in Hampshire.[134] Elsewhere it was known as bee-sookies, 'due to its nectar-filled flower-tubes',[135] hinney-flooer and sookies[136] in Shetland, bog honeysuckle in Ireland,[137] and honey-cup and wild honey in County Donegal.[138] Children also sucked the flowers of cowslips, but the name honeysuckle does not appear to have been extended to them:

> I'm nearly 75 . . . [during my childhood we] pulled the flowers out of cowslips to suck out the sweet drops of nectar.[139]

Boys looked around for tobacco substitutes:

> I was born in Chesterfield, Derbyshire, in 1921 . . . when I was about 10 I and some pals thought we would try smoking. Our pipes were hollowed out acorns, and grass for the stem. The 'tobacco' was mugwort. It was so dreadful that I was cured of smoking for ever.[140]

Similarly, near Truro, Cornwall, in the 1930s, mugwort, known as mugger – was smoked by schoolboys.[141] It appears that in earlier times mugwort was also smoked by adults. Murdoch McNeill, writing of Colonsay in the Hebrides in 1910, noted that mugwort leaves were smoked by old people,[142] possibly suggesting that mugwort was used as a substitute by anyone who could not afford the real thing. Similarly:

> An old lady, born c. 1870, from Crewkerne, Somerset, called mugwort (*Artemisia vulgaris*) moggle. She said the leaves, after being hung to dry, made substitute tobacco. My grandfather tried this during World War II, but was not overly impressed.[143]

Probably the most widespread tobacco substitute used by children was wild clematis, also known as traveller's joy, or old-man's beard:

> As a boy in the Croydon [Surrey] area, I knew the wild clematis as whippy-wood, and young gentlemen used to smoke it; its stem is like that of elder inside.[144]

In Sussex wild clematis was known as Tom-bacca or boys' bacca, 'because the boys cut the small wood in pieces to smoke like cigars'.[145]

In the 1960s Norfolk boys:

> Always smoked elder leaves when money was not available for tailor-made cigarettes. We spent much time in the woodland of Thetford Chase, where on our regular walks we would break down, but not completely snap off, small sprigs of elder. We found that if we severed the supply of sap completely the leaves on the sprig would dry out resulting in a hot strong smoke. We found that if the leaves remained just slightly damp they were quite a pleasant smoke. It was obviously trial and error, sometimes they remained too wet to burn properly. We would stuff the leaves very lightly into the stems of various umbellifers . . . We actually preferred these cigarettes to the tailor-made, but they were not available during winter.[146]

Soon after schools reassemble for the autumn term, horse-chestnut trees receive their annual assault from boys who cannot wait for conkers to fall naturally:

> Is it possible for horse-chestnut trees to have the fruit doctored, but keep the tree healthy? . . . Where I live we have such a tree and we are plagued each year with children throwing large sticks, stones and even house bricks to knock down the horse-chestnuts. This year has been exceptionally bad. The children come over our garden fence, damage the fence, and pull parts of the wooden structure away as missiles.[147]

The horse chestnut, native to the Balkans, was introduced to the British Isles in about 1615,[148] but it seems as if the use of its seeds in the game of conkers did not become popular until much later. Britten and Holland in their *Dictionary of English Plant-names* (1878–86) give only three references to the game. Although Britten organized boys' clubs and Holland was the father of a large family, they appear to have had little, if any, first-hand knowledge of conkers:

CONQUERORS – The fruit of *Aesculus hippocastanum* L. – Ches[hire], where children thread them on strings and strike them one against each other. The one remaining unbroken is the conqueror.

KONKER-TREE – *Aesculus hippocastanum* L. – Som[erset], 'A game known as Konkers is played with the fruits.'[149]

A further entry, under the name *oblionker*, is derived from *Notes & Queries*:

Having heard this word [oblionker] as being in common use at Ledbury in Herefordshire, I wrote to Mr Piper of that town . . . His reply was: – Oblionker is a game played by boys with horse-chestnuts: each of the contending players passes a piece of string a foot or so in length, and having a knot at the end to prevent escape (a with of yellow willow answers equally well), through a chestnut. They then strike alternately at each other's nut whilst held suspended, and he who succeeds in breaking that of his adversary is the winner. The first who utters the following rhyme has the right to begin:

'Obli, obli, O,
My first go.'

And on striking it is customary to say:

'Obli, obli, onker,
My nut will conker.'

The chestnut that has demolished the greatest number of its congeners acquires proportionate reputation, and the successes theretofore scored by the vanquished opponent are added to the achievements of the victor.[150]

This name, as obly-onker, continued in use in Worcestershire until the late 1940s, when children 'preceded the game with the solemn chant:

> Obly, obly-onker
> My best conker,
> Obly-obly O,
> My best go!'[151]

Although 'conker' may be a corruption of 'conqueror', an alternative theory is that the game is a descendent of an earlier one in which snails' shells were crushed; hence its name is derived from 'conch'.[152] Another earlier game was known as cob-nut. In Leicestershire:

> Strings are passed through nuts, by which to use them in play-ing. Each player, in turn, holds his cob-nut up by the string to be 'cobbed' at by the other, and the player who first breaks his adversary's nut is the winner of the game.[153]

By the second decade of the twentieth century the game of conkers seems to have become popular and widespread. In 1914 it was noted that horse-chestnut trees 'have such an extraordinary fascination for small boys in furnishing material for the game of "conkers" (conquerors) that the value of the species in some districts is seriously diminished by their efforts with sticks and stones to bring down the nuts before they naturally fall'. This problem can be overcome by planting the variety 'Baumanni', 'which has double flowers which are long lasting and don't produce nuts'.[154]

Methods of procuring a winning conker varied. In Ayton, North Yorkshire, it was believed that a nut that was caught as it fell from the tree would be a 'hundreder'.[155] In the Northam area of Southampton in the 1930s:

> Recipes for hardening winners were varied: it might be to part-bake the conker, or soak it in paraffin. Ginger Blake, Ken's friend, said his Dad recommended soaking them in the 'Po' overnight before baking. Ken confided in me that he didn't really want to win Ginger's current prize conker.[156]

According to Jeff Cloves' *Official Conker Book*:

> Baking and vinegar are the oldest known methods of hardening your potential Conqueror and are as old as the game. In the days when everybody had a fire in their hearth, conkers were left by the fire for a few days or shoved up the chimney. With care, they

wouldn't look any different from 'seasoners' [i.e. conkers which had stored for a year]. The same applied to baking conkers in the oven. This had to be done in a low oven for about half an hour. The other method was to pickle them in vinegar.[157]

Alternatively:

I recently caught my seven-year-old son using a microwave oven to harden his conkers.[158]

However, most schoolboys use fresh, untreated nuts, as at Shipley, West Yorkshire, in the 1940s:

In October most boys collected horse-chestnuts or 'conkers'. The term 'conking' covered both casually looking for them and undertaking exhaustive searches at weekends. On these expeditions much expert knowledge of the peculiarities of local trees and park-keepers was amassed. Trees with pink flowers tended to produce the inferior 'water conk', which was useless for the game of 'conkers', having nothing but fluid inside. Most park-keepers or 'parkies' objected to small boys in general, and the sport of knocking conkers off the trees with stones and sticks, or 'throwing for conks' in particular. Conkers were collected partly for their own sake; they are attractive objects and anyway small boys will collect almost anything. But they were collected ostensibly for the sake of the game. For 'conkers', large conkers had holes driven through them, and were threaded on strings. One player challenged another and perhaps claimed the right to begin by calling 'fuggy smack'. The opponent then held up his conker, dangling on its string, for the first player to aim a smack at it. They continued, aiming alternate smacks and probably watched by an excited crowd, until one conker disintegrated. The winning conker was then nominated a 'oner'. If it won again it became a 'twoer', and so on. Any score accredited to a beaten conker was passed on to the winner; thus, if a 'twoer' beat a 'fiver', it became an 'eighter'. In this way champion conkers sometimes built up large if somewhat exaggerated scores. They were carefully examined for signs of wear and tear, and maybe re-threaded to make them more secure. If the outer shell had been largely knocked off, but the kernel remained, it might be soaked in vinegar to make it harder than ever. These champion conkers could be swapped for quantities of sweets or marbles, bits of liquorice root, and so forth, but they were usually preserved by their owners. Crowds gathered to watch games in which such battered relics were concerned. As with all games there were ways of cheating at conkers. The most diabolical was to aim at your opponent's string, rather than his conker, in the hope of pulling it out of his hand and dashing it to the ground. Such treatment would obviously do no good, and one could always claim it had been an accident. Sometimes unfair play of this kind was penalised; if the offended party called 'strings' he was rewarded a free smack. There was an understandable but mistaken feeling that it was an advantage to have the smack; if your conker was cracked it would as soon break up from hitting as being hit. Sometimes, as bits of scattered conker flew everywhere, you thought you had won, only to find on looking at your string that it was your conker that was finished. Sometimes both players let go of their strings in the excitement, especially if they had become entangled; and then a dispute would arise, very serious to the players but amusing to the crowd, over which fragments belonged to which party . . . Some far-sighted boys would store champion conkers for next season, when they would be brought out as 'last-yearers', 'eighteeners' or whatever, very hard and venerable.[159]

Occasionally the game of conkers is taken up by adults who organize championships. The World Conker Championships have been held at Ashton, Northamptonshire, since 1965, when a group of anglers, frustrated by the cancellation of a sea-fishing trip, took consolation in playing conkers.[160] The championships, which take place on the second Sunday in October each year, consist of a men's competition with 256 competitors and a much smaller women's competition. Conkers are supplied by the organizers, and the winner of a round draws a new conker for the next round. Since 1965 the event has raised over £359,000 for charities for the blind and visually impaired.[161]

Smaller, but apparently well-established, events are held at Miskin, near Cardiff,[162] in mid Suffolk,[163] between the Military Knights of Windsor and the boys of St George's School, Windsor,[164] and Hampstead Heath, London.[165]

It is said that the game of conkers is known only in the British Isles.[166] *La Fédération Française de Conkers*, based in Bandiat, in the Dordogne, where it was founded by British expatriates in 1991, holds an annual championship.[167]

However, games similar to conkers are known elsewhere. Thus a woman who lived in the Western Australia township of Brown Hill between 1908 and 1917 recalled:

Another game the older boys liked to play was to thread a quandong (native peach) stone on the end of a string and compete by hitting at each other's stones until one was smashed.[168]

The same game, known as 'bullies', was being played in western New South Wales and South Australia until at least 1970.[169]

Conkers were also used in other children's games:

> They came in very handy for making furniture for my dolls' house. A plump, shiny chestnut was an excellent seat for a dining-room chair, while very long pins with glass heads formed legs and slats for the backs interwoven with wool. I was very proud of my work (age 7).[170]

> Over 40 years ago, at around the age of 10 . . . beside the usual fun of conkers, we also put them to use as stink-bombs. The local park contained a large pond which was surrounded by horse-chestnut trees. The majority of the wind-falls would land on the ground, but . . . many would end up floating in the water. As with the natural process of time, these would blacken and become brittle, allowing the water to seep through and turn the centre into a putrid yellow liquid. We would gather small quantities of these fragile blackened conkers, throw them on the ground, the brittle skin cracking and releasing its odorous liquid contents to the disgust of unsuspecting passers-by.[171]

Other fruits that were widely gathered by children were the hips of dog rose, which were used to produce an unpleasant itching powder:

> A school prank in east Hertfordshire, 1945–50 . . . the most awful material was made from rose hips – the hairs on the seeds being put down someone's neck – a bath and complete change of clothing being the only cure. [172]

In November 1991 similar practices were recorded from County Durham, Dorset in the 1970s, Blackpool, Lancashire in the 1950s, and Sutton, Surrey in the late 1930s.[173]

In the past plants provided children of all abilities with a free, readily available range of playthings. However, with an increase in the availability of mass-produced toys, a fear of allowing children to play unsupervised on open ground, a belief that the picking of any wildflower is wrong, and a lack of knowledge of which plants are harmless and which are harmful, it's probable that many of these pastimes will cease.

7

HISTORY AND LEGEND

Plants that displayed unusual characters, or grew in unusual situations, often became the focus of legends which explained these features. However, very often the 'unusual' was not spectacularly evident, giving the impression that at one time someone had looked closely, noticed an oddity and created a tale, which for some reason other people liked retelling so it entered oral tradition, local guidebooks and popular publications.

A County Galway legend, recorded in 1937, explained why the tips of rushes become withered and brown:

One night as St Patrick went to bed he warned his servant lad that if he talked in his sleep he might be impolite. The servant was warned to listen to all that the Saint said. After sleeping for a while the Saint shouted: 'Bad luck to Ireland!' The listening boy responded: 'If so, let it be on the tips of the rushes!' After sleeping a little longer the Saint shouted again: 'Bad luck to Ireland!' The boy answered: 'If so, let it be on the highest part of the white cows!' After another short sleep the Saint shouted: 'I'll say again what I've said already: "Bad luck to Ireland!"' The boy answered: 'If so let it be on the bottom of the furze!' On waking the Saint asked his servant if he had said anything during his sleep, and, if so, what. The boy replied that he had said 'Bad luck to Ireland!' three times. 'And what did you say?' asked the Saint. The boy explained what he had said. Ever since the tips of the rushes have been withered, the tips of the horns of white cows have been black, and the lower parts of gorse bushes have been withered, and every priest should have a boy serving him at Mass.[1]

Alternatively, in County Longford:

St Patrick got a piece of a dog to eat in a house one day. When he found out what it was he cursed the place. When he had cursed it he was sorry, but he couldn't take back the curse . . . without putting it on some other thing, so he put it on the tops of the rushes.[2]

Butterwort, which grows on damp moorland, was also associated with the activities of early Christian missionaries:

> One piece of lore first mentioned to me by an aunt on the Island of Soay (Skye) . . . [which] referred to a little heath flower that grew among the peat heather . . . The saying went that where the flower grew was where St Moalrudha touched the ground with his staff. I suppose that was meant to signify the extent of St Moalrudha's travels, which were, indeed, very wide.
>
> Professor Charlesworth [1889–1972] . . . once told me that when he was young in Antrim the flower was known as St Patrick's spit, or St Patrick's staff, attached to which was the story that while crossing a wide bog St Patrick lost his staff and unable to find a tree came upon one of these plants whose stem had grown so long and strong that he was able to use it as a staff. The flower on the head (which is shaped with a curve like a staff) never faded and afterwards wherever the staff touched the ground the flower sprang up.[3]

Since butterwort grows on desolate, unproductive areas, perhaps these legends suggest not only the saints' wide travels but also their concern for the most impoverished members of a community.

Lungwort was associated with the Virgin Mary, mother of Christ. This herb, which is frequently found in old-fashioned gardens, and is sometimes naturalized, has characteristic creamy-white spots on its leaves, and its flowers, which are pink when young, become blue with age.

> Lungwort is associated with the Virgin Mary because it has blue and pink flowers – these two colours being the colours of the Virgin's clothes in medieval paintings.[4]

Britten and Holland in their *Dictionary of English Plant-names* give an anecdote from Salisbury, Wiltshire, in which an old lady weeding a garden refused to pull up lungwort: "'Do ee know Sir, what they white spots be?" "No, I don't" "Why they be the Virgin Mary's Milk! so don't ee turn em out, for it would be very unlucky!"'[5]

Names that relate to this legend include the Monmouthshire Virgin Mary's milk-drops, and the Cheshire, Lady's milk-sile (sile = soil).[6] A particularly elaborate legend was recorded from Osmington, Dorset, where

> there is a survival of a sweet, simple, old-world piece of folklore about spotted liverwort. The cottagers like to have it in their gardens, and call it Mary's tears. The legend is that the spots on the

leaves are marks of the tears shed by St Mary after the crucifixion. Farther . . . her eyes were blue as the fully opened flower, and by weeping the eyelids became red as the buds.[7]

Good Friday plant, a Somerset name for lungwort,[8] presumably refers to a similar legend.

Plants with dark spots on their leaves are sometimes said to have been stained when Christ's blood dripped on to them at his crucifixion. In north Wales there was said to be a 'popular superstition' that the leaves of lords-and-ladies (also known as cuckoo pint or wild arum) acquired their spots in this way.[9] Similarly:

> One species of orchis, which in Cheshire is called Gethsemane, is said to have been growing at the foot of the cross, and to have received some drops of blood on its leaves: hence the dark stains by which they have ever since been marked.[10]

and:

> I was told by Mrs D (a devout Catholic) of Chillington, Ilminster, in the 1950s, that the red spots on the leaves of orchids are where the blood dropped from Christ when he was on the Cross.[11]

The single blotch on leaves of redshank, sometimes known as persicaria, can be dark and distinctive when plants grow in dryish exposed places, but becomes much less noticeable on plants that grow in the shade. In Gaelic-speaking areas of Scotland, redshank was known as Am boinne-fola (the blood-spot) or Lus chrann ceusaidh (herb of the tree of crucifixion): 'the legend being that this plant grew at the foot of the Cross'.[12] Similar beliefs have been recorded from west Cornwall,[13] and County Cork.[14]

Elsewhere redshank was associated with the Virgin Mary, or an unnamed murderess. In Oxfordshire it was said:

> The Virgin was wont of old to use its leaves for the manufacture of a valuable ointment, but that on one occasion she sought it in vain. Finding it afterwards, when the need had passed away, she condemned it, and gave it the rank of any ordinary weed. This is expressed in the local name: She could not find it in time of need. And so she pinched it for a weed. The mark on the leaf is the impress of the Virgin's finger and the persicaria is now the only weed that is not useful.[15]

Presumably the Shropshire name Virgin's thumb-mark,[16] refers to a similar legend.

Herbe traitresse . . . this name originates in a Guernsey legend to the effect that a woman who had committed a murder, wiped her blood-stained fingers on the leaves of the plant, which betrayed her, and led to her detection. Ever since the leaves have been marked in the centre by a dark spot.[17]

A Norfolk name, devil's arse-wipe,[18] suggests yet another explanation.

The Holy, or Glastonbury, Thorn is a variety of the common hawthorn which is unusual in that it flowers twice each year; in winter and at the usual time, in May. What appears to be the earliest mention of the Thorn can be found in a lengthy poem, *Here begynneth the Lyfe of Joseph of Armathia*, which is thought to have been written early in the sixteenth century. The poem states that three thorn trees growing on Wearyall Hill, just south of Glastonbury, in Somerset:

> Do burge and bere grene leaues at Christmas
> As fresihe as other in May when ye nightingale
> Wrestes out her notes musycall as pure glas.[19]

However, there are hints that the Thorn was known much earlier. J. B. Phipps, who has spent much of his professional life studying hawthorns, speculates:

> Only about 16 kilometres from Glastonbury is the village of Hallatrow, whose name is a corruption of the Saxon *Helgetrev* or Holy Tree. Helgetrev already existed in 1087 as it is mentioned in the Domesday Book. Is it not possible that the holy tree of Helgetrev was a twice-flowering hawthorn and that, after its remarkable and perhaps miraculous winter-flowering characteristics had been fully appreciated and assessed, it was moved to Glastonbury Abbey?[20]

At Appleton Thorn, Cheshire, an event known as Bawming the Thorn is held each year. Basically, this consists of decorating a hawthorn tree that grows in the centre of the village,[21] and according to tradition, a tree has stood on this site since 1125, when an offshoot of the Holy Thorn was planted there.[22]

The *Lyfe of Joseph* provides no information on the trees' origins and does not mention the production of winter flowers. Fifteen years after its publication and four years before the suppression of Glastonbury Abbey, the Christmas flowering of the Thorn is first recorded. On 24 August 1535 Dr Layton, the visitor sent to the Abbey, wrote to Thomas Cromwell, enclosing two pieces of a tree that blossomed on Christmas Eve:

7. Holy thorn, drawing by Margaret Tebbs, 1979.

I send you Relicks: First two flowers wraped in white and black sarsnet, that on Christen Mass Even . . . will spring and burge and bare blossoms.[23]

During the reign of Elizabeth I the Thorn growing on Wearyall had two trunks:

> when a puritan exterminated one, and left the other, which was the size of a common man, to be viewed in wonder by strangers; and the blossoms thereof were esteemed such curiosities by people of all nations that Bristol merchants made traffick of them and exported them to foreign parts.[24]

According to another account, presumably of the same activity, the puritan was discouraged from cutting down the second trunk because he had been 'miraculously punished . . . by cutting his leg, and one of the chips flying up to his head, which put out one of his eyes'. However, both parts continued to grow and blossom for about 30 years. A few years later one piece 'was stolen away, not known by whom or whither'.[25]

During the reign of Elizabeth's successor, James I, the Thorn enjoyed some popularity as a garden curiosity. Members of the aristocracy, including the King's consort, Anne of Denmark, paid large sums for cuttings.[26] It is possible that this fashion of growing Thorns in private gardens saved the plant from extinction, for during the civil unrest later in the century the surviving trunk of the original tree was destroyed by a Roundhead, who 'being over zealous did cut it downe in pure devotion'.[27] In 1653 it was lamented that: 'the white thorn at Glastonbury which did usually blossome on Christmas Day was cut down: yet I did not heare that the party was punished.'[28]

In 1645 John Eachard described the Holy Thorn, then much mutilated by visitors who had removed bits for souvenirs, as being the kind 'wherewith Christ was crowned'. An elaboration of this belief is that St Joseph of Arimathaea brought two treasures to Glastonbury: silver containers holding the blood and sweat of Christ and a thorn from Christ's crown of thorns, which grew and proved its holiness by flowering annually at the time of Christ's birth.[29]

Seventy years after Eachard wrote, a Glastonbury innkeeper explained how the Thorn had grown from a staff carried by St Joseph of Arimathaea.[30] According to tradition, the Apostles divided the world between them with St Philip being sent to Gaul, accompanied by St Joseph. After some years St Joseph left the Apostle and accompanied by 11 others set out for Britain, arriving at Glastonbury, where in AD 63 he founded the first church to be built on British soil.[31] When Joseph reached Glastonbury he rested on Wearyall Hill, thrusting his staff into the ground, where it grew and became the original Holy Thorn.[32] Some writers have asserted that it was this miracle that persuaded Joseph to settle in Glastonbury.

Another version of the legend tells how Joseph landed on the Welsh coast, or possibly at Barrow Bay in Somerset, but found the natives hostile. He continued his wanderings and eventually reached the land of King Arviragus. Although Joseph failed to convert the monarch, he made a sufficiently good impression for land at Ynyswitrin – Glastonbury – to be granted to him and his companions. Initially, the local inhabitants showed little enthusiasm for the new faith, but when Joseph fixed his staff in the ground and prayed, whereupon it immediately blossomed, people began to pay serious attention to the missionaries' preaching.[33] Sometimes it is claimed that Joseph performed this miracle on Christmas Day and hence the Thorn has flowered on this day ever since.[34]

Some writers have suggested the Thorn originated from stock brought from the Holy Land, or at least a country bordering the Mediterranean.

The then vicar of St John's, Glastonbury, in a pamphlet produced in 1977 claims: 'Whatever the legend may say, a Thorn has been growing here for 2,000 years and it came from Palestine'. More convincingly, a botanist who has made a study of hawthorns states that some North African populations of hawthorn, which are 'morphologically fairly similar to the Holy Thorn', produce late autumn and early winter flowers.[35]

When the calendar was reformed in 1752 the Holy Thorn attracted attention as people gathered to see if the trees would produce their Christmas blossoms according to the new or old calendar. The *Gentleman's Magazine* of January 1753 reported that on Christmas Eve, 24 December 1752, hundreds of people gathered in Glastonbury to see if the several trees growing there would produce flowers. No flowers appeared, but when the crowds reassembled on Old Christmas Eve, 5 January 1753, they were rewarded and the trees blossomed, thus confirming their doubts about the validity of the new calendar. However, later in the year, a correspondent to the *Magazine* reported that according to the vicar of Glastonbury the trees had blossomed 'fullest and finest about Christmas Day New Style, or rather sooner'.[36] Holy Thorns continued to be visited on Old Christmas Eve at Sutton Poyntz, Dorset in 1844, Woolmingston, Somerset in 1878, and Wormesley, Herefordshire, in 1908.[37]

Other trees that supposedly have grown from staffs include a walnut tree, which formerly grew in Glastonbury and always budded on St Barnabas Day (11 June) but never any earlier.[38] Like the Holy Thorn, this tree was said to have grown from a staff carried by St Joseph.[39] Congresbury, in Somerset, is said to have been founded by the sixth-century St Congar, who founded an oratory there after his staff, which he had placed in the ground, grew into a yew tree.[40] For many centuries this tree was known as Congar's Walking Stick, but its remains are now enclosed within a beech tree: 'the old pieces of yew spill out on the ground below the spreading beech branches'.[41]

A fig tree that grows from the south wall of St Newlyn East church, in Cornwall, is said to have sprouted from a staff carried by St Newlina, an obscure virgin martyr. According to a tradition recorded (or possibly invented) by the village's vicar in the 1930s, Newlina, a Christian princess, sailed from Ireland, landed at Holywell, and walked to where St Newlyn East now stands. On arriving at the site where the church is now built she thrust her staff into the ground and said, 'Let a church be built'. Her staff took root and grew into a fig tree. It is locally believed that the tree still enjoys Newlina's protection. A postcard on sale in the late 1970s depicts the tree, and gives the verse:

> In ancient days Newlina came,
> The saint who gave this place its name.
> Her staff she planted and she prayed,

'Let here a church to God be made.'
This fig tree is her staff folks say;
Destroy it not in anyway,
Upon it lies a dreadful curse,
Who plucks a leaf will need a hearse.

On 1 June 1958 the *Sunday Express* reported:

Four Cornishmen have defied a 'curse of death' and lived. Warning of the 'curse' is printed beside a fig tee which grows out of the wall of the ancient parish church of St Newlyn East, near Newquay. It says death will follow within a year if any man so much as plucks one leaf from the tree.

Twelve months ago four men of the village pruned the tree. One of them . . . said yesterday: 'When I was asked if I would prune the tree I said "Certainly. I'm not superstitious." But soon afterwards, when I went to fell some trees one fell on me putting me off work for three months.'

Does he believe in the 'curse' now? 'Not a bit. I think it was invented to make a good yarn.'

Nevertheless, in January 1978 the vicar of St Newlyn East recorded that 'from time to time the tree has to be pruned, but, by a remarkable number of coincidences, some of those who have done so have met with misfortune and death'.

In his *British and Foreign Trees and Shrubs in Cornwall* (1930) Edgar Thurston provides a photograph of the tree, but fails to mention the St Newlina legend. As Thurston had an interest in folklore, which led to the inclusion of material irrelevant to trees in his work, perhaps his omission of the legend is significant: did he fail to collect it, or was it invented, rather than collected, by the parish's incumbent a few years later?

Also in Cornwall, a fig tree grows from the south-west wall of Manaccan parish church, but this tree has no legend associated with it. In August 1998 a former vicar of the parish noted: 'I have personally cut large chunks from it and no harm has come to me, other than [that which is] natural to man!' It has been suggested that both the St Newlyn East and the Manaccan trees were planted by the Cornish historian Richard Polwhele, who was vicar of Manaccan from 1794 to 1821 and of St Newlyn East from 1821 to 1838.[42]

An isolated sycamore, known as the Lone Tree, used to grow near Dover:

A soldier of the garrison at Dover is said to have slain a comrade with a staff, and as the two men were alone he struck it into the ground, exclaiming that his crime would never be discovered until the dry staff took root. He served abroad for many years unsuspected; but when once again stationed at Dover he visited the spot, driven by morbid curiosity, and found that his staff had taken root, and was a flourishing tree. Stricken with horror, he avowed his crime, and suffered for it on the gallows.[43]

An account published in 1956 provides another version of the legend. Here the tree is identified as an elm, 'surrounded by other trees, but [a] 100 years ago it stood alone on a barren hill', rather than a sycamore, and the protagonists are identified as two Scottish soldiers, companions from childhood who, in the mid-eighteenth century, fell in love with the same girl. One evening one of the soldiers, Donald MacDonald, beat his rival and left him for dead. The stick with which he did this was covered with blood, so fearing discovery he thrust it deeply into the ground. Many years later he was horrified to find that the staff had sprouted and grown into a flourishing tree:

> He knew he would find no relief for his conscience until he confessed so went straight away into Dover and gave himself up. Inquiries were made and eventually it was established that the man Donald thought he had killed was alive and well. So the man who thought he was a murderer was allowed to go. He returned to Scotland a different man and lived to be almost 95. He told the story of the Lone Tree to his minister in the tiny Highland village where he lived, just before his death in 1843.[44]

In 1913 three atheists' tombs were described in Hertfordshire. One of these was an altar tomb on the south side of St Mary's church in Watford. This tomb had no inscription, but had a well-developed fig tree growing from it. Legend suggests that the tomb was that of an old lady, or according to the parish magazine of September 1898, one Ben Wangford:

> He did not believe in a hereafter and wished, when buried, to have something placed with his remains that might grow and prove to his relatives that his soul was alive; if nothing appeared, they would know that he had been right all along. What, if anything was placed in the grave with him has gone unrecorded, but a fig tree duly appeared and became much talked of, so that people travelled for miles to see it.
> The tree died in 1960s, but numerous postcards which depict it still exist, suggesting the appeal of this curiosity.[45]

The trees associated with the other two atheists' tombs still exist. At

Aldenham three sycamores grow from the grave of William Hutchinson (d. 1697) and his wife Margaret (d. 1706). William is said to have declared his disbelief in the Resurrection, and ordered a heavy stone tomb enclosed in iron railings; if a tree grew from the tomb future generations would know that there was life after death. In Tewin churchyard the tomb of Lady Anne Grimston (d. 1713) has an ash tree, which is said to have seven distinct stems growing from it. The dying Lady Grimston is said to have gathered her friends around her and told them: 'Bear witness, my friends, what I say. If there is any truth in the Word of God, may seven trees grow from my grave'.[46]

Westwood and Simpson, in their *Lore of the Land*, note that similar legends have been recorded from Cheshunt, also in Hertfordshire, Chislehurst, in Kent, Perivale, in Middlesex, and Passenham, Northamptonshire, where an unbelieving lady was buried with a gooseberry in her coffin, saying that if there was a living God a gooseberry bush would spring from her tomb, as so happened.[47]

Although the Aldenham and Tewin graves were considered to be sufficiently interesting for postcards of them to be produced, one wonders why they ever attracted such attention. Both are enclosed within substantial iron railings which protect them when the churchyards were mown or grazed, thus encouraging the growth of trees upon them. Ash and sycamore with their wind-borne seeds can readily take advantage of such situations, and it is easy to imagine a mower taking a swipe at the Grimston ash tree, inadvertently coppicing it so that it produced seven trunks.

Some plants are said to have sprung up where blood was spilt in ancient battles, usually against Danish invaders. One such species is the pasqueflower, which is restricted to calcareous grassland in central and eastern England:

> traditionally associated with the Danes. It is supposed to grow only where their blood has been shed and is known in Hampshire as Danes' blood. One of the few places where its purple bell-like flowers can be seen is on the Downs dividing Hampshire from Berkshire – curiously enough, the site of King Alfred's battlefield.[48]

Alternatively, in the 1950s pasqueflowers on the Berkshire Downs and Oxfordshire border were said to have been planted by the Danes where they fell in battle.[49]

However, the plant most often said to have grown from the blood of Danes is dwarf elder – also known as danewort or Danes'-blood – an ancient introduction to the British Isles and a robust scruffy plant that grows on waste ground and roadsides. John Aubrey (1626–97) wrote of Wiltshire:

Danes-blood (*ebulus*) about Slaughtonford in plenty. There was heretofore a great fight with the Danes, which made the inhabitants give it that name.[50]

Similarly, writing of South Creake, Norfolk, in 1722, Edmund Gibson speculated:

This must have been the scene of war between Danes and Saxons, for in the fields there is a Saxon fortification and the way that goes from it is to this day called 'bloodgate' as a mark of the dismal slaughter. Hereabouts is also great plenty of the herb called by the inhabitants 'Daneblood' as if it were the product of the blood spilt there.[51]

During his travels in southern Sweden in May 1741 Carl Linnaeus examined a plant known as *Mannablod*:

a plant which is much talked about . . . for it was said that it grows in no other place in the world but Kalmar Castle, where it once grew up from the blood of Swedes and Danes, killed in warfare on this field. We were much taken aback when we realised that the plant was nothing but the common Ebulus or Sambucus herbacea . . . which grows wild in the greater part of Germany, around Vaxjo and in gardens.[52]

However, according to the herbalist John Parkinson, writing in 1640, dwarf elder 'tooke the name Danewort from the strong purging quality it hath, many times bringing them that use it into a fluxe, which then we say they are troubled with the Danes'.[53]

Geoffrey Grigson, writing in *Country Life* of 16 January 1953, states that the first author to use the name danewort, as danwort, was William Turner in 1548. But Turner did not associate his danwort with the Danes, leading Grigson to speculate that the name might be derived from 'dain', which meant stink. Thus danewort perhaps means stinkwort or stinkweed.[54] Grigson's article stimulated some discussion, including one writer who noted:

At Ailsworth, Northamptonshire, along the old Roman Road – where this plant is known as Blood Elder – local tradition asserts that it grew from the blood of Romans buried at the side of the road. No doubt Danes were buried here and the story gradually changed through oral transmission.[55]

One wonders how the writer could be so certain with his 'no doubt'.

A second correspondent thought the simplest explanation of the name danewort was the probability that Jutes settling in England brought the plant with them as a valuable herb.[56]

Borough Hill in Northamptonshire was supposedly associated with the Danes, and for local people this was proved by the presence of a plant known thereabouts as Dane-weed. Daniel Defoe in his *Tour Thro' the Whole Island of Great Britain* (1724–7) noted:

> The roads hereabouts . . . being overgrown with Dane-weed, they fancy it sprang from the blood of Danes slain in battle; and that if, upon a certain day of the year, you cut it, it bleeds.

This 'Dane-weed' was not dwarf elder, but the much rarer field eryngo, which, according to Anne Elizabeth Baker in her *Glossary of Northamptonshire Words and Phrases* (1854) grew only by the old Roman road and was more usually known as Watling-Street thistle.[57]

Westwood and Simpson note that in some places clustered bell-flower and fritillary were also thought to have grown from the blood of Danes, but conclude:

> It is debatable if remembrance; is involved in *any* tradition concerning Danes. That flowers may be born of blood is an idea found almost worldwide.[58]

When the six-year-old Dorothy L. Sayers moved to her new home, Bluntisham Rectory in the Huntingdonshire Fens, in January 1897, she was amazed by the carpet of winter aconites, which made the ground 'all yellow like the sun'. Later her father told her that these flowers grew in England only where Roman soldiers had shed their blood, and Bluntisham contained the remains of a Roman camp.[59] Assuming this was a genuine tradition, rather than an invention of the Revd Henry Sayers, it is difficult to imagine what stimulated the legend. Winter aconites are native to southern Europe, which might associate them with the Romans, but they are believed to have been introduced to the British Isles late in the sixteenth century, and their bright yellow flowers do not suggest any association with shed blood.

Lilies-of-the-valley in St Leonard's Forest, West Sussex, have reputedly grown from the blood of St Leonard, who slew a 'strange and monstrous serpent (or dragon)' thereabouts. 'The battle was long and ferocious, and as a reward for Leonard's courage, Heaven granted that wild lilies-of-the-valley would spring up for ever wherever his blood has sprinkled the earth.'[60]

In Hartland, north Devon, foxgloves are associated with the obscure St Nectan, to whom the parish church is dedicated. According to what appears to be a comparatively recent tradition, St Nectan and his sister arrived in Cornwall from Wales, and made their way towards Hartland. At Stoke they were attacked by robbers, and the Saint was decapitated. However, he picked up his head and their journey was not delayed. Wherever a drop of his blood fell from his wounds a foxglove sprang up.[61] In 1927 the incumbent of Hartland arranged a Foxglove Procession after Evensong on St Nectan's Day (17 June), and since then the event has been observed 'with great gusto', usually on the Sunday nearest the patronal feast.[62]

Sometimes absence of vegetation indicated places where blood had been spilt, evil deeds have been committed, or the Devil had walked. St George is said to have slain a dragon on Dragon's Hill, near the famous white horse hill-figure at Uffington, Berkshire, and where the dragon's blood was spilt, no grass has ever grown.[63]

A letter dated 17 July 1778 records the legend of the Brothers' Steps in London:

> They are situated in a field about half a mile from Montague House, in a North direction; and the prevailing tradition concerning them is, that two brothers quarrelled about a worthless woman, and . . . decided it by duel. The print of their feet is near three inches in depth, and remains totally barren . . . Their number I did not reckon, but suppose they may be about ninety. A bank on which the first fell, who was mortally wounded and died on the spot, retains the form of his agonising posture by the curse of barrenness, while grass grows around it. A friend of mine showed me these steps in the year 1686; but it is generally supposed to have happened in the early part of the reign of Charles II. There are people now living who well remember their being ploughed up, and barley sown, to deface them; but all was labour in vain; for the prints returned in a short time to their original form.[64]

Jennifer Westwood, writing in 1985, stated that the Brothers' Steps can still be seen in the south-west corner of Tavistock Square Gardens, near the tree planted in 1953 in honour of Mahatma Gandhi, and was 'happy to report that there are bare patches there which could be taken for footprints'.[65]

Heathland vegetation flourishes, but trees were said to never grow in Ashdown Forest, East Sussex:

> All attempts to restock it with trees have failed; this dates from the time when the first cannons were cast, because the trees were used for charcoal for iron smelting and whereas they were quite willing to help make tools and other objects of a peaceful nature,

they refused to let themselves be used for making weapons. It is thought that gypsies, who wanted the Forest to remain open, deliberately started fires at about Easter time each year to prevent the growth of trees.[66]

In Ulster bare patches persist on the grave of a rioter who was shot in 1845, the bare earth in this case presumably bearing testimony to his innocence:

> A young man, John Boyle, was shot dead in a riot in Armagh on 12 July 1845. His grave is much visited and has always been an object of wonder. There are a number of bare round depressions on the grave, about four inches in diameter, on which grass never grows. Traditionally people say that these are signs of the wounds he received (although he received only one wound). The grave has been re-dug a number of times, as recently as last year when the whole graveyard was cleared and re-sown. Still these patches appeared.[67]

Sometimes showy plants that are relatively uncommon become the focus of legend. During the summer the purplish-pink flowers of everlasting pea create a flamboyant display along a roadside hedge at Whitegates Farm, Rushton in Northamptonshire. In about 1965 the farmer gathered seeds from a local railway embankment and sowed them along his hedge:

> People come for miles just to see them when in flower during the first week in August. Some people call them Pharaoh's peas. The story is that a person from the nearby village of Weebly went to Egypt and brought home some seeds which were said to come from a royal tomb in a pyramid.[68]

Everlasting pea is native to southern Europe, and has been cultivated as an ornamental in the British Isles since the fifteenth century, but has not been recorded from Egypt.

Ancient trees, or their supposed descendants, have been associated with a variety of historical people. Perhaps the most bizarre of these is the association of an extremely ancient yew tree growing in the churchyard at Fortingall in Perthshire which is said to be 'incontestably the most ancient specimen of vegetation in Europe', which is possible. Less likely is the belief that as a baby Pontius Pilate had been suckled beneath the tree when his father was a legionary during an early Roman expedition.[69] Alternatively, Pontius Pilate was said to have been born near the yew tree.[70] Neither legend is true. Pilate served as Roman governor of

Judaea from AD 26 to 36, approximately 35 years before the Roman army ventured into Scotland.

Yew seems to have attracted people's imagination to the extent that a great deal of nonsense has been written about them. Thus in 1998 the botanist David Bellamy wrote:

> We also know that ever since people arrived in force upon these shores they have been in the habit of planting yew trees in acts of sanctification, close to where they eventually hoped to be laid to rest.[71]

Similarly, the label on a yew tree at the Royal Botanic Gardens, Kew, in 1993, read:

> The Druids regarded yew as sacred and planted it close to their temples. As early Christians often built there churches on these consecrated sites, the association of yew trees in churchyards was perpetuated.

Needless to say these statements lack the sort of evidence that one would expect from scientists, and much of what has been written on yews is best ignored or forgotten.

Probably the most sane account of yew in the British Isles is Robert Bevan-Jones's study published in 2002, where, after surveying the evidence accumulated over many years and 'from many quarters', concludes that large old yew trees 'frequently exceed a thousand years growth'.[72]

Bevan-Jones believes that some of the oldest yews found in English and Welsh churchyards mark the sites of the hermitages or cells of early saints, but these trees were planted by the cells, rather than the cells being built near an already existing holy tree.[73] Perhaps an argument against this idea is that Cornwall, the English county in which memory of early saints persists strongest in church dedications, lacks ancient yews.

The reason for yews being planted in churchyards has never been satisfactorily explained. In 1307 Edward I decreed that yews should be planted in churchyards to protect their churches from gale damage. Robert Turner, writing in 1644, suggested that yew absorbed vapours produced by putrefaction.[74] In 1791 John Collinson, writing of Somerset, thought that yew trees were preserved in churchyards because their evergreen foliage was 'beautifully emblematical of the resurrection of the body'.[75] Other people have suggested that yew trees were planted in churchyards to provide wood for making bows,[76] or, being poisonous to livestock, they were planted in churchyards so that farmers did not allow their cattle from straying on consecrated ground,[77] or they warded off evil spirits.[78] More imaginatively:

Yew tree is distinctly red and white, especially when the trunk is freshly cut. The heartwood is red, the sapwood . . . white. The colours were used to symbolize the blood and body of Christ.[79]

Recently the idea that yew wards off evil has led to it being used in topping-out ceremonies. These ceremonies, which celebrate the completion of a building – 'a logical counterpart of the foundation stone ceremony'[80] – were revived, or largely created, in the 1960s. In its early form the ceremony involved the placing of a leafy branch on a high point of the finished building. More recently it appears that this branch must be of yew. When the new Sadler's Wells Theatre was completed on 20 November 1997 a photograph published in the *Independent* on the following day showed 'building worker JS Hunda Singh praying at yesterday's topping-out ceremony . . . With him is Fr Victor Stock, rector of St Mary-le-Bow, who is holding a piece of yew to be mixed with concrete to ward off evil spirits'. In its January 1999 edition, the *Railway Magazine* reported:

Celebrity steeplejack and steam fanatic Fred Dibnah has performed the topping-out ceremony for the National Railway Museum's new workshop in the traditional manner – with a sprig of yew tree, used by builders for centuries to ward off evil spirits.

In 2003 when the London Borough of Barnet's new arts building was completed:

In keeping with the tradition of planting a yew tree at the highest point of the building for luck, a giant yew branch was swung around the theatre space on a crane to bring good luck to future productions.[81]

Yews are frequent in churchyards, and may be associated with early saints, but there are surprising few gospel yews. There are numerous gospel oaks, under which various saints preached, or under which the gospel was read when a parish's bounds were beaten. Bevan-Jones mentions without comment or explanation a gospel yew 'on the Bromyard to Ledbury road',[82] which is probably the one at Castle Frome, Herefordshire. A website that mentions this yew states:

There are various gospel yews, oaks and ashes scattered about the country, where the local parsons used to hold occasional services.[83]

It appears that this is an exaggeration. The Castle Frome tree was described in 1896 as 'a vulnerable yew of great antiquity, which has been known, time out of mind, as the Gospel Yew',[84] but there is no record of religious services being held under it. No other gospel yews are known.[85]

Most gospel trees are oaks. One of the most famous of these stood near the church at Polstead, Suffolk. According to tradition, in the mid-seventh century Saxon missionaries, led by St Cedd, preached under this tree.[86] What is believed to be St Cedd's tree collapsed in 1953, but it has been replaced by a young tree, which is assumed to be self-sown from the original tree. Since 1910, or possibly earlier, an annual Gospel Oak Service has been held beside the oak tree on the first Sunday in August. Music is provided by the local Salvation Army band, there is a guest preacher, and an expected congregation of 70 or more.[87]

A gospel oak at High Ercall, Shropshire, was used as a Methodist preaching site from early in the nineteenth century until the mid 1850s.[88] Other oaks, 'under which passages from the gospels were recited, imploring the blessing of the Almighty on the fruits of the earth and for the preservation and rights of the parish' were recorded at Avington in Hampshire, Huntingfield Park and Lavenham in Suffolk, Stoneleigh in Warwickshire and Lapworth in Worcestershire.[89]

As oak trees are the most long-lived of British broad-leaved trees they have become associated with various historic figures. Queen Elizabeth I (reigned 1558–1603) seems to have oak trees associated with important moments in her life, and to have enjoyed eating under the shade of oaks. As a child she danced beneath the boughs of an oak in Greenwich Park, London. This tree became hollow as it aged 'and for three centuries afterwards offenders against park regulations were locked up in it'. It died in the 1870s. In November 1558 she was informed of her accession to the throne while reading under an oak, which was reduced to a decaying stump in 1972.[90] At an unknown date she is said to have dined (and narrowly escaped death from a stag at bay) under the Crouch Oak – 'a venerable tree even in decay' – in Addlestone, Surrey.[91] In 1573 she dined beneath an oak tree at Northiam, Sussex.[92] During the last year of her life the Queen dined under an oak tree in One Tree Hill in Camberwell, south-east London.[93] Other oaks were pointed out as being places from which the Queen shot a deer. At Huntingfield Hall, Suffolk, there stood a tree, 'which has borne the name Queen's Oak ever since the day she shot a buck with an arrow from the cover of its 33ft girthed bole'.[94]

It is said that history records what happened, and legends record what should have happened. A plant that appears to be unusual – a tree that appears to be exceedingly ancient, or a herb with odd markings on its marked leaves – soon attracts the attention of creative members of the community, who invent stories, some of which survive and get passed on.

8

NOTES ON NAMES

Throughout Great Britain and Ireland plants have been given a huge number of names, relating to their appearance, uses, habitat and whatever else might have attracted people's attention. The great time for recording these names was the last decades of the nineteenth century and the early years of the twentieth century. The English Dialect Society had a short but productive life between 1873 and 1896, leading to Joseph Wright's *English Dialect Dictionary* published in six volumes between 1898 and 1905. Thereafter local enthusiasts continued to collect local plant names. Early in the 1920s A. S. Macmillan appealed in the columns of the *Somerset County Herald*, with such success that in 1922 he was able to publish a list running to over 290 pages of plant names known in Somerset and surrounding counties.[1] Other useful lists, which usually lack any explanation of the names, can be found in the *North Western Naturalist* between 1937 and 1954.

Many people regard Geoffrey Grigson's *The Englishman's Flora*, published in 1955, to be the greatest compilation of plant names, but, although Grigson gathered together a great many names from many sources, his primary source, which he seems to have deliberately played down, was James Britten and Robert Holland's *A Dictionary of English Plant-names*, published by the English Dialect Society in three parts between 1878 and 1886.

Unsurprisingly, many of the names collected during these years appear to have become extinct. However, an extraordinary number of names are still known. Some of these have been invented since and others escaped the attention of early collectors. Some were considered to be too obscene to be recorded in print. Victorian compilers of dialect dictionaries were reluctant to list any word that might possibly cause offence (though sometimes words were misunderstood and thus slipped through).

What is perhaps surprising is how some species attracted a great many local names, and others seem to have never gathered more than a few. Some, indeed, seem to have remained unnamed. When discussing local names it is often difficult to give an exact number of recorded names. The same name can have been written down differently by different recorders; for example craw-taes, craw-tees and craw-toes have all been listed as names for bluebell.

Musk mallow with its conspicuous pink flowers and attractive deeply cut leaves is widespread but rarely abundant throughout the British Isles. Isolated plants occur on hedge banks, pastures and grassy places. Thus, it might have acquired a lot of local names, but only three alternative names have been recorded. Two of these – jagged mallow and vervain mallow[2] – appear to be 'book' names, which probably never strayed far from the printed page. The third, buttons, recorded from South Petherton, Somerset,[3] could be based on a misidentification, and perhaps common mallow was the plant intended. One wonders how widely the name musk mallow was used by the average country dweller who had no great interest in plants, and one suspects that it was often referred to as 'that pretty pink flower'.

Conversely, bluebell, a widespread, conspicuous and much-loved flower with a well-known descriptive name, has acquired approximately 70 names. Some of these, such as the Somerset adder's flower,[4] cuckoos on the Isles of Scilly,[5] and cuckoo's stockings in Derbyshire, Northamptonshire and Staffordshire,[6] refer to its time of flowering, when adders emerge and cuckoos return. Others, like the standard name, describe the flower: the widespread blue bottle, blue bonnets in Somerset,[7] and wood bells in Buckinghamshire.[8] Another range of names which cannot easily be explained associates bluebells with crows. Such names include craw-taes in Scotland,[9] crow-flower in Devon,[10] Hampshire, Somerset[11] and Wiltshire,[12] and crow-picker in County Donegal.[13]

Many species were given 'crow' names. Thus in Orkney bogbean was known as craw-shoe,[14] in County Donegal common sorrel was crow-sorrel,[15] in Wiltshire shepherd's purse was crow-pecks[16] and on the Isle of Wight the now near-extinct shepherd's needle was known as crow's needles.[17] It appears that 'craw' or 'crow' in plant names implies 'wild', or possibly 'toy'.

Some of the names given to bluebells were shared with the early purple orchid, another plant that flowers at about the same time of year, can occupy similar habitats, and has some morphological similarities. Adder's flower has been recorded as a name for both bluebell[18] and early purple orchid in Somerset,[19] but appears to be used only for the orchid in Hampshire and Cornwall.[20] Occasionally bluebell would be differentiated from early purple orchid by being described as blue rather than red. Thus in Cornwall bluebell was known as blue googoo, while red googoos was a name for early purple orchid.[21]

Almost 100 names have been recorded for early purple orchid. As is the case with bluebells, some of these names relate to the plant's time of flowering. Thus it was known as adder's flower in Cornwall, Hampshire and Somerset (where it shared the name with bluebell),[22] adder's tongue in Devon, Dorset,[23] and Cheshire, cuckoo-cock in Essex, and cuckoo-bud in Northamptonshire.[24] Another range of names refer to goslings, presumably because its flowers were produced when the first batches of goslings hatched. A Wiltshire name was simply goslings;[25] a Somerset name was goose-and-goslings.[26] Other names seem to refer to the purple spots on the orchid's leaves, or possibly the resemblance of its inflorescence to a bloody finger. Such names include bloody-man's fingers in Cheshire, Gloucestershire, and Worcestershire;[27] butcher in Herefordshire,[28] and red butcher in Kent.[29] It is probable that the name Gethsemane, given to 'a species of orchis in Cheshire',[30] was given primarily to the early purple orchid, although some other orchids have similarly spotted leaves.

The name orchid is derived from the Greek *orkhis*, meaning testicle and referring to the paired root tubers of many ground-growing orchids. One of these tubers is the one that survived during the past winter, the other is forming to sustain the plant during the next winter. Consequently, one tuber is usually larger than the other. Adam-and-Eve, a widespread name for early purple orchid is said to refer to its 'male' and 'female' tubers.[31]

In their *Flora of Ashdown Forest*, Tim Rich and colleagues record stinkers as a name for early purple orchid, 'from the tom-cat smell of the flowers after fertilisation, or at night after it has been picked'.[32]

Other plants that have accumulated a large number of local names include lords-and-ladies (also widely known as cuckoo-pint and wild arum), greater stitchwort and bird's-foot trefoil.

Lords-and-ladies is the only native British species of the Araceae, a family which is far more diverse in tropical regions. In Britain and Ireland the altar, or arum, lily, native to South Africa, associated with Easter, and formerly associated with funerals, or, less frequently used in wedding bouquets, is probably the best-known cultivated member of the family. From its similarity to the cultivated altar lily, lords-and-ladies has acquired such names as cuckoo-lily in Cambridgeshire,[33] lily in Wiltshire[34] and wild lily in Devon.[35]

Lords-and-ladies has a characteristic, exotic-looking inflorescence which appears early in the year and consists of a membranous sheath (known as a spathe) partially enclosing an erect organ known as a spadix. Vivid orange berries appear after the leaves have withered. The spathe which is usually pale yellowish-green, can have dark spots, and the leaves, which can be pure dark green, are frequently purple-spotted. The spadix can be dull purple or pale yellow. Thus it is easy to imagine how lords-and-ladies attracted attention, leading to a variety of names.

It would appear that the name lords-and-ladies refers to the fact that the spadix can be yellow or purple. Similar names which relate to this feature include the widespread Adam-and-Eve,[36] angels-and-devils in

Somerset,[37] bulls-and-wheys in Westmorland and Yorkshire,[38] kings-and-queens in County Durham, Lincolnshire and Somerset,[39] and white-and-red in Dorset.[40]

The semi-sheathed spadix has given rise to such names as preacher-in-the-pulpit in Somerset,[41] parson-in-his-smock in Lincolnshire,[42] and Jack-in-the-box in Buckinghamshire, Somerset and northern Ireland.[43]

Cuckoo-pint, a common alternative name for lords-and-ladies may, as in the case of the 'cuckoo' names given to early purple orchid, refer to the fact that the plant flowers at about the time that the cuckoo starts to call. Other 'cuckoo' names given to lords-and-ladies include cuckoo-flower in Northamptonshire,[44] cuckoo-pin in Plymouth,[45] cuckoo-babies on the Isle of Wight[46] and cuckoo-spit in Lancashire.[47]

The 'pint' part of the name is said to be derived from pintle, meaning penis, and refers to the stiffly erect spadix. Related names include pintelwort,[48] and, in Cumberland, Derbyshire, County Durham and Lincolnshire, priest's pintle.[49]

Greater stitchwort, which produces its showy blossoms on hedge banks and woodland borders in late spring, has attracted over 130 folk

8. Greater stitchwort (Joachimus Camerarius, *Epitome Matthiolii*, Frankfurt, 1586).

names. Some of these names simply refer to the white flowers. Thus one of many Somerset names was lady's chemise,[50] Cornish names included lady's white-petticoat,[51] children in north Hampshire in the 1940s used the name little dicky shirt-fronts,[52] wedding-flowers was a Gloucestershire name,[53] and star-of-the-wood was used in Devon and Somerset.[54]

Other names refer to the time of year at which stitchwort flowers bloom. Such names include Easter-bell[55] and, Whit-Sundays in Devon,[56] and Whitsuntide in northeast Hampshire.[57] Like lords-and-ladies and early purple orchid, greater stitchwort has been given a number of 'cuckoo' names, presumably because it flowers at about the same time as the cuckoo starts calling. A Buckinghamshire name was cuckoo's meat,[58] and a west Yorkshire name was cuckoo-wort.[59]

Possibly the various 'snake' names, such as the Yorkshire hagworm (i.e. adder) flower,[60] the Hampshire snake-grass,[61] and the widespread snake-flower,[62] could relate to the fact that stitchwort flowers appear when snakes and slow-worms fully emerge from hibernation. However, in Cornwall and in the Yeovil area of Somerset, children believed that if they picked stitchwort flowers a snake would 'run' after them.[63] Other names that suggest stitchwort might be dangerous are devil's flower, which was used in Somerset,[64] and piskie, pixie or pixy, which was used in the Plymouth area of Devon, where in the 1880s children believed that if you picked the flowers you would be pixy-led – hopelessly lost, even in an area that you knew well.[65]

Once the globular seed-capsules had formed it appears that greater stitchwort was no longer feared and young children found popping these capsules a popular amusement. Names that refer to this pastime include snap-crackers in Essex,[66] snapper-flowers in Sussex,[67] and snap-jacks in Dorset[68] and on Dartmoor, Devon.[69]

Many, if not most, of the 100 or so names given to bird's-foot trefoil refer to its fruiting state. 'Bird's-foot' itself refers to the four or five slender seed-capsules that develop in such a way that they resemble the foot of a song-bird. Similar names include chicken's feet in Cheshire,[70] craw's (crow's) toes in Scotland,[71] and craa-taes or craa's foot in Northumberland.[72] Other names that may refer to the seed-pods include the widespread fingers-and-thumbs,[73] cat's claw in Buckinghamshire and Somerset,[74] five-fingers in East Anglia,[75] devil's claws in Somerset,[76] fisherman's baskets in Radnor,[77] granny's toenails and pig-toes in Kent,[78] and horse yakkels (molars) in Shetland.[79] The petals of bird's-foot trefoil are bright yellow when young but become orange or reddish as they age. Hence the plant has received such names as the widespread eggs-and-bacon, cheese-cake grass in northern England, buttered eggs in Cumberland and, in Yorkshire where rashers of bacon were known as collops, eggs-and-collop.[80] Other names refer to the shape of the flower: boots-and-shoes in southern England,[81] Dutchman's clogs,[82] goody-two-shoes on the Isles of Scilly,[83] grandmother's slippers in Hampshire,[84] Lady Margaret's slipper in Wimbledon, south London,[85] lady's slippers in Yorkshire,[86] and pattens-and-clogs in Gloucestershire, Somerset and Sussex.[87]

Bellies-and-bums-fingers-and-thumbs was a name given to bird's-foot trefoil around Hadleigh in Essex.[88] Such multi-syllable names seem to have become forgotten during the twentieth century, but recorders of plant names early in the century and in the late nineteenth century collected many such names, especially for wild and garden pansies.

It appears that many of the names given to pansies resulted from stories with which adults entertained children:

> My grandmother had a pansy game or story which goes like this: There were these five lovely daughters and they all went to the ball in the most lovely velvety ball gowns. My grandmother would pick off the five petals and hand them to me to admire the gowns. Then she would say – but they left their old mither (she was a Scot, my gran!) all alone sitting with her two legs in one stocking! Then she would show me the two spindly plant parts from which she had pulled a little green covering. I was always fascinated that this was so. And even now, I often pull apart a fading flower just to repeat my gran's story![89]

No name is recorded in connection with this story, but many names given to pansies seem to suggest forgotten tales: kiss-me-love-at-the-garden-gate in Devon,[90] meet-her-at-the-entry-kiss-her-in-the-buttery in Lincolnshire,[91] meet-me-love-behind-the-garden-door,[92] three-faces-under-a-hood in Northamptonshire,[93] Kitty-run-the-street in Wiltshire,[94] and the 'old name' Jack-jump-up-and-kiss-me.[95]

In Dorset the name welcome-husband-though-never-so-late was given to houseleek and welcome-home-husband-though-never-so-drunk was given to biting stonecrop.[96]

A name given to greater stitchwort in Buckinghamshire and Suffolk was bachelor's buttons, said to refer to the plant's 'button-like capsules'.[97] Of all British plant names, bachelor's buttons seems to have attached itself to the greatest number of species. Approximately 30 plants share this name. In the case of burdock, sometimes known as bachelor's buttons in Devon and Somerset,[98] one can imagine an undomesticated bachelor attempting to hold his clothing together using burdock burs. Many ornamental plants that produce small, multi-petalled flowers have been given the name: the double-flowered form of sneezewort in Northamptonshire,[99] tansy and an old-fashioned variety of chrysanthemum 'bearing bunches of small-button-shaped dark red or yellow flowers'[100] in Somerset, a 'small rose not much bigger than a daisy' in north Lincolnshire,[101] and kerria in Dorset[102] and Wiltshire.[103] One wonders if at one time the wearing of these flowers hinted at the 'artistic sensibilities', which in the 1890s were associated with green carnations by Oscar Wilde and his circle.[104]

Other plants that were called bachelor's buttons often have symmetrical, colourful flowers. Such plants included corn-cockle,[105] marsh marigold in Dorset, Somerset[106] and the Isle of Wight,[107] cornflower in Derbyshire and Yorkshire[108] (and the United States),[109] shining cranesbill in Lancashire,[110] herb robert in Kent,[111] white campion in Gloucestershire,[112] Sussex and north Yorkshire,[113] and water avens in Northumberland.[114]

Few other names have been applied to more than ten species.

Fingers-and-thumbs seems to have been a particularly popular name in Somerset and surrounding counties in the first decades of the twentieth century. Of the 12 species which were given this name 11 have irregular (zygomorphic) flowers. These include horseshoe vetch, yellow corydalis and yellow toadflax. The only species with regular flowers is red campion.[115]

Approximately 15 species have been given the name cuckoo-flower, and most of these come into blossom at about the time the cuckoo starts to call. Cuckoo-flower is now the standard name for the pink-flowered *Cardamine pratensis*,[116] also frequently known as lady's smock. Other species widely called cuckoo-flower included early purple orchid,[117] red campion[118] and ragged robin,[119] toothwort in Hampshire,[120] and wood anemone in Buckinghamshire, Cheshire and Yorkshire.[121]

Bird's-eye was a name given to plants with small bright flowers. Most often the name was given to species of speedwell, especially the bright blue hedgerow species, germander speedwell.[122] In Somerset, children said that if you picked germander speedwell 'the birds will come and pick your eyes out',[123] but it seems that the name led to the superstition rather than the superstition giving rise to the name. Other blue-flowered species that were called bird's-eye included forget-me-nots in Buckinghamshire, Northamptonshire, Nottinghamshire,[124] and Somerset,[125] and green alkanet in west Somerset.[126] Plants with flowers of other colours that were given the name included scarlet pimpernel in Buckinghamshire, Oxfordshire,[127] and south-west Wiltshire,[128] herb robert in many areas,[129] bird's-eye primrose in Yorkshire,[130] and London pride in Devon.[131] An anomaly is bird's-foot trefoil, which was known as bird's eye in Somerset, where it was 'more generally known as fingers-and-thumbs'.[132]

Sixteen species have been given the name billy-buttons. Some of these, such as burdock – known as billy-buttons in Cornwall,[133] and Devon[134] – were also known as bachelor's buttons, but on the whole the name appears to have been given to attractively coloured flowers that children might have used to decorate their clothing. Such plants include hollyhock[135] and marsh marigold[136] in Somerset, wood anemone in west

Lancashire,[137] ox-eye daisy in Shropshire,[138] and the double-flowered garden form of meadow saxifrage.[139]

Occasionally a plant spreads rapidly, but knowledge of its name spreads less rapidly, so people create new local names for it. One such plant seems to have been rosebay willowherb. Although its showy pink flowers are now familiar to people even in urban areas, until the early nineteenth century it appears to have been of restricted upland distribution. Now it is widespread in disturbed areas, woodland clearings and on burnt ground. Some writers believe that the development of a railway network encouraged its spread; others suggest that the introduction of a more vigorous adaptable form from overseas may have led to the plant becoming widespread.[140]

William Curtis, writing in 1798, considered rosebay willowherb to be a noteworthy rarity:

> In the third [1724] of Ray's *Synopsis*, this plant is said to have been growing wild near Alton in Hampshire: in confirmation of this, I have myself found it in a wild unfrequented wood near the same place . . . Mr Hudson in his *Flora Anglica* [1762] mentions it growing in Maize Hill, beyond Greenwich.[141]

About 70 years later, the Worcester botanist Edwin Lees observed:

> Rosebay willowherb has become numerous in several parts of the Vale of Severn, and promises to spread, incited to take possession of new-made roads and embankments.[142]

Rosebay willowherb's leaves somewhat resemble those of some narrow-leaved willows. Thus it has been given names such as blooming sally in Cumberland,[143] and Ireland, flowering withy in Berkshire, French saugh in Lanarkshire,[144] and blooming willie in County Tyrone.[145] Names which are less easy to explain include blood-vine in Hampshire, cat's eyes in Shropshire,[146] plum jam in Dorset,[147] red buffer in Shropshire,[148] and romping molly in Craven, Yorkshire.[149]

Rosebay willowherb's ability to rapidly, sometimes spectacularly, colonize burnt areas and bombsites led to it being called fireweed:

> Rampant in Northumberland . . . it is a moot point whether it is called fireweed because it spreads so rapidly and its flowers are purplish pink, or because in the days of steam engines it was often ignited on railway embankments by flying sparks from the engines.[150]

> An older generation than ours called rosebay willowherb bomb-weed because it was the first to grow on bombsites.[151]

A B C

D E F

1. Cigarette cards, issued 1939:
   A. bluebell
   B. cowslip
   C. lords-and-ladies
   D. marsh marigold (king cup)
   E. periwinkle
   F. poppy.

2. World Conker Championships poster, 1990.

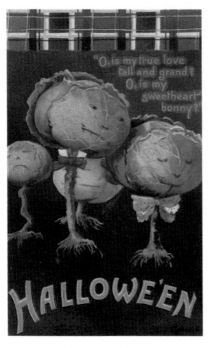

3. Postcard depicting divination using cabbage, posted Altoona, Pennsylvania, October 1910.

4. Postcard depicting lucky four-leaved clover, posted Dilton, Wiltshire, June 1911.

5. Postcard depicting shamrock, posted Chelmsford, Essex, August 1909.

6. Floral tributes to train-robber Buster Edwards, at the South London Crematorium, December 1994. Photograph by A. R. Vickery.

7. Garland, Bampton, Oxfordshire, Spring Bank Holiday, 1981. Photograph by J. M. Mullin.

8. Well-dressing, Wirksworth, Derbyshire, June 1993. Photograph by A. R. Vickery.

9. Christmas tree, Streatham, London, 1994. Photograph by M. E. Vickery.

London pride – the pink flower that was remembered coming up everywhere in London after the War.[152]

I come from Twickenham in Middlesex and have always known fireweed as London's ruin, as it was said that it only bloomed in London after the Great Fire of 1666 and the blitz.[153]

A visitor told me recently that her aunt was totally convinced that rosebay willowherb seeds were actually put into German bombs – because they grew so rapidly after the blitz.[154]

In 2002 when the charity Plantlife International asked people to select 'County Flowers', rosebay willowherb was chosen as the flower for London.

Beyond the London area:

Clydebank was bombed during the last war and one of the casualties was the Singer Sewing Machine factory. On the bombsite a profusion of rosebay willowherb sprang up, which locals of that vintage now call Singer weed.[155]

Westwood lily – my wife learnt this name [for rosebay willowherb] in Sheffield [25–30 years ago]; it is a purely local name and refers to a district in their village (High Green) which is called Westwood and where these flowers grew in profusion.[156]

Another species that spread rapidly, collecting names as it did so, was red valerian (often known in older wildflower books as spur valerian). This species, native to the Mediterranean region, has been cultivated in British gardens since late in the sixteenth century, and was first recorded in the wild, in Cambridgeshire, in 1763,[157] now it is widespread, and spreading, on shingle beaches, cliffs and old walls.

Some people compared red valerian with the better-known lilac. Two names that recognized the plant's foreign origin were the Devon American lilac,[158] and the Lincolnshire German laylock.[159] Other 'lilac' names included wall lilac in Somerset,[160] and ground laylock in Lincolnshire.[161] Some names associated red valerian with drunkenness: drunkard's nose in Minehead, Somerset,[162] drunkards – 'the flower heads sway about in the wind' – in Devon[163] and Somerset,[164] drunken sailors in Devon,[165] and drunken willy in Devon and Somerset.[166] 'Neighbour' names given to red valerian are difficult to explain, but good neighbours was recorded in west Somerset,[167] Gloucestershire, Oxfordshire and Wiltshire,[168] good neighbourhood in Wiltshire,[169] Gloucestershire and Oxfordshire,[170] and quiet neighbours in Wiltshire.[171]

Several local names given to red valerian refer to places in which it is particularly showy and abundant. Thus near Plymouth, Devon, it was known as Bovisand soldier, the plant being 'very abundant' in that locality.[172] In Portland, Dorset, where red valerian was associated with the local prison, it was known as convict grass.[173] More usual were 'pride' names: Devon pride,[174] pride-of-Fowey (or maids-of-Fowey) in Cornwall,[175] and Ventnor pride on the Isle of Wight in about 1940.[176]

Other plants that received a variety of names were garden ornamentals that were passed around between neighbours. One such plant is *Limnanthes douglasii*, native to California and cultivated in Britain from 1833,[177] which has the unsatisfactory standard English name of meadowfoam.

In 1893 T. F. Elworthy reported Sebastopool daisy as a Devon name for *Limnanthes*. He considered this name to be 'clearly a modern invention . . . without the redeeming quality of truth, *L. douglasii* having been introduced from California'.[178] Presumably Elworthy was thinking of the British bombardment of Sebastopool (now Sevastopol) during the Crimean War, but there is, in fact, a town of Sebastopool in California. This developed during the 1850s and grew during the Californian gold rush, so it is possible that the *Limnanthes* grown in Devon late in the nineteenth century could have descended from seeds brought back from California by a gold prospector.

The names American buttercup, poached eggs and fair-maid-of-France were recorded at Kirton-in-Lindsey, Lincolnshire, in 1900, and ham-and-eggs was recorded from Broadway, Worcestershire.[179] Today *Limnanthes* is usually known as poached-egg plant.[180]

The variegated form of reed canary-grass is another plant which was passed around between cottage gardeners and attracted a variety of names. These include bride's laces in Northamptonshire,[181] gardener's garters,[182] lady's garters in Roxburghshire,[183] match-me-if-you-can in Kent,[184] ribbongrass in Cheshire, Nottinghamshire and Berwickshire,[185] sparked grass in southwest Wiltshire,[186] and tailor's garters in Scotland.[187]

Some of these cottage garden plants were collected as wild plants from the surrounding countryside, and later thrown out when they became invasive in gardens. Thus they moved in and out of cultivation. One such plant was monk's-hood, known as bear's foot in Nottinghamshire,[188] Adam-and-Eve – 'when the hood [of the flower] is lifted up there is an appearance of two little figures' – in Great Yarmouth, Norfolk,[189] bird-of-paradise in Somerset,[190] cuckold's cap in East Anglia,[191] dumbledore's (i.e. bumblebee's) delight,[192] granny-jump-out-of-bed in Wiltshire,[193] and Venus'-chariot-drawn-by-doves in Berkshire, Devon and Essex.[194]

Another such plant, popular in gardens and also found in the wild, is columbine, also commonly known as granny's bonnet. The 50 or so names that columbine has attracted include Cains-and-Abels in south-east Wiltshire,[195] folly's flower in Dorset and Somerset,[196] lady's shoes in East Anglia[197] and Somerset,[198] and two-faces-under-a-hat in Sussex.[199]

While it is perhaps surprising that such a well-known plant as blue-bell should attract a large number of local names, it is also surprising that some well-known plants share their names with other species. Cowslip (*Primula veris*), a conspicuous plant whose flowers were used in love-divination,[200] sucked by children to extract their nectar,[201] and gathered by country wine-makers,[202] shared its name with seven other plants. These include two other members of the genus *Primula*: oxlip in Essex,[203] and, more widely, false oxlip (the hybrid between cowslip and primrose). [204] Other 'cowslips' listed by Britten and Holland include wood anemone in northern Scotland, fritillary in Hampshire, daffodil in Devon, and early purple orchid in Rutland.[205] Macmillan adds to the list buttercup in Devon,[206] and Grigson contributes foxglove from the same county.[207]

Oak, which has been adopted as the national tree of the Irish Republic,[208] and is often considered to be the national tree of England, shares its name with the much smaller field maple.

Writing of Devon in 1882 Hilderic Friend noted:

I have been astonished to find how constantly the maple is called oak. On Whit Monday, which this year was Oak-apple Day as well (May 29th), I took an early walk into Bradley Woods. Here I met a number of children decorated with maple, and asked them what it was for. 'It's Oak-apple Day sir, and if you ain't got a piece of oak-apple they'll pinch you, or sting you.' 'Will they?' I replied, 'then I must get a piece.' 'Here's a piece sir,' said a bright lad. It was a sprig of maple, as was all the rest they had. I said, 'This is not oak, is it?' to which they replied, 'It's *oak-apple*, sir.' I could give illustrations from conversations with grown people showing the same error.[209]

At about the same time in Nottinghamshire, field maple was distin-guished from oak by being called dog (i.e. spurious) oak, and was worn on Oak Apple Day, if the real thing was not obtainable.[210] As late as the 1940s Derbyshire children wore field maple as oak on 29 May, 'on pain of being nettled for non-compliance'.[211]

So plant names can move around from species to species and can cause a great deal of confusion. Furthermore, some species have attracted many names. However, the collection and study of these names can yield a great deal of information about how plants were used, viewed and generally thought of by our ancestors.

9

THE CHANGING SCENES OF LIFE

Our ancestors saw signs in the natural world that predicted births and deaths, and used everyday objects to foretell if and when they would marry.

Particularly in Victorian England villagers believed that an abundance of hazelnuts in the autumn would lead to many babies the following spring. According to Christina Hole's 1961 revision of E. and M. A. Radford's *Encyclopaedia of Superstitions*:

> In many English counties still, a plentiful crop of nuts in any parish is said to foretell numerous births there during the coming year. 'Good nutting year, plenty of boy-babies' is a well-known country saying, to which is sometimes added a rider that if the tree[s] bear an unusually large crop of double nuts, a correspondingly large number of twins may be expected.[1]

However, such beliefs appear to have been forgotten later in the century.

If the child was unwanted there were various plants which could be used to produce an abortion. In Ireland houseleek was sometimes used.[2]

Until World War I, pennyroyal syrup was valued as an abortifacient by the poor of Salford,[3] and in a North Riding sword-dance play collected in 1926, a man-woman who is killed, simulates labour and is revived after being dosed with 'oakum-pokum pennyroyal'.[4] In the 1940s a nurse training in a London hospital found that one of her patient's records showed that she had suffered a miscarriage after swallowing pennyroyal pills.[5] About 15 years later pennyroyal extracts were resorted to by Halifax telephonists. If there was a strong smell of mint in the workroom, someone would be sure to say 'Hello girls, who else has been got now?', for bottled pennyroyal was commonly used as 'a standby for girls who missed a period', and worked in some cases, 'when it probably would have worked anyway'.[6]

In Cornwall, where pennyroyal was known as organ, in the nineteenth century women enjoyed organ tea: 'women in the last century were usually well versed in herbal lore . . . so were these modestly held gatherings to drink tea really a way of trying to control the size of one's family?'[7]

According to a London woman in 1982:

> If you want to bring on your period put a sprig of parsley inside your vagina for 12 hours – your period should start 24 hours later.[8]

In the Fens, 'village girls who became pregnant before marriage had faith in parsley, eating it three times daily for three weeks'.[9]

Bastard-killer was a Somerset name for juniper,[10] a shrub that was widely used to produce abortion. According to legend, a Scottish queen Mary had four ladies-in-waiting called Mary in her court. One of these, Mary Hamilton, was made pregnant by the king and resorted to juniper – savin – as an abortifacient. In the words of a ballad telling of this episode, it was unsuccessful:

> She's gane to the garden gay
> To pu' of the savin tree;
> But for a' that she could say or do,
> The babie it would not die.[11]

Sometimes the name savin became corrupted as saffron. The Pitt Rivers Museum in Oxford was presented with an item that consisted of 'about five sprigs of saffron [i.e. juniper], around 4.5 inches in length' in 1914. Its donor explained:

> *To prevent conception.* When a woman notices that she has missed a period she puts about the same quantity of saffron as this envelope contains into a pint jug; pours half a pint of *boiling* water on to it, covers the jug's mouth with muslin and puts a saucer on the top. She leaves the saffron to soak, and, when cold, strains it through the muslin and drinks a wineglass-full for four consecutive mornings. She puts one sprig of saffron into each boot and wears it for *nine* days. The idea of this being that as the feet get hot the saffron soaks through the stocking into the foot. The sprigs here contained have been worn in the boots [of an] Oxford [woman].

Although large families brought their problems, childless marriages were regarded as strange, and herbs could be used to stimulate fertility. In East Anglia the eating of tansy salad was thought to increase fertility, while the drinking of mandrake tea (prepared in rural England from the rootstock of white bryony) was also considered to be effective.[12] The use

of mandrake to induce fertility was widespread and can be traced back to Old Testament times.[13]
According to William Coles, in his *Art of Simpling* (1656):

> The seeds of docke tyed to the left arme of a woman doe help Barrenesse.

More recently, in County Donegal:

> No woman may fear to be barren who carries a bag filled with docken seeds under her left oxter.[14]

Once a woman knew she was pregnant and the date of birth had been calculated her thoughts would turn to guessing the sex of her child. It was widely thought that if household herbs – parsley, rosemary and sage – thrived in the parents' garden the wife was dominant and such women were likely to produce daughters. So if a boy was wanted the growth of such herbs was restricted.[15]

> A simple method of determining the sex of an unborn baby was for a Fenland couple to sleep with a piece of horseradish under each of their pillows. If the husband's horse radish turned black before his wife's, then the expected child would be a boy, and vice-versa.[16]

Any talk of the human reproductive system was taboo, so false explanations were used to explain the arrival of a new baby to older siblings. Throughout Britain the most frequently used of these explanations, which can be traced back to the seventeenth century,[17] was that babies were found in parsley beds. In Guernsey in the 1880s children were told that babies were either brought over in band-boxes from England, or dug out of parsley beds using a golden spade[18] – an implement that no child would be able to obtain. Another popular source of babies was the gooseberry bush.[19] In July 1975 a botanist working in London who complained that his gooseberry bush had produced only three fruits was humorously reminded that he could not expect the bush to be more productive, as he had just had an addition to his family. Other impenetrable places that produced babies included currant bushes,[20] which produced babies of both sexes, and nettle beds, which produced only boys.[21] A more sentimental explanation was that baby girls were found under rose bushes.[22]

Precautions had to be taken to ensure that the child would be born free of physical or mental defects. In Wales it was thought that if a woman came into close contact with strongly scented flowers during pregnancy her child would have a poorly developed sense of smell.[23] More widespread was the belief that the eating of strawberries during pregnancy would result in the baby being born with a strawberry-like birth mark.[24]

The pains of labour could be eased by drinking a tea prepared from raspberry leaves, a preparation of which was sold in Bradford herbalists' shops under the name of 'Mother's Friend'.[25] Similarly in the 1970s Mary Newsam, of Dore, Sheffield, considered such tea to be something of a cure-all:

> Raspberry leaf tea: 1oz raspberry leaves (wild or cultivated) to two cups of water.
> Dose: 2 cups a day during the last month of pregnancy to give an easy delivery.
> Also mentioned in the Sheffield area for preventing mis-carriage, increasing mother's milk, for painful menstruation, diarrhoea, and as an eye-wash for sore eyes. After being soaked to the skin, to avoid a cold take raspberry leaf tea and go to bed.[26]

On the Hebrides women put their faith in clutching a sea bean in their hands when giving birth. Sea beans include the seeds of a number of tropical species that are carried across the Atlantic and are occasionally found on the western shores of the British Isles. It appears that the beans that were most highly valued by midwives and others were those of *Merremia discoidesperma*, a member of the Convolvulus family, which

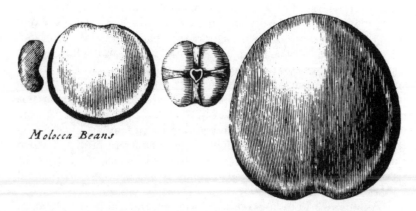

Molucca Beans

9. Sea beans, from left to right: *Erythrina, Mucuna, Merremia, Entada* (J. Wallace, *An Account of the Isles of Orkney*, London, 1700).

have characteristic cross-shaped markings. A Lieutenant-Colonel Feilden presented such a seed, which he had acquired some 20 years earlier, to the Royal Botanic Gardens, Kew, in 1891. The seed's Gaelic name meant Mary's Bean, and in Roman Catholic communities in the Outer Hebrides it was believed that if it was clenched in the hand of a woman in labour it would ensure an easy delivery.[27] According to Alexander Carmichael, the great collector of Hebridean folklore, every nurse had a *Merremia* seed, which she placed in the hand of a woman in labour, 'to increase her faith and distract her attention'.[28]

Newborn babies, particularly before they were baptized, were carefully watched to ensure that no harm befell them, so it is hardly surprising that traditional protective items, such as four-leaved clovers, were carefully hidden under cradle-mattresses.[29]

However, some babies failed to thrive, and it was suspected that such infants were changelings – sickly fairy babies left in place of healthy human ones. Various tests were attempted to prove that a poorly child was a changeling. In County Leitrim:

> If you have a peevish child, or one that from being in good health becomes sickly, and you have reason to believe it is a fairy child, the following plan may be tried in order to ascertain whether this is the case. Take lusmore (foxglove) and squeeze the juice out. Give the child three drops on the tongue, and three in each ear. Then place it at the door of the house on a shovel (on which it should be held by someone), and swing it out of the door on the shovel three times, saying: 'If you're a fairy away with you!' If it is a fairy child, it will die; but if not, it will surely begin to mend.[30]

As Jeremy Harte has pointed out:

> The concentrated juice of foxglove contains digitalis, which can cause death by heart spasm; about a tenth of an ounce of dry leaf is fatal for an adult, while a malnourished child would respond to a lesser dose.[31]

At least one case has been recorded, from Caernarvonshire in 1857, of a supposed changeling being killed by foxglove poisoning.[32] Thus it seems as though the use of foxglove (and other ordeals to which supposed changelings were subjected) might have been a form of acceptable infanticide.

Another worry for a new mother was that she might not be able to produce sufficient milk to satisfy her baby. Among the educated elite lettuce, borage, fennel, aniseed, mint and chamomile were recommended to help nursing mothers,[33] but few, if any, of these remedies seem to have entered the oral tradition.

Breasts that become sore as a result of breastfeeding are treated using cabbage leaves:

> Earlier this year my daughter had a baby and about a week later her breast became very sore. A friend . . . advised her to put cabbage leaves in the freezer and when cold place them on the breast. She did apply the cabbage leaves that evening and by the morning she was much more comfortable. She continued with the cabbage leaves for a few more days till back to normal. She is convinced that the cabbage leaves worked![34]

Once the baby is weaned its mother wants her milk to dry up, and in Gloucestershire 'within living memory, a way of doing this was to place large foxglove leaves on the breasts'.[35]

Before long, children start to wonder about the future, and for girls this inevitably involved pondering about when and who they would marry. Ash leaves, cowslips, daisies and rye-grass were all used by girls to foretell their matrimonial prospects.[36] Other plants used in such divination included ivy. In Lanarkshire in the mid-twentieth century, school girls would place a piece of ivy next to their hearts and repeat:

> Ivy, ivy, I love you,
> In my bosom I put you.
> The first young man who speaks to me
> My future husband he shall be.[37]

The peeling of an apple (or more rarely orange)[38] so that its peel forms one long strip, which is thrown over the shoulder to form the initial of a potential husband on the ground, was a widely recorded activity at Hallowe'en.

> 'At midnight', says a 14-year-old in Aberdeen, 'all the girls line up in front of the mirror. One by one each girl brushes her hair three times. While she is doing this the man who is to be her husband is supposed to look over her shoulder. If this happens the girl will be married within the year.'
>
> 'After they have done this', continues the young Aberdonian, 'each girl peels an apple, the peel must be thrown over her left shoulder with her right hand. This is supposed to form the initial of her husband-to-be.'[39]

Such activities were probably instigated and supervised by adults, but other forms of Hallowe'en divination using apples were probably more spontaneous. In Cornwall:

> Allantide was still a popular occasion in my Newlyn childhood, and extra-large Allan Apples were much in demand. The older girls put them under their pillows to dream of their sweethearts.[40]

An apple pip flicked into the air indicated the lover's home, so long as this verse was used:

> North, south, east, west,
> Tell me where my love does rest.[41]

In Lancashire:

> In order to ascertain the abode of a lover, the anxious inquirer moves round in a circle, squeezing an apple pippin between finger and thumb, which, on pressure being employed, flies from the rind in the supposed direction of the lover's residence. The following doggerel is repeated during the operation:

> > Pippin, pippin, paradise,
> > Tell me where my true love lies;
> > East, west, north or south,
> > Piling brig or Cocker-mouth.

> That the reply may be corroborated, the inquirer afterwards shakes another pippin between the closed hands, and, on ascertaining the direction of the point of the pippin to the point of the compass, the assurance is supposed to be rendered doubly sure, if the charm works as desired, but not otherwise.[42]

In the same county in the 1980s:

> I remember twisting off apple stalks, each time the apple is turned a letter of the alphabet was said, when the stalk broke that letter was the initial of the christian name of the one you were to marry. The broken stalk was then poked into the apple, counting letters again, when the skin broke that letter was his surname initial.[43]

Such activities were probably light-hearted pastimes rather than serious divination rites. However, as girls became older, such things became less frivolous. It seems that the sowing of hempseed was a seriously undertaken ritual. First recorded in the late seventeenth century and surviving until early in the twentieth,[44] the sowing of hempseed on Midsummer's Eve formed a pivotal event in Thomas Hardy's 1887 novel *The Woodlanders*. In Guernsey in the 1880s:

> A vision of your future husband can . . . be obtained by the sowing of hemp seed. The young maiden must scatter on the ground some hemp seed saying:
>
> > Hemp-seed I sow, hemp-seed grow.
> > For my true love to come and mow.
>
> Having done this she must immediately run into the house to prevent her legs being cut off by the reaper's sickle, and looking back she will see the longed-for lover mowing the hemp, which has grown so rapidly, and so mysteriously.[45]

Hardy's Hintock maidens chose the dark seclusion of the local woods for their hempseed sowing, but it seems as if the churchyard was a more frequently favoured location.[46] What is surprising perhaps is the variety of dates on which girls sowed hempseed. Midsummer's Eve seems to have been most widely favoured;[47] other dates included St Valentine's Eve (13 February) in Derbyshire and Devon,[48] and St Mark's Eve (24 April) in parts of East Anglia.[49]

In north-east Scotland another fibre plant, flax, was similarly used. On Hallowe'en a girl would sow flax seed in a field, and 'on looking over the left shoulder she saw an apparition of him who was to be her mate crossing the ridges, as it were, in the act of pulling flax'.[50] In Ireland:

> Bravest of all was the girl who made her way to the crossroads as the night wore on and there sprinkled flax seed on the road or laid a *súgán* [straw- or heath-rope] across it, for at the very hour of midnight her future husband would be seen stepping across it.[51]

Also at Hallowe'en, in Ireland, boys and girls would pull cabbage plants and examine them to learn about their future mates:

> If there is a bit of clay on it he will get a rich wife. If it has a long straight stalk she will be tall. If it is a short stalk she will be small. If it is crooked then so will she be.[52]

In County Down, after the stems or 'runts' had been pulled and examined they:

> were hung above the door; each was given a number and the name of a boyfriend, for an example Barney might be the name given to

the third runt. If Barney was the third person to enter the house on the night, this was considered to be a good omen.[53]

Yarrow was widely used in attempts to find the identity of future partners. On the Isle of Man young women would greet a yarrow plant with the words 'Good morrow, green yarrow, good morrow to thee', and believed that if they gathered it by moonlight and placed it under their pillows they would dream of their future husbands.[54] In 1869 a 'simple serving woman' in Dublin explained to her employer that on May Day, or the preceding night, women would put a stocking filled with yarrow under their pillows, and recite:

> Good morrow, good yarrow, good morning to thee;
> I hope 'gain the morrow my lover to see,
> And that he may be married to me;
> The colour of his hair, and the clothes he does wear;
> And if he be for me may his face be turned to me;
> And if he be not, dark and surly he may be,
> And his back turned to me.[55]

For those who preferred not to place themselves in the uncertain hands of fate, and wanted to take practical steps to ensure the success of their courtship, other traditional practices were available.

Shetland Islanders believed that nettles gathered at Hallowe'en and placed between the blankets of a loved one's bed would ensure the return of affection.[56]

In Sussex good luck in courtship was thought to accompany young men who provided themselves with a 'honeysuckle stick' – a stem of hazel that had been disfigured by having honeysuckle twining around it, so that it appeared to have been twisted.[57] Such curiosities were probably never common, so unless the young man was lucky enough to inherit one, he either had to diligently search through the local woodlands to find one, or tend a stick for several seasons to produce his own.

Enid Porter, curator of the Cambridge and County Folk Museum, collected several traditional practices which a shy village lad could use to convey his emotions to a girl of his choice. In the Norfolk Fens he would place a bunch of southernwood in his buttonhole before he set out for an evening stroll with his friends. The village girls, who would also be strolling along the main village street, would observe the button-hole and choose to either ignore its wearer, or make it clear that they had noticed his buttonhole. If the latter, the lad would summon up his courage and offer the southernwood to his chosen girl. If she accepted they would leave their friends and set off together for the first stroll of their courtship.[58]

Many of the local names given to southernwood relate to similar practices: boy's-love-and-maiden's-ruin,[59] girl's delight,[60] kiss-me-and-go,[61] lad-love-lass in the Wakefield area of Yorkshire in the 1890s,[62] maiden's delight in Cornwall,[63] and maiden's ruin in Devon.[64]

Alternatively, a small bunch of flowers, a true lover's knot made of straw, or a token made of three ears of wheat, were presented to a girl as a symbol of her suitor's feelings. She would show these to her parents who would decide if the match was acceptable and if courtship should proceed.

The token of wheat ears had a more elaborate ritual attached to it. The young man made one token to give to his girl and another that he kept to himself and wore inside his jacket with the ears pointing towards his heart. On the Sunday after he had presented the girl with his token, he would pay a visit to her home. If she was wearing it on the right side of her dress, he knew that she had discussed him with her parents and had decided to reject him, but if it was pinned to the left side, over her heart, he knew he was accepted and their official courtship could begin. The tokens would be worn throughout the courtship, which would, it was hoped, end in marriage, before the wheat grains began to fall.[65]

In the nineteenth century books were published on the so-called Language of Flowers, which, in theory, could be used to express sentiments by the selection of suitably chosen blossoms. Thus flowering almond symbolized hope, 'bachelor's button' celibacy,[66] candytuft indifference,[67] gorse 'love for all seasons' or anger,[68] and so on. However, although these books seem to have enjoyed a great deal of popularity, they seem to have been little used. One problem must have been that different books ascribed different meanings to the same flower. According to the book consulted, passionflower could mean faith, meditation, or religious superstition.[69] Also it was necessary for the recipient of a bouquet to carefully examine it: was that poppy red, in which case it meant consolation, or scarlet, meaning fantastic extravagance?[70] One of the few known examples of the Language being used is in Dublin in May 1868, when Rose La Touche whose parents had forbidden her to write to John Ruskin sent him a package of flowers. He was able to understand what was meant by 'a rose enfolded in *erbe della Madonna*', but unable to decipher the rest of the message.[71]

A series of postcards produced in the first decade of the twentieth century that depicted couples in appropriate poses, a flower and a caption, such as 'heliotrope – devotion' or 'forget-me-not – true love', allowed no room for confusion.

In rural areas more direct methods were preferred:

In Herefordshire, in the 1870s, my uncle attracted my aunt by firing a [ribwort] plantain seed-head at her. It must have worked, they got married.[72]

Similarly, according to Mont Abbot, a farm labourer born at Enstone, Oxfordshire, in 1902, when he was a young man he and his companions would cycle to neighbouring villages on summer evenings, and view the girls, who were 'scattered about like daisies':

> We foreigners 'ud pull up on our bikes within winking or aiming distance, picking the Daisy we fancied from the bunch by looping the pliant stem of plantain into a catapult and pinging her bare neck with its . . . seedhead.[73]

Some plants were thought to stimulate lust rather than love. In rural Oxfordshire in about 1920, broadbean flowers had such a reputation: 'there ent no lustier scent than a beanfield in bloom'.[74] In Suffolk between the two World Wars:

> Best of all traditional aphrodisiacs was the scent of the bean flower, for this not only stimulates passion in the man, but extreme willingness in the girl.[75]

The novelist Barbara Cartland (1901–2000), recalling her time as a young woman in fashionable London, wrote of Lord Wimborne, who

> was incurably romantic, to him love must always be *une grande passion*, otherwise it was not interesting. He always sent bunches of tuberoses (believed by the Edwardians to incite desire) to any woman he fancied.[76]

True love did not always run smoothly. There was room for anxiety and doubt; poorly substantiated gossip could lead to concern about a lover's constancy.

On Midsummer's Eve a Herefordshire girl might test the faithfulness of her lover by making a 'Midsummer Man'. This was a fleshy stem of orpine (known in Somerset[77] and Sussex[78] as life-long-love-long) placed upright in moist clay on a piece of slate or pottery. The following morning she would examine the stem to see if it was leaning to the right or to the left, thereby indicating whether or not her love would prove true.[79]

In Sussex Midsummer Men were made by pushing pieces of orpine through two empty cotton-reels, which girls took to bed with them. One reel was given the name of a boyfriend and the other represented the enquirer. In the morning they were examined, and if the stems had fallen towards each other the prospects were good; if they had fallen apart the lover would be unfaithful.[80]

Such practices date back at least to the seventeenth century, when they were recorded by John Aubrey in his *Remaines of Gentilisme and Judaisme*.[81]

In addition to providing details of a future lover, yarrow and apples could be used to find out if a lover was faithful. A widespread name for yarrow was nosebleed,[82] and its leaves were used medicinally both to treat and to cause nosebleeds, thus relieving migraines and headaches.[83] In the second half of the nineteenth century a widely used method of finding out if a lover was constant was to push a piece of yarrow into a nostril and rotate it several, usually three, times. If the lover was faithful the enquirer's nose would bleed. A Suffolk rhyme that was recited while performing this method of divination ran:

> Green 'arrow, green 'arrow, you bears a white blow;
> If my love love me my nose will bleed now;
> If my love don't love me, it 'ont bleed a drop;
> If my love do love me 'twill bleed every drop.[84]

An apple pip placed in, or near, the fire could also be used to test fidelity. If it burnt noisily the lover was true, but if it burnt silently the lover was unfaithful. A couplet repeated when making this enquiry was:

> If you love me pop and fly,
> If you hate me lay and die.[85]

In Sussex in the 1860s a similar form of divination, using hazelnuts, was practised at Hallowe'en,[86] while in Ireland walnuts, chestnuts and grains of wheat were similarly employed.[87] Lovers living on the Shetland Islands would place two short straws, one of which had a node or joint, on the glowing peat of an open hearth. Soon the heat would cause the straw with the node to jump, but only if it moved closer to the other straw would marriage take place.[88]

However, in this, as in many other superstitions, the folk were sometimes uncertain as to how omens can be interpreted. What might be thought an omen of good fortune in one area might be considered to be an omen of misfortune elsewhere. Thus, although the pip that burnt silently was usually taken to indicate a lover was unfaithful, the opposite was sometimes considered the case. In Golspie, Sutherland, a Hallowe'en custom was to place two nuts, one representing the enquirer and the other representing a prospective spouse, side by side near the fire. If the nuts burnt quietly beside each other, the two would marry, but if they burnt vigorously and sprang apart, the omen was unfavourable.[89]

A method described as being popular among children in the late 1950s utilized a more exotic fruit, the banana. The tip of the fruit was cut off with a sharp knife, if the dark central flesh resembled a 'Y' for yes, the boyfriend was faithful, while a circular blob betrayed unfaithfulness.[90] Sometimes this means was used to predict the outcome of any other activity that required a simple yes or no answer.[91]

Before World War I, east London girls might try to regain a wandering sweetheart by boiling tormentil roots at midnight on a Friday. This was believed to so discomfort and worry the young man that he would be compelled to return.[92] Tormenting root, an Ulster name for the plant,[93] might suggest that the rite had been practised elsewhere, but it could, of course, simply be a corruption of the standard name.

The unsteady joys of courtship can culminate in marriage, a time when flowers are often abundant. In earlier times people had little to make an event memorable. If colour was required, their scope was limited, and it was mainly through the use of flowers and foliage, the one abundant source of bright colours available, that a vivid visual impact could be achieved. Thus it seems flowers were originally included in marriage celebrations as an easily obtainable source of colour; later they became part of tradition and acquired symbolic roles.

At country weddings, where the bride and groom walked to church, their path might be strewn with flowers, rushes and wheat ears.[94] In Guernsey the yellow iris was a favourite plant for strewing and was much sought after for this purpose.[95] Sometimes strewing might prove an embarrassment to the bridal couple, for a jilted lover might choose the occasion to make grievances known. Writing in 1912, Ella Mary Leather described how this had been done at Cusop, Herefordshire, a few years earlier. A girl who had been jilted waited in the church porch, and when the husband emerged she threw a handful of rue at him, saying 'May you rue this day as long as you live.' As she had gathered her rue from a plant that grew in the churchyard, and thrown it 'between holy and unholy ground' (between church and churchyard), it was believed that the curse would come true.[96]

On the Isle of Man, peeled wands of osier were carried as emblems of office by attendants of the bride and groom.[97] In some country areas an arch of evergreens,[98] or covered in mosses,[99] was erected at the entrance to the churchyard.

The bridal bouquet, which is carried in various forms by many brides around the world, has a long history, but does not seem to have been an essential accessory of British brides until the eighteenth century. Over the centuries, the flowers favoured by brides have undergone gradual change, but usually there has been a preference for fragrant white flowers – lilies, carnations, myrtle and orange.

It is inevitable that records of how poorer classes celebrated their

131

weddings are scanty. Presumably brides carried small bunches of whatever seasonal flowers were available.

Tudor brides carried garlands of wheat ears.[100] In the seventeenth century it was customary for brides to weave rosemary, a symbol of fidelity, into their wreaths, and sprigs of rosemary were used to deck the bridal bed.[101]

In the nineteenth century myrtle became popular, following a custom supposedly started by Queen Victoria in 1840.[102] However, contemporary newspaper reports make no mention of myrtle being used at the Queen's wedding:

> Her majesty's dress will be of rich white satin, trimmed with orange-flower-blossoms, head-dress – a wreath of orange-flower-blossoms, and over this a beautiful veil of Honiton lace.[103]

The first British royal wedding at which the use of myrtle was recorded was that of Princess Augusta of Cambridge to Frederick, Grand Duke of Mecklenburgh-Strelitz, at Buckingham Palace on 28 June 1843. Augusta's dress, head-dress and wedding cake were all decorated with myrtle – 'being introduced with the orange flowers as the emblematic flower of Germany'.[104] Thereafter royal brides commonly carried myrtle.[105] In March 1863, when Princess Alexandra of Denmark married Edward, Prince of Wales, her bouquet was

> of the most beautiful description, being composed of orange blossoms, white rose buds, rare orchidaceous flowers, and sprigs of myrtle, with a trimming of Honiton lace. The myrtle was by express command of Her Majesty [Queen Victoria], sent from Osborne, and was taken from plants reared from the sprigs used in the bridal bouquet . . . [of] her Royal Highness the Princess Royal.[106]

However, old myrtle bushes are still pointed out as being descendents of myrtle carried by Queen Victoria:

> When I was a child I lived in an old house on the outskirts of Belfast, and on a south-facing wall outside my nursery there grew a fine myrtle bush which flowered freely. According to local tradition this bush grew from a sprig from Queen Victoria's wedding bouquet.[107]

Royal brides carry myrtle supposedly descended from Victoria's bouquet. Thus when Princess Anne married Captain Mark Phillips on 14 November 1973 her bouquet contained 'a sprig of myrtle grown from myrtle used in the wedding bouquet of Queen Victoria'. Its supplier commented: 'We do not find that myrtle is asked for very much these days'.[108]

In Wales it is said that myrtle was 'much esteemed' and if it grew on each side of the door 'the blessings of love and peace will never depart from the house'.[109] More recently, in 1995, nurserymen attempted to sell myrtle as 'the herb of Venus': 'The custom of brides carrying a sprig of myrtle in their bouquets, indicates the plant's long association with love.'[110]

Another Victorian innovation was the use of white heather as a bridal flower. At the wedding of the Princess Royal to Crown Prince Frederick William of Prussia in January 1858, the bridesmaids' garments were decorated with white heather.[111] Thereafter it became a favourite flower for royal brides.[112] However, the flower most frequently used by Victorian brides, including Victoria herself, was orange blossom. According to some versions of the Language of Flowers such blossom symbolized chastity,[113] and it is claimed that the use of a crown of orange blossom as a symbol of purity, chastity and eternal love was introduced to Europe during the crusades.[114] Alternatively, since orange trees bear flowers and fruits at the same time, they are said to be associated with fertility.[115] Both orange blossom and white heather, often artificial, continue to be associated with weddings. Thus a woman living in Lilliesleaf, in the Scottish borders, interviewed in 1990 recalled:

It's lucky to have white heather in the bouquet. I did have a bit of wild heather growing in the garden and if someone was getting married, I often cut a piece and sent it to her. I like the white heather, and I could give it to a bride because I know a lot of them feel that it is lucky; but I cannae see that it would bring you any more luck than what is happening.[116]

In addition to the bride, groom, and principal guests wearing flowers, it became fashionable for churches to be decorated for weddings. In 1890 the florists Wills and Segars announced in their catalogue:

Church Decorations for Weddings

We devote special attention to this particular branch of our business, always having on hand a large stock of graceful Palms and Foliage Plants of all sizes specially grown for this purpose up to twenty feet high . . . We shall be pleased at any time to meet our patrons at the Church, to receive their commands, make suggestions, and furnish estimates. The price of a Wedding Decoration may range from Five to Fifty Guineas.

The accompanying illustrations, of wedding decorations at St Margaret's Westminster, show a jungle-like profusion of palms and precariously placed pots of lilies and other flowering plants.[117]

In the late nineteenth and early twentieth centuries huge 'shower' bouquets, held together by the extensive use of wiring, and extending 'from a bride's bosom to her toes' became popular. These consisted of white flowers – including carnations, lily of the valley, roses and stephanotis – backed by asparagus fern.[118] Later, in the 1920s, a 'sheaf', often of Madonna or altar lilies, cradled on the bride's arm, became fashionable.[119]

Although white flowers have obvious associations with purity and virginity, they also had the advantage that they looked good in black-and-white photographs. The use of a wider range of colours in bridal bouquets coincided with the advent of colour photography, which itself coincided with the acceptance that many brides were not virgins. As in other aspects of life the 'traditional' is no longer considered to be the only way of doing things, and present-day brides often seek bouquets that express their personalities. According to an early twenty-first century advisor on wedding etiquette:

> The bride's bouquet is very much according to personal taste and the style of the dress. A large bouquet would complement a long, lacy dress with flowing train and veil, whereas a small posy or even a single bloom would look better with a simple, shorter dress. The bride's flowers always used to be white, but now they can be any colours of the rainbow. It's usually a good idea to think of the colour scheme you want for the bridesmaids and pages first, then choose flowers that blend with this.
>
> For the bridesmaids, small posies are most popular picking up the colours of the bride's bouquet and those of the church or other venue.[120]

A common custom in North America is for the bride to throw her bouquet into the air, and whoever catches it will be the next to marry.[121] In Britain it is more usual for the bouquet to be placed on the grave of a dead parent or grandparent.[122]

Not only the bride and bridesmaids are decked with flowers, it is usual for the groom and best man and other principal guests to wear button-holes, often of carnations. The button-hole on the left lapel of men's jackets was first introduced in the 1840s to hold such decorations.[123]

> Traditionally buttonholes were white or red carnations, but now it's more usual to choose single flowers in a colour to match the wedding bouquets. The groom and both fathers can have double

flowers if you like. It is not considered good etiquette for them to contain any foliage . . . Corsages should be worn by the bride's and the groom's mothers, to complement their outfits. They should not be too flamboyant.[124]

At weddings of fairground show people bouquets are presented to the mothers of the bride and groom, grandmothers and other important female guests.[125] Not surprisingly, this is a custom that florists are keen to encourage. Thus items in the 'Flowers and Favours' price list distributed by an exhibitor at a wedding fair in Wandsworth, London, in 1996 included brides' posies, priced at £25–30, and bouquets, 'starting at £10', for the mothers of the bride and groom. A few years later wedding planners were told 'don't forget to include . . . a bouquet each for the bride's and the groom's mother (to be given at the reception)'.[126]

Flowers abound at Jewish weddings. The approaches to the *chupah*, and the *chupah* or canopy itself, receive special attention, while flowers placed elsewhere ensure that the whole synagogue resembles the Garden of Eden; many rabbis having compared marriage to the admission to paradise.[127]

On leaving the church, today's brides are sometimes showered with pastel-cloured paper confetti, although in recent years this has been thought of as littering the churchyard and has been discouraged. Sometimes rose petals are substituted for confetti. The custom of showering important people or religious statues with rose petals dates back to Roman times, and on 12 June 1928, the *Daily Mail* recorded that when the daughter of the singer Dame Clara Butt was married in London she was greeted by a shower of thousands of rose petals. These, however, were not natural petals, but were of 'softly tinted tissue paper' as supplied by the Disabled Men's Industries for most big society weddings, including those of Princess Mary and the Duchess of York.

Paper confetti has replaced the grain formerly thrown over brides to ensure prosperity and fruitfulness. Until late in the nineteenth century wheat was still thrown in some country districts, but later rice became popular.[128] In recent years rice, which is considered to be more environmentally friendly, is sometimes used instead of confetti. At Jewish weddings, nuts and raisins are occasionally placed in the bride's veil and tossed into the air,[129] an ancient custom that was possibly reinforced in the mid-nineteenth century when the selling of nuts and dried fruit in London was largely controlled by the Jewish community.[130] Baring-Gould (1834–1924), who was parson of an isolated Devon parish for over 40 years, recorded that Devon brides would be offered a basket of hazelnuts as they left the church.[131] On the Brendon Hills in Somerset an onion was thrown after the bride in the hope that she would mother many children.[132] In Castleton, Derbyshire, sods of earth, horse beans, and corn, were thrown. The sods were supposed to ensure good luck with produce of the soil, and the beans and corn plenty of children.[133]

A well-known rhyme that describes a bride's apparel is:

> Something old, something new,
> Something borrowed, something blue.

Near Cheltenham in Gloucestershire:

> The 'some thing blue' that a bride wears is the blue periwinkle. One informant told me that it must be worn in the garter for fertility.[134]

In Wiltshire periwinkles found along the hedge banks of old cottage gardens are said to have been planted by newly married couples in the belief that the plant ensured a happy, lucky marriage.[135] Similarly, in the Cambridgeshire fens it was believed that if a couple planted periwinkles in the garden of their first home their marriage would be a happy one. Many Cambridgeshire people believed that periwinkles worn as a button-hole would wither rapidly if the wearer was flirtatious or unchaste.[136]

Popular works of the sixteenth and seventeenth centuries mention periwinkles as a promoter of love. First published in English in c. 1550, *The Book of Secrets*, falsely attributed to the German philosopher and theologian Albertus Magnus (d. 1280), states that when periwinkle is 'beaten unto a powder with worms of the earth wrapped round it, and with an herb called *Semperviva*, in English houseleek, it induceth love between man and wife, if it be used in their meats'.[137] A little more than a century later Nicholas Culpeper explained that as periwinkle is a plant of Venus, 'the leaves eaten by man and wife causeth love between them'.[138]

As has been noted elsewhere,[139] where culinary herbs thrived the wife was dominant, as Monmouthshire people said:

> Where mistress is master
> The parsley grows faster.[140]

A belief said to be still current in some Hertfordshire villages in the 1970s was that a thriving rosemary bush in the garden indicated that the wife was dominant:

> 'That be rosemary sir,' said a cottager . . . 'and they do say that it only grows where the missus is master, and it do grow here like wildfire.'[141]

In Buckinghamshire in the 1880s it was believed that sage flourished where the wife rules, and:

> A farmer recently informed me that the same plant would thrive or decline as the master's business prospered or failed. He asserted that it was perfectly true, for at one time when he was doing badly, the sage began to wither; but as soon as the tide turned the plant began to thrive again.[142]

Similarly, in Devon, over a century later, it was believed that as a sage bush thrived so does the family.[143]

In 1982 it was recorded:

> In Worcestershire, in the Bromsgrove area, there is a belief that stag's-horn sumach, if growing in the garden of a house, is sure to bring marital strife to the family living in the house. This was related to me by an old gardener, who died in 1973 full of years. He lived until he was about 90 years of age . . . It was [a belief] firmly held by other gardeners of my informant's generation.[144]

If a marriage in anyway offended local opinion, there were ways of expressing disapproval. When a husband was suspected of wife-beating, a widespread practice was to scatter chaff, a by-product of threshing, on the couple's doorstep.[145] Early in nineteenth-century Cheshire, May Birchers would visit houses after dark on May Eve and leave a sprig of tree on the doorsteps. The next morning the householders would discover what people thought of them, according to a code based on rhyme:

> Nut for a slut, pear if you're fair, plum if you're glum, bramble if you ramble, alder (pronounced 'owler') for a scowler, and gorse for whores. There was also hawthorn, which did not rhyme with anything, but counted as a general compliment.[146]

In nineteenth-century west Dorset, if older brothers or sisters remained unmarried on the wedding day of a younger sibling they were expected to dance, 'bare-footed (I think)', over gorse bushes placed on the floor.[147]

Perhaps not surprisingly there were more folk beliefs associated with death than with either birth or marriages. Death stalked every home, always waiting to receive another victim. The elderly helplessly slipped away and children were liable to suddenly sicken. Death came to the home, for the terminally ill were not removed to hospitals.

It was thought that the picking and bringing indoors of certain blossoms would cause a death in the family, most usually of the mother. Flowering hawthorn – may blossom – was the most widely feared plant,[148] and cow parsley was the plant most frequently associated with causing the death of mothers,[149] and possibly due to misidentification the superstition also attached itself to similar-looking members of Apiaceae.[150] Other species that were given the name mother-die include hogweed in the Midlands,[151] rosebay willowherb in Shropshire,[152] and white campion in Cumberland.[153] Particularly in hospitals, having red and white flowers mixed together in a vase could lead to a death.[154]

In *Notes & Queries* of 13 December 1873 it was recorded:

On the death of a friend in the summer, an old lady, a relative, who was on a visit of condolence to the widow, went quietly into the garden and counted the flowers on the peonies . . . [she said] there was an odd number on each plant, which was a sure sign of death in the house before the year was out.[155]

Certain landed families had prophetic trees, which foretold deaths in the family by shedding a branch, growing on their property.

One of the oldest, if not the oldest cedars of Lebanon in England is that standing in Bretby Park, Derbyshire . . . planted in February, 1676 . . . This tall cedar has lost many limbs, and is now scantily provided. The stump of every limb has been carefully sealed with lead, and each remaining branch is supported by chains.

There is a legend that a limb of this tree falls at the death of a member of the family . . . The family history is a mournful one. The last Earl died a young man and childless on returning home after a visit. His sister was the wife of Lord Carnarvon, and her death will be remembered. The fall of these recent limbs has left the tree a wreck – a lofty and noble trunk, almost naked, except a few remaining branches on the top, supported by artificial means.[156]

J. H. Wilks, a tree-surgeon writing rather less than a century later, recorded that the tree had its main branches chained and braced to prevent the collapse of any part of it; 'the last fall of a limb is said to have taken place on the death of Lord Carnarvon after his discovery of the tomb of Tutankhamun'.[157]

The occupiers of Manor Farm, at Deverill, Wiltshire, believed that if a limb was blown off one of a nearby clump of ash trees a member of their family would die.[158] Similarly, a 'prophet elm' in the grounds of Credenhill Court in Herefordshire, formerly property of the Eckley family, was believed to foretell each death in the family by shedding a branch.[159] In Fife feudal barons used trees, known as joug trees, as their gallows, and these trees became ominous, for when they shed a branch a member of the laird's family would die.[160] Less worrying was an oak tree at Dunsford, Devon. This tree has twisted bole; when the Fulford family cease to own the property on which it stands, the bole will untwist.[161]

Sheila St Clair has collected two instances of phantom trees that appear before a death. Near Redruth in Cornwall a tree appeared to be planted in the grass near the front door, where no one could remember a tree ever having grown. In Ireland a bush, which resembled a holly, was observed from an upstairs window. Both the tree and the holly-like shrub were believed to foretell death.[162]

A very widespread belief was that a green and grassy churchyard at Christmas foretold a large number of deaths during the following year. The usual explanation being that mild winters failed to kill off germs.[163]

Equally widespread was the belief that if apple or other fruit trees flowered out of season death was foretold:

> A blossom on the tree when the apples are ripe
> Is a sure termination of somebody's life.[164]

In Northamptonshire it was believed that twigs that produced such blossoms had been touched by the devil.[165] In the Basingstoke area of Hampshire it was believed that when fruit trees flowered at unusual times war was foretold.[166]

However, regardless of whether or not it is foretold, death is inevitable, and at most funerals flowers abound. In north Shropshire wallflowers, roses and other blooms were arranged in the coffins of the poor,[167] while in Monmouthshire rue, hyssop or wormwood, all considered to be symbolic of repentance, were sometimes placed in coffins.[168] Early in the 1920s every herb which grew in the garden, with the exception of thyme, was used to line coffins in some Oxfordshire villages.[169]

It is apparent that most of the plants used to line coffins were strongly scented, and it seems probable that their original purpose was simply to mask the odour of decaying flesh. In her novel *Wuthering Heights*, Emily Brontë, a clergyman's daughter, provided a short description of the mourning practices of Yorkshire gentry early in the nineteenth century. When the elder Catherine Linton died in the early hours of a Monday morning her body was placed in an open coffin, strewn with flowers and scented leaves, and left in the drawing room of her home until her funeral on Friday.[170] About a century later, a promising young boxer died in South Shields, Co. Durham. Towards the end of her life his widow recalled the days following his death:

> That was the finish now. Exceptin' old Mrs Hancock from the market. She brought me a sandwich and a pot of tea up. The only

thing to heat with in the room was the fire, so I couldn't even boil
a kettle. I daresn't light it in case it would turn poor Johnny. I had
already poured two bottles of whiskey down his throat, but he was
still turnin' . . . during the days Johnny lay in that room waitin' to be
buried, hardly a soul came near . . . I hardly knew what I was doin'
or what day it was as I waited with 'im for the hours to tick away.
I slept in a chair because the bed had been taken down to make
room for the flowers and wreaths which arrived by the score.[171]

Particularly explicit is a verse in the folk song *The Unfortunate Rake*, also
known as *The Young Sailor Cut Down* or *The Streets of Laredo*, which was
probably written early in the mid-eighteenth century.[172] According to a
typical version of the song:

> And now he is dead and laid in his coffin,
> Six jolly sailor boys carry him on,
> And six pretty maidens all carry white roses
> So that no one might smell him as he passes along.[173]

At funerals in the north of England a tray of box twigs was placed outside
the door of the house. Each mourner would take a twig as he went out,
and later drop it in the grave. A *Daily Telegraph* reporter covering the
aftermath of the 1868 colliery disaster at Hindley Green, near Wigan,
wrote:

> I find an old Lancashire custom observed in the case of this
> funeral. By the bedside of the dead man, the relatives, as they took
> their last look at the corpse, have formed a tray or plate, upon
> which lay a heap of sprigs of box. Each relative has taken one of
> these sprigs, and will carry it to the grave, many of them there
> dropping it upon the coffin. Ordinarily the tray contains sprigs of
> rosemary or thyme: but these poor Hindley people not being able
> to obtain those more poetical plants, have, rather than give up an
> old custom, contented themselves with stripping several trees of
> boxwood: hence it is the mourners carry the bright green sprigs
> which I have seen.[174]

Box leaves have been found associated with Romano-British burials in
Berkshire and Cambridgeshire.[175]

Late in the nineteenth century, mourners in Shropshire were given
a sprig of rosemary when the funeral procession set out, and, after the
coffin had been lowered, dropped these into the grave.[176] Christina Hole,
writing in 1940, observed that 'sprigs of rosemary wrapped in white paper
are still thrown into the grave in many districts'.[177]

Evergreens such as cypress, laurel and yew, were used at eighteenth-century funerals. Writing of Somerset in 1791, John Collinson described how branches of yew, which he considered 'beautifully emblematical' of both the resurrection of the body and the immortality of the soul, were placed under the deceased during the funeral ceremony.[178]

In Cornwall,[179] north Devon,[180] and some other areas, pot plants were decked in black crepe when death occurred. In her *Walks about St Hilary* (1879), Charlotte Pascoe wrote:

> I saw with my own eyes a little black flag attached to our church-woman's bits of mignonette, which she assured me had begun to quail since her poor grandson was burnt to death, but had revived after she had on it the piece of mourning.[181]

Floral tributes such as we know today came into use during the second half of the nineteenth century. Charlotte Burne records that wreaths were not commonly used at funerals in Shropshire until the early 1870s.[182] Early in the 1880s Hilderic Friend noted with approval:

> The pretty custom of sending wreaths for the coffins of deceased friends is also growing, and it is certainly a delicate, expressive, and touching method of paying tribute to their memory. The Queen and Royal Family have set us an example again and again in this matter, and it is an example which we have not been slow to imitate.[183]

However, by the close of the nineteenth century the art of making floral tributes had reached its apex, and florists were adept at producing elaborate designs such as pearly gates, hearts, broken columns, books and empty chairs, in addition to a wide range of wreaths and posies. Even the poor had elaborate and costly flowers at their funerals. In his 1886–1903 inquiry into poverty in London, Charles Booth records how a pious Roman Catholic woman and her two daughters occupied a first-floor room in one of the poorest streets. When one of the daughters died, neighbours showed their respect by covering the coffin, and almost filling the room, with costly wreaths and vast quantities of flowers.[184] According to Booth, fish sellers and cats'-meat dealers were particularly fond of showy funerals.[185]

The flowers produced for the funeral of Queen Victoria in February 1901 are reputed to have cost £80,000, and produced a display of unparalleled extravagance:

> The Queen Regent of Spain sent a wreath seven feet high; the business firms of Queen Victoria Street presented a Royal Standard

five feet by nine composed entirely of violets, geraniums and mimosa. Australia's large wreath was of finest orchids, while the King Scholars of Westminster offered a wreath of pink and white flowers measuring twelve feet.[186]

Contrasting with such extravagance were the funerals of the rural poor. According to an Oxfordshire farm labourer recalling funerals in the early years of the twentieth century:

There waren't no money for wreaths; the coffin were often bare or, at times, strewn with a few wild flowers.[187]

At about the same time, in Glen Gairn, Aberdeenshire, when anyone died, the minister's wife,

made a wreath of flowers from the garden to place on the coffin whenever she had the opportunity, arranging the lilies and other flowers in their season, round a circle of wire, with moss and greenery as a base. For a baby's funeral she made a little posy of snowdrops, cowslips or violets with a background of ivy leaves. Her simple tribute was often the only one.[188]

With a great increase in cremation during the second half of the twentieth century, many people now prefer the money formerly spent on flowers to be donated to a favourite charity. Of the 24 death announcements in the *Shropshire Star* of 4 February 1993: 14 requested family flowers only and suggested donations to various charities, two mentioned flowers or donations, and the remaining three did not mention flowers. More recently it seems as if 'family flowers only, but donations to' a favourite charity is most usually requested.[189]

Elaborate floral tributes can still be seen at the funerals of some conservative communities, travellers, and criminals. A gypsy woman buried at Castor-on-Sea, Norfolk, in May 1965, had her coffin surmounted by two wreaths of flowers in the shape of bow-topped caravans drawn by horses. A few months later in Flintshire, the coffin of a gypsy woman was bedecked with floral tributes representing a dog, a bird-cage, a box of matches and cigarettes, a chair, a cushion, a cooking tripod, a boar's head and a horse collar.[190] Almost 12 years later, the *Balham and Tooting News* of 8 April 1977 reported the south London funeral of a respected gypsy leader. The funeral procession was headed by a horse-drawn hearse, and followed by a long line of cars, lorries and flat-back trucks displaying flowers, many of the wreaths being in the shape of horses and dogs.

Similar floral tributes, representing footballs, pets, teddy bears and cans of favourite lagers – all usually composed of (or at least covered by) dyed or sprayed chrysanthemums – can be seen in urban cemeteries.[191]

Throughout much of the twentieth century, fairground showmen, another group of travelling people, produced elaborate floral decorations for their burials, and the tributes sent to funerals were listed at length in their weekly newspaper, *The World's Fair*.[192] Obviously it is often impractical for showmen to attend funerals, so showy wreaths are sent instead.

Members of criminal communities may also find it difficult to attend funerals. Some of them may be locked away; others may not want to be seen. Consequently extravagant flowers appear at their funerals. Thus in November 1994, following the funeral of the train-robber Buster Edwards, hundreds of wreaths were displayed at the South London Crematorium. Among these was at least one small train-engine, made mainly from chrysanthemums, and a model flower-stall, Edwards having worked on such a stall towards the end of his life.[193] A few months later the funeral procession of the East End gangster Ronnie Kray consisted of six black-plumed horses pulling a flower-covered hearse, followed by over 20 limousines, their roofs covered with wreaths:

> Outside English's Funeral Parlour, the day began with the arrival of one vanload after another of flowers that almost blocked the pavement, Underworld floral tributes are an art form all their own. Atop the hearse was a wreath fashioned like a boxing ring and another like a boxing glove.[194]

Similarly, when Kray's brother Charlie died in 2000, his hearse was decorated with 'two giant boxing gloves from his "friends" in Parkhurst jail, a huge white carnation teddy bear to "grandad" and a display of white roses that spelt "Gentleman"'.[195] When the last of the Kray brothers, Reggie, died later in 2000, his funeral was a relatively restrained affair, but nonetheless the pavement outside the undertakers was covered with floral tributes, and his coffin was decorated with a giant crucifix of red and white roses, from his widow.[196]

According to *Ms London* of 27 March 2000, at the funeral of Shirley Pitts 'the uncontested Queen of Shoplifting' who died in 1992, most of the floral tributes celebrated her crimes by being shaped in the logos of her favourite shops.

During the twentieth century massive displays of flowers were produced following disasters, or deaths that have captured popular emotion. In 1966 when part of a coal tip slid down on the mining village of Aberfan, south Wales, killing 144 people:

> Above the two 80ft trenches that served as graves lay a 100ft tall cross made from hundreds of wreaths from all over the world – one came from South African miners.

There was a wreath made in the shape of Panteglas school, which was destroyed by the avalanche of coal waste, white and pink carnations formed the walls and laurel leaves the roof.[197]

Similarly, in 1989, after the Hillsborough football stadium disaster, in which 95 fans were killed, the home ground of one of the clubs involved was transformed:

Day by day they have poured in to Anfield – the proud ground that is home of Liverpool Football Club. And with their flowers gradually covering the pitch they have turned Anfield into a shrine.[198]

This event received a great deal of attention in the popular press. Before it happened there was a growing custom of placing flowers at the site of tragic deaths, or at places associated with people who have died in tragic circumstances. After it had happened it became almost essential to do so; lack of flowers implies an uncaring community and an unloved victim.

Early in September 1997 the death of Diana, Princess of Wales, in a car crash in Paris, dominated the media, the press coverage included numerous pictures of flowers left at town halls, embassies and places associated with her. The main focus for these tributes was Kensington Palace, the Princess's official London home. On 3 September, three days after her death, *The Times* reported:

Florists have brought in extra staff to cope with the demand for floral tributes following the death of Diana, Princess of Wales. Telephone requests and personal callers left many florists in Kensington and around Buckingham Palace unable to cope with the demand. The owners of Watkins & Watkins, near St James's Palace and Buckingham Palace, received a call from Interflora at 6.30 a.m. Sunday [a few hours after the announcement of the Princess's death] asking them to open early . . . The manager said: 'We are doing four times in excess of Mother's Day business, which is the busiest day of the year. It has been absolutely unbelievable.' The florist . . . has received orders from mourners in dozens of countries. It has employed four cars to deliver the flowers to the palaces, whose entrances have become a sea of bouquets. White roses and lilies, the traditional symbols of grief, are especially requested.

On 4 September, *The Sun* reported:

An amazing £30 million worth of flowers have been laid around Britain in memory of Diana. Weeping mourners have left hundreds of thousands of wreaths and bouquets at the Royal Palaces in London and at shrines throughout the country. To meet demand, blooms are being rushed in from around the world . . . Wholesale prices have rocketed by up to 25 per cent.

During the journey of the Princess's corpse to its burial place at Althorp, the Northamptonshire home of her family:

Single stems and beautifully wrapped bouquets rained down on the black Daimler hearse. There were so many that the driver had to use his windscreen wipers at times to clear aside the flowers and petals.[199]

The placing of flowers at sites of tragedies was a practice that the Princess encouraged:

The Princess of Wales yesterday won the hearts of people on a crime-ridden housing estate by asking for flowers to be laid at a makeshift shrine to a man who died as he confronted vandals. Her convoy, on the way to a Barnardo's family centre in Cardiff's Ely estate, slowed as it passed the spot where father-of-three Mr Les Lee, aged 45, died 18 days ago. She asked police to put bouquets received from wellwishers on a makeshift memorial.[200]

In the 1970s and particularly the 1980s, it became common to place flowers at the scenes of road accidents and other places where people met with violent deaths.

The heartbroken family of two teenage friends killed in a car crash in Ealing [west London] has transformed the tragic spot where they died into a blaze of colour.

Best friends, Wayne Dunne, 18, and his friend Stephen Wesley Shakespeare, 18, were killed when their car hit a tree on Gunnersbury Avenue, Acton, last Monday.

This week, their families have turned the tree into a memorial for the pair by bedecking it with flowers and messages.[201]

In many urban areas, and along some roads and riverbanks, it is impossible to travel far without coming across bouquets commemorating spots where people have died as a result of traffic accident, violent crime, or suicide, and at least one local authority has felt it necessary to try and restrict this activity. In 2003 Wakefield, West Yorkshire, council considered bouquets and memorabilia to be distracting to drivers, and accordingly banned them.[202]

After burial the various floral tributes are left on the grave, to be removed by the family or the cemetery's caretaker when they have decayed. Later bunches of, often artificial, flowers or pot plants are placed on the grave, or it may be planted as a small garden. It is apparent that many people derive great solace from such activities. At crematoria, gardens of remembrance are common and it is possible to have a standard rose bush, or, more rarely some other small shrub, planted in memory of a loved one. Despite the disapproval of the gardens' managers, these closely planted, uniformly labelled rose bushes are often treated in much the same way as graves, and cut flowers are frequently placed at the base of them, or tied to their spindly trunks.[203] The memorial gardens of the City of London Cemetery and Crematorium contain approximately 600 rose beds containing about 20,000 bushes, some of the most popular varieties being Alec's Red, Summer Holiday (National Trust), Peace, Mischief (Blessings), Silver Jubilee, Susan Hampshire (Prima Ballerina) and Goldstar.[204]

Depending on the mourners' feelings, graves continue to have flowers placed on them, especially on the birthdays and anniversaries, Christmas, Easter, Mothering Sunday, Father's Day, Flowering (Palm) Sunday in parts of Wales,[205] and All Souls' Day (2 November) among Polish and some other Catholic communities.[206]

For the famous, the tending of memorials may, of course, exceed the few years that the graves of the more humble are likely to receive. The equestrian statue of King Charles I, in Whitehall, London, is decorated with wreaths and posies in commemoration of his execution in 1649.[207] King Charles was canonized by the Church of England in the 1660s, and although most of the flowers placed against the statue's plinth are modest offerings, the sentiment expressed on the accompanying cards suggest that for some people the King is worthy of his titles of Saint and Martyr. Another seventeenth-century notable still commemorated is the diarist Samuel Pepys, who was buried in St Olave's church in the City of London, in 1703. On or near 26 May, the anniversary of his death, a commemoration service is held, at which the Mayor or another dignitary places a wreath in front of the memorial.[208]

The railings in front of Kensington Palace usually bear a few bouquets in memory of Diana, Princess of Wales, and outside Stockwell underground station, in south London, flowers are still placed at the informal memorial that commemorates Jean Charles de Menezes, a young Brazilian carpenter, who on 22 July 2005 was shot by a policeman who mistook him for a terrorist.[209]

Throughout life plants, especially flowers, are used to convey a wide range of emotions, ranging from joy and hope to grief and remorse.

While we are unlikely to push a yarrow leaf up a nostril to test a lover's fidelity, or count the number of flowers on a peony to see if death is foretold, society is unlikely to let weddings and funerals pass creating opportunities for selling flowers. And, if a tragedy occurs, only the most hard-hearted neighbourhoods would dare let it go unmarked by not producing piles of flowers at the scene.

10

GARLANDS AND NOSEGAYS

Traditional customs have attracted much attention from folk music enthusiasts and people seeking to reconnect with what they imagine to be the pre-Christian religions of the British Isles. Most recently they have been documented for England by Steve Roud,[1] while the writings of Ronald Hutton have brought new rigour to the study of their origins.[2] As in the celebration of critical times in the human life cycle, plant materials were used by communities celebrating their annual cycle of festivals. Again, these plants were probably chosen simply because they provided colour at the appropriate time. Later they became part of the tradition; became *the* plants to be used. Their availability was reassuring, all was right with the world. If they were unavailable, because it was an exceptionally early or late season, it was a matter for unease and concern. Today, with worries about human-induced climate change, early seasons cause particular concern.

It is not possible here to attempt a comprehensive account of all of those customs which use plant materials. Instead an attempt is made to indicate some of the many ways in which plants feature in a variety of customs.

During the late nineteenth and early twentieth centuries burning the ashen faggot – a faggot made from ash saplings – was a widespread custom in parts of Devon and Somerset, on 5 January (Old Christmas Eve) or thereabouts. According to C. H. Poole, writing in 1877, it was 'an ancient ceremony transmitted to us from the Scandinavians who at their feast of Juul were accustomed to kindle huge bonfires in honour of Thor'.[3] Hutton has found records of logs being burnt during the Christmas period in the first half of the seventeenth century, but has not been able to find any records of burning ashen faggots before 1795.[4] In the first half of the nineteenth century Ashen Faggot Balls were held in some Somerset towns, the one at Taunton in 1826 being 'most respectably attended by the principal families of the town and neighbourhood'.[5]

By the mid-twentieth century the burning of ashen faggots had almost died out, although it survived at the King William IV public house in Curry Rivel, Somerset,[6] and occasionally has been revived elsewhere. A particularly healthy revival is that at the Squirrel Inn, near Winsham, on the Dorset-Somerset border. This revival took place in 1974,[7] and the event continues to attract a good crowd:

> The Squirrel's ash faggot has been made by Thorncombe farmer Mike Turner for over 20 years. It is tied together by 12 hazel bonds, which Mr Turner believes represent the months of the year, and the customers traditionally drink a toast to each one as it breaks in the fire, There is a competition to guess how long the faggot takes to burn. It was placed in the fire around 8 p.m. and finished burning five hours, four minutes and five seconds later.[8]

Although most reports of the event mention the drinking of toasts whenever a bond snaps, this does not appear to be so. On 6 January 2009, although the bar was almost full, few people paid any attention to the faggot, and most simply chatted near the bar. However, it was said that if a woman stepped over the faggot she would become pregnant. Two women who had done this in 2008, one of whom had 'been trying for three years', had produced babies.[9]

At the same time of year apple trees were wassailed. In the mid-nineteenth century:

> In certain parts of this country superstitious observances yet linger, such as drinking health to the [apple] trees on Christmas and Epiphany eves, saluting them by throwing toasted crabs or toast around them, lighting fires, etc. All these ceremonies are supposed to render the trees productive for the coming season.

I once had the occasion to pass the night preceding Twelfth Day at a lone farmhouse on the borders of Dartmoor, in Devonshire, and was somewhat alarmed at hearing, very late at night, the repeated discharge of fire-arms in the immediate vicinity of the house. On my inquiring in the morning as to what was the cause of the unseasonable noise, I was told that the farm-men were firing into the apple-trees in the orchard, in order that the trees might bear a good crop.[10]

Although the wassailing of apple trees was often thought of as a West Country custom, it 'was actually common in some form or other across the southern and western counties and elsewhere'.[11] It seems that wassailing persisted longest at the Butchers Arms, at Carhampton, Somerset, which claims to be the only place to continue the unbroken tradition,[12] but revivals have taken place elsewhere. In 1974 the Taunton Cider Company promoted a wassailing, complete with Wassail Queen, at Norton Fitzwarren, also in Somerset.[13] A revival which has continued for many years is that started by the Chanctonbury Ring Morris Men, in Sussex, in 1967. The event uses the local name of Apple Howling, but is based on a compilation of traditions from different parts of the country.[14] The 1978 programme proceeded from a 'cacophonous noise' to signal the start, through a series of traditional activities, which include placing a spiced wassail cake in a fork of an apple tree 'to ensure the goodwill of robins and other birds', to a 'general hullabaloo', followed by three cheers for the orchard's owner, and concluding with the distribution of wassail cake and cider from the barrel. Apple Howling continues in much the same way, usually on the first Saturday in January each year, at Old Mill Farm, Bolney.[15]

Towards the end of January, or in February, Chinese communities in London and elsewhere hold their New Year festivities. It is believed the first public celebrations of the Chinese New Year were held in Gerrard Street and the neighbouring area, in Soho, London, on Sunday 31 January 1971, and, since 1973, they have become an annual event.[16] Various activities have been added to the celebrations over the years, some of these have become regulars, others occur infrequently, but lion dances are considered essential. A lion consists of a large multicoloured grotesque mask with a young man inside, surrounded by a number of men with bamboo poles who attempt to maintain adequate space for the lion. Music is provided by a small gang of percussionists, and the party is completed with a costumed character who guides the lion from one offering to the next. Offerings consist of bank notes, and lettuce and other vegetables, tied on lengths of string hung from the windows of shops and restaurants. After eating one offering, the lion moves on to the next.

> The highlight of the dance is Choi Cheng, which means 'Picking the Green'. The 'Green' is a bunch of lettuce leaves tied up with a red packet of lucky money, and is traditionally hung above the doorway of a house or shop. The head dancer stands on the shoulder of the second to reach out for the bunch and swallow it with the lion's jaws. At this point the drums roll furiously to create an exciting atmosphere. The lion then tears the lettuce into small pieces and spits it out. This act symbolises the acceptance of the reward or thanks from the household for the luck and prosperity the lion may bring; the lion eats the lettuce, thus tearing it to pieces, and when it spits the lettuce out it shows there will be plenty of everything for the coming year.[17]

Other plants associated with the Chinese New Year include Chinese plum and tangerine. Twigs of flowering Chinese plum (often called peach) are offered for sale, and decorate shops and restaurants:[18]

> It is the custom for Chinese families to go out into the market on New Year's Eve to buy peach blossoms to decorate their homes.

151

The blossoms signify spring, which also means the beginning of the New Year in the lunar calendar.[19]

It is said that the tangerine is associated with New Year celebrations because of the similarity of its name with the word for 'blessing' or 'fortune'.[20] At the celebrations in London small potted tangerine (and similar citrus) shrubs with abundant fruit are offered for sale, and tangerines are often offered to the lions.[21]

St Valentine's Day (14 February) in its present commercialized form does not have a long history; the use of Valentine's cards, after several false starts from about 1820 onwards, failed to get established until the 1950s.[22] Since then it has become an important source of income for florists, who sell millions of red roses to people who want to convey their love to their partners, or potential partners, on this day. At one time the gift of a single red rose was considered to be a sufficiently romantic gesture, but now any fewer than a dozen suggests miserliness. As red roses are the flowers for Valentine's Day, and the day is celebrated in many parts of the world, it is inevitable that they become much more expensive in the time running up to 14 February. Thus on 14 February 1991 the *Daily Mail* reported that:

At Sally's, in Dulwich, southeast London, a dozen red roses had soared 300 per cent from £9 to £36. The assistant was frank. 'It's Valentine's now, so everything has gone right up.'

While in 1995 it was reported that at this time of year the maximum price of a dozen long-stemmed roses delivered by Interflora increased from £25.50 to £35.[23]

On 1 March the Welsh celebrate St David's Day, by wearing leeks or daffodils. Why the leek became associated with St David and Wales is unknown,[24] but dates back to the Middle Ages.[25] In Anglesey in 1877 it was the custom for boys to wear leeks before midday on St David's Day, while girls were 'supposed to deck themselves' with leeks in the afternoon. Should a boy fail to wear a leek in the morning, or be seen wearing one after midday, he would be mercilessly pinched, and similar punishment would be dealt out to girls who wore leeks before midday.[26] A favourite press photograph on 2 March is of a small girl in Welsh costume presenting a leek to a tall member of the Welsh Guards.[27] It appears that the use of daffodils, which are more decorative and easier to wear, was a later innovation. As well as being worn on St David's Day both daffodils and leeks feature on a wide range of goods sold in Welsh souvenir shops, and are worn by supporters of the Welsh rugby team.

St Patrick, the patron saint of Ireland is commemorated on 17 March, when the Irish and their supposed descendents overseas wear shamrocks.

Sixteenth-century references to shamrock imply it was an edible plant, possibly watercress.[28] However, in 1597 John Gerard stated that shamrock was a species of clover.[29] It has been claimed that the earliest association of shamrock with St Patrick occurs on a copper coin minted 'for the use of the Confederate Irish in the Wars of Charles I', in Kilkenny. This coin supposedly depicted St Patrick 'displaying a trefoil to the assembled people'.[30] However, no such coin appears to have been produced during the reign of Charles I (1625–49), but an attractive halfpenny piece minted during the 1670s accurately fits this description.[31] By 1681 or thereabouts shamrock was being worn, at least by 'the vulgar' on St Patrick's Day. According to the English traveller Thomas Dinely:

> The 17th day of March yeerly is St Patrick's, an immoveable feast when ye Irish of all stations and condicions wear crosses in their hats, some of pins, some of green ribbons, and the vulgar superstitiously wear shamroges, 3-leaved grass, which they likewise eat (they say) so cause sweet breath.[32]

Since then the wearing of St Patrick's Day crosses has declined,[33] while the wearing of shamrock has become prevalent. By the end of the seventeenth century shamrock had become firmly established as an emblem of Ireland and the Irish,[34] but it was not until 1726 that Caleb Threlkeld recorded the tradition that St Patrick used the three-leaved shamrock to demonstrate the nature of the Trinity.[35]

The identity of the plant that St Patrick used has been a matter of controversy, and writers have suggested species of clover or medic, and wood sorrel. Irish tradition is unhelpfully vague:

> First of all the mystic plant is not a clover, in the next place it never flowers, and finally it refuses to grow on alien soil.[36]

The suggestion that wood sorrel, which is eaten by children,[37] was shamrock was promoted by the English botanist James Bicheno, who in 1831 conceded that although white clover was the plant then known as shamrock, wood sorrel was the plant originally known by this name. When Ireland's woodlands became depleted, wood sorrel became scarce, leading to the use of clover as a substitute.[38] Perhaps another reason why clover replaced wood sorrel as the plant for wearing on hats or in buttonholes is that the leaves of clover are much more robust and wilt less rapidly than those of wood sorrel.

Early in the 1890s Nathaniel Colgan, a clerk with the Dublin constabulary, requested people to send him rooted bits of shamrock, which he grew on until they were sufficiently mature for identification. On examination, he found that four species were represented. White clover and lesser yellow trefoil were the species most often considered to be shamrock, while red clover and black medick were less frequently favoured as such.[39] Some years before Colgan's investigations James Britten examined bunches of shamrock on sale in London, found that most of them consisted of lesser yellow trefoil,[40] and Colgan eventually concluded that this species was probably the true shamrock. In 1988 Charles Nelson attempted to repeat Colgan's work and received 221 shamrock plants that grew to maturity. On examination these proved to be much the same mixture of species as that sent to Colgan: 46 per cent of the plants were lesser yellow trefoil, and 35 per cent of the plants were white clover. Nelson concluded that 'very little significant change evidently has taken place during almost one century in the folk concept of shamrock'.[41] As a characteristic of shamrock is that it never flowers, perhaps it is significant that although lesser yellow trefoil plants are compact and bright green early in the year, when they flower they send out sprawling stems, so that mature plants look quite different from younger ones.

It is usual for a member, or representative, of the Royal Family to present shamrock to the Irish Guards on St Patrick's Day, and this was a favourite custom of Queen Elizabeth, the Queen Mother, who carried it out every year from 1965 until her death in 2002.[42]

On the whole St George's Day (23 April) has been largely ignored by the English, some churches fly the St George's flag in the day, and a few people, including television newsreaders, wear red roses. However, in 1986 when the Labour Party adopted the red rose as its symbol there were protests. At a meeting of the Common Council of the City of London:

A motion was tabled by Mr Brian Boreham that all Common Councillors should wear a red rose provided by the Corporation for their meeting on St George's Day. However, Mr Norman Harding said that he would be voting against the motion since the red rose was now an emblem of a political party.[43]

Two years later, a Mr Meloy, of Tunley, Avon, wrote to *The Times*:

It has been my custom, in previous years, to wear a red rose on April 23 – a custom shared with many of my fellow countrymen and women. However, I am a Civil Servant, and as such must show no tendency to favour any individual political party.

Given that the rose has become the symbol of one of our major political parties I wonder if any of your correspondents could suggest what, if anything, would be appropriate to wear on St George's Day?[44]

Perhaps more widespread than the wearing of red roses on St George's Day was the practice of collecting dandelion flowers for home wine-making.[45]

In some areas of England it was customary for schoolchildren to wear ash twigs on Ash Wednesday, the first day of Lent.[46]

When I was at school, on the Hampshire, Sussex and Surrey borders, you had to have an ash twig tucked into your sock on Ash Wednesday, until 12 o'clock; if you had one after 12 you were punished by having your feet stamped on. I assume the custom came to an end when schoolboys stopped wearing short trousers.[47]

Mothering Sunday (now often known as Mother's Day), the fourth Sunday in Lent, is another busy time for florists. During the first half of the twentieth century it became usual for churches to hold Mothering Sunday services at which posies, often of wild flowers, were distributed to mothers.[48] In 1979 at West Coker, Somerset, 'the children received a card and a candle to present to their mothers and flowers were distributed by the Sunday-school teachers'. Elsewhere in Somerset, every mother present at St Mark's Methodist church in Yeovil received a bunch of heather, at Stoke-sub-Hamdon carnations were presented to mothers, and at Aller 'each child received a Mother's Day card and a posy of flowers',[49] which were presumably given to mothers. Later the day became greatly commercialized, so that in 1996 it was reported that £50 million (of which daffodils accounted for £10 million) was spent on Mothering Sunday.[50] Ten years later it was said that on Mothering Sunday 'the UK's sales of cut flowers and indoor plants increase by 40% on a normal day's trading'.[51] Unlike Valentine's Day, when red roses are by far the most important flower, on Mothering Sunday no particular flower seems to be in special demand, thus in 1994 Sainsbury's Homebase offered a variety of 'Mother's Day gifts', ranging from a 'teddy bear arrangement' at £2.99 to a 'planted large hooped basket' priced at £16.95.[52]

Palm Sunday, the Sunday before Easter, commemorates Christ's entry to Jerusalem: 'some people carpeted the road with their cloaks, while others spread brushwood which they had cut in the fields; and those who went ahead and the others who came behind shouted "Hosanna! Blessings on him who comes in the name of the Lord!"'[53] Just as the tree in the Garden of Eden is commonly interpreted as an apple, so in tradition 'brushwood' has become palm. In northern Europe where there are no native palms substitutes had to be found. Throughout England the twigs of goat willow (also known as pussy willow or sallow) with male catkins were most frequently used as palm:[54]

Sallow catkins and branches are the only plant material permitted in church during Lent. These are known as palm or pussy palm and represent the palm branches strewn on the road as Christ entered Jerusalem for the last time.[55]

In Ireland cypress[56] or yew were commonly used. Indeed, many Irish-speakers knew Palm Sunday as *Domhnach an Iuir* (Yew Sunday).[57]

> Yew tree branches are used in Catholic church ceremonies on Palm Sunday and afterwards distributed to the congregation. It may be worn and afterwards some is placed in the dwelling house and byres to bring good luck.[58]

In recent years imported dried palm fronds, tied in the shape of a cross, have largely replaced native 'palms' in most churches.

In parts of Wales Palm Sunday was known as *Sul y Blodau*, or Flowering Sunday, on which it was the custom to decorate graves. Although the name *Sul y Blodau* was recorded as early as the fifteenth century, it does not appear to have been restricted to Palm Sunday until the latter half of the nineteenth century.[59] Late in the nineteenth century the custom became so popular in some urban parts of south Wales that in 1896 a writer described how thousands of people 'wend their way to the Cemetery, the roads thereto presenting an appearance like unto a fair'.[60] During the twentieth century the custom steadily declined, although in 1983 it was recorded that in many parts of Wales graves continue to receive special attention, usually by having bunches of daffodils placed on them, on Palm Sunday.[61]

On Maundy Thursday, the last Thursday in Lent, the Queen presents Maundy gifts to elderly people.[62] In recent years this ceremony takes place alternately in Westminster Abbey, London, and a provincial cathedral. In its original form monarchs or their representatives washed the feet of the elderly people, but now the monarch presents bags of specially minted coins instead. Not surprisingly it was considered necessary for precautions to be taken before monarchs came into contact with their decrepit subjects, so it became usual for posies to be carried to ward off unpleasant odours and disease. Today the carrying of posies continues, and although they are largely decorative they contain a high propor-tion of highly scented plants. Thus in 1994 it was recorded that each of the larger posies contained: 'nine daffodils, 11 pieces of white stock, 15 narcissus cheerfulness, 14 bunches of violets, 12 bunches of primroses, 20 pieces of cupressus, 14 sprigs of rosemary and 12 of thyme'.[63]

Many churches maintain the tradition of having no flowers during Lent, and Good Friday is a day devoid of decorations, but on the fol-lowing day flower-arrangers get busy so that churches are abundantly decorated on Easter Sunday. Lilies, often bought in commemoration of dead parishioners, are usually given pride of place. In the mid-twentieth century arum lilies (now more usually known as altar lilies) were usual:

> In 1947–8 the Rev. George Grove became Vicar of Thorncombe [Dorset] and suggested to me that in order to achieve flowers in nice numbers cheaply for Easter parishioners might like to donate arums (the cost of them) in memory of someone known to them. This idea has continued ever since, though nowadays the cost of even one bloom can be too much for an individual, so we tend to ask people to give what they can towards flowers . . . We used to get about 50 flowers, and still achieve between 30 and 40.[64]

More recently the fragrant *Lilium longiflorum*, known as Easter lily, has largely replaced the arum lily.[65] Thus at Easter 2002 Holy Trinity parish church at Llandrindod Wells, Powys, was filled 'with the scent of over 150 lilies' donated by members of the church community in memory of their loved ones.[66]

Even non-churchgoers are likely to celebrate Easter by having Easter eggs. During the twentieth century these were usually made of chocolate, but in earlier times they were often simply boiled, sometimes dyed, hens' eggs. In the British Isles the two favourite vegetable dyes used for Easter eggs were onion skins[67] and gorse (whin) flowers.

> On Easter Sunday we collected all the weans of the village and took them up to a field with a big hill on it. We made our tea after lighting a fire and got all the eggs in a big saucepan to boil them hard. Unknown to the kids we put whin blossom in the water while they were boiling and they came out a lovely yellow colour. The kids thought it was magic. Then up to the top of the hill and roll the eggs down.[68]

The fortieth day after Easter is celebrated as Ascension Day, and marks the traditional start of the well-dressing season in the Derbyshire Peak District. This popular custom is commonly supposed to have started in pre-Christian times, when 'wells were honoured with religious ceremonies and dances, and decorated with flowers and green branches at the greater festivals'.[69] Naylor and Porter in their 2002 study of well-dressing make an association between the custom and the decorating of clootie, or cloutie, wells. These are wells, often named after a local saint, which have pieces of cloth – clouties – tied as offerings to nearby trees.[70] Perhaps another custom to which well-dressing might be usefully compared is the production of Corpus Christi floral carpets.[71]

However, the earliest records of well-dressings date only from 1748, when it was recorded that on Holy Thursday (presumably the day now better known as Maundy Thursday) at Tissington, springs were adorned with garlands.[72] This was said to be an annual event, suggesting that by that time springs, or wells, had already been dressed for a decade or more. However, Peak District well-dressing does not consist of decking water supplies with garlands, but with erecting boards covered with elaborate floral pictures behind or near them, and the first record of such boards – 'screens' – dates from 1817.[73] In its present form:

> Wooden trays, c. 2.5cm deep and up to 3.7m in length, are filled with moist clay onto which is pressed natural, mostly plant, materials to form vivid mosaic-like pictures, usually depicting religious themes or ecclesiastical buildings. Materials commonly used include petals, sepals of hydrangea, fruits of alder (*Alnus glutinosa*), various seeds, parsley leaves and lichens. When the picture is completed the tray is placed in an erect position at a village well, the well remaining dressed for about a week.[74]

Although the well-dressing year traditionally started on Ascension Day, at Tissington, where a population of about 200 manages to dress five wells, in recent years the start of the season has moved forward, partly because the custom has become so popular that there are insufficient dates available between Ascension Day and the Late Summer bank holiday, at the end of August, which, at one time, marked the last well-dressing of the year, at Eyam. Despite the tremendous amount of work involved in preparing the screens, gathering the flowers, designing the pictures, pressing the plant materials into the clay, and transporting and erecting the finished work, well-dressing continues to become ever more popular and spread beyond its traditional boundaries. The list of well-dressings prepared by the Peak District National Park Office in 1974, included only 11 towns and villages.[75] Nineteen years later the 1993 Wirksworth well-dressings programme listed 48 dressings, taking place between 3 May and 18 September, while in 2009 a website listed over 70 dressings between 4 May and 20 September.[76] Many years ago the number of screens prepared exceeded the number of water supplies available for dressing, so often they are erected at any focal point in the village where visitors can safely stop and admire them. In recent years the increase in dressings has resulted not only in summer weekends becoming crowded with well-dressing events, but also in screens being prepared in some places where the necessary skills appear to be lacking.

Outside the Peak District and its vicinity well-dressing screens intermittently appear elsewhere. In 1995 St Chad's church in Lichfield, Staffordshire, marked the 50th anniversary of the foundation of Christian Aid by 'reviving the custom of well-dressing at their harvest festival'.[77] Since the custom was previously unrecorded from Lichfield, perhaps 'introducing' would have been more accurate than 'reviving'. However, since 1995 it seems to have become a regular event.[78] Since 1985 a well-dressing has been held at Froome, in Somerset, each year:

> The well is dressed by petals, seeds, etc., pressed into a clay foundation to create an appropriate design – different every year. The flowers used are a mixture of wild and garden flowers, some provided by a local florist, depending upon the colours needed to produce the design. The work is placed in position early in the morning of the chosen day, and the clergy and town mayor, accompanied by the wardens, servers and choir, process from the church to the well or spring . . . where a short service of blessing – of the spring and of the town – is held. The event takes place on the Saturday nearest St Aldhelm's Day (25 May). Aldhelm was the founder, in 685 AD, of the church and of the settlement which became Frome.[79]

Even further afield, Tom Shaw, who was born in Derby in 1916 and migrated to Australia in 1956, produced three well-dressings in Perth, Western Australia, in 1985.[80]

Since 1863 Bisley, in Gloucestershire has dressed its wells on Ascension Day. After a service in the church there is a procession to the wells where children from the village school attach garlands and wreaths to metal frames.[81]

The seventh Sunday after Easter is known as Whitsun or Pentecost, and commemorates descent of the Holy Spirit on to Christ's disciples. Many of the customs formerly associated with Whitsun have migrated to the Spring Bank Holiday. Churches often use red and white flowers in their Whitsun decorations – 'the symbolism of the fire and the wind of the Holy Spirit'.[82] A formerly widespread custom, 'dating from time immemorial',[83] involved decorating churches with branches of birch on Whit Sunday. Charlotte Burne noted that in Shropshire the only local custom associated with Whitsun was decorating churches with birch branches that were stuck into holes in the tops of pews:

> Hordley Church was thus adorned up to the year 1857; at St Mary's Shrewsbury, the custom was kept up until about the year 1865; at St Chad's it was continued up to 1855, and probably later.[84]

The bringing of birch branches into churches at Whitsun seems to have died out in most places in the second half of the nineteenth century, but it survives at the church of St John the Baptist, in Froome, Somerset:

> We are allowed the top of young silver birch trees in the woods

of Longleat each year and we fix the resultant five or six foot branches to the pillars which separate the nave from the north and south aisles. We believe that the significance of the branches is twofold: being young growths, they represent the renewal of life; and the stirring of leaves resulting from the moving air currents in the church represent the sound of the 'rushing mighty wind' as the Holy Spirit descended on the Apostles. We have however nothing but tradition by word of mouth to support this interpretation nor can we say when the custom began, except to say we know it was in operation by 1836, since we have amongst our church records a contract by which the verger undertook to obtain holly to decorate the church at Easter and birch branches at Whitsun.[85]

The last moveable feast to be considered in a plant-lore context is Corpus Christi, celebrated on the Thursday after Trinity Sunday, the eighth Sunday after Easter. This feast celebrates the institution by Christ of the Holy Eucharist, and in Catholic churches the Body of Christ (Corpus Christi) is carried in procession as a public witness to the belief of Christ's presence in the Eucharist. In some places specially prepared floral carpets cover the processional route. In England the Roman Catholic Cathedral in Arundel, West Sussex, produces the most well-known of these floral carpets. Here:

> The tradition of the carpet of flowers was taken from the village of Sutri outside Rome and introduced . . . by the 15th Duke of Norfolk in 1877. It seems not to have been carried on during the First World War, but was revived in 1919 and has continued ever since; the whole work being undertaken by parishioners.[86]

In recent years the carpet, which is six feet wide and runs the length (97 feet) of the cathedral's aisle (97 feet), is laid on the Tuesday before the feast day, and is on display all day on Wednesday and until 5.30 p.m. on Thursday, when Mass is celebrated. Following the Mass, its celebrants carry the sacrament down the aisle and thus destroy the carpet. A different design is employed each year, but the plants employed remain the same: mainly chrysanthemums to give large splashes of bright colour, carnations to provide more intricate highlights and Lawson's cypress, which provides a sombre background.[87]

At Arundel the carpet designs are abstract or include Christian symbols and simple wording. For example in 2006 it incorporated a white dove and the words 'Pray for world peace'. However, quick examination of various websites that depict carpets in other parts of Europe show that they include images of biblical scenes, and thus they closely resemble some Derbyshire well-dressings.

At least two of London's Anglo-Catholic churches prepare Corpus Christi carpets for the Sunday after the feast day. At All Saints, Notting Hill, a carpet similar to the Arundel one has been prepared every year since either just before or just after World War II:

> Flowers are bought – as the feast is variable the flowers are usually akin to the season. Most of the flowers are stripped of their petals and these petals are what make up the design. It doesn't last long. Usually it is made the day before and by the next evening you can usually see the signs that it is beginning to go. The carpet's primary function is to be the carpet for the beginning of the Blessed Sacrament procession and it is not walked upon until that stage at the end of the Mass (after which it is destroyed by those who walk upon it in the procession).[88]

A rather different carpet is prepared at St Mary's, Bourne Street, in Belgravia. Here, where the Corpus Christi procession 'goes back beyond living memory':

> Rose petals are scattered by little girls in front of the procession of the Host, but the carpet on the floor is of leaves and herbs. The herbs are sweet smelling, but most of them are straight kitchen herbs and then occasionally the odd sprig of verbena or scented geranium gets included . . . the church is like something in an especially aromatic wood.[89]

While the church follows its own arcane ways, the secular calendar continues through the year.

May Day, 1 May, was the traditional day on which children prepared garlands and took them around villages hoping to get gifts. In the 1920s at Desborough, Northamptonshire:

> The older school-girls would go out at dawn to pick primroses, violets, bluebells, wood anemones. These were taken in a covered clothes-basket from door-to-door, where the drape was lifted, with the hope that the housewife would give a penny or two. Later the headmistress arranged that this celebration should be done in school.[90]

This late memory describes a rather rudimentary form of 'garland'. Earlier garlands were more elaborate, 'ranging from a simple bunch of flowers tied to the top of a long staff, or a pole wreathed in flowers, to the elaborate double-hoop garland, densely covered with spring flowers of every kind, or the less usual pyramid, also thickly covered by blossoms, and usually very tall, rising to a height of 5 or 6ft'.[91] A sentimental-ized account from the garland-carriers' viewpoint in rural Oxfordshire in the late nineteenth century is given by Flora Thompson in her semi-autobiographical *Larkrise*.[92] A slightly later account, from another vantage point, is provided in the memoirs of Princess Alice, Duchess of Gloucester (b. 1901). At Boughton, Northamptonshire, one of her childhood homes, children would come in turns from the four villages that stood at the edge of the park:

> the girls garlanded and the boys holding bunches of spring flowers as they carried their May Queen on a throne smothered in blooms and leafy branches. After singing songs they would dance around the maypole and then to the delight of all, we showered them with well-polished pennies, thrown as far as possible to cause the greatest chase and scramble.[93]

Early in the 1950s Iona and Peter Opie found that May garlands were still carried in parts of Oxfordshire and by girls who looked 'the Marsh or gypsy type' at Ashford in Kent, although related customs still survived elsewhere.[94] Since then the custom of children making and carrying garlands appears to have died out.

In places where garlands are made it is usual for adults to do so, and they are carried on dates other than May Day. The best known of these garlands are those carried at Abbotsbury, Dorset, which since the cus-tom's first known description in 1867, have been carried on 13 May, and are believed to be linked with the local fishing industry. Only children of fishermen were allowed to participate, and the number of garlands carried equalled the number of village families that owned boats. In the 1920s an average of about eight garlands seems to have been produced each year and in the 1930s about five. Since the 1960s only two garlands have been produced, one supposedly of wild and the other of garden flowers. The Abbotsbury garlands represent the survival of a custom that was once common in local villages, including Burton Bradstock where garlands were carried on 12 May until 1940, Puncknowle on 13 May until 1946, Swyre until 1922 and Wyke Regis on 1 May until about 1921.[95]

Following the closure of Abbotsbury School early in the 1980s the garland carrying has been moved to early evening. Until that time the children have no contact with the garlands, which are prepared by local women during the afternoon. In 1983 two rigid plastic frames were first covered with elder leaves before generous bunches of flowers were added. Each bunch contains only one species, and the decorators work downwards from the top of the frames. The wild flower garland con-tained bluebells, cow parsley, cowslips, pendulous sedge, primroses (only available when the season is late – 'only twice since I've been making them'), and some cultivated flowers, including apple blossom, flowering currant and lilac. The 'garden garland' contained camellias, lilac, pieris foliage, rhododendron, stocks and wallflowers. At about 5.30 p.m. the children assembled and divided into two groups, one to carry around each garland. Each group consisted of about eight children aged from about 8 to 15 each, and without adult supervision they set out around the village, visiting all the houses. This occupied about three hours, during which time the garlands became increasingly limp and dishevelled. Donations from householders varied from a few pence to a couple of pounds.[96]

Thirteen years later the procedure was similar, but the village seemed to lack pride in the event. The garden garland was accompanied by about 20 children, mostly of primary school age, and three women. Two or three of the older children would dump the garland outside a front door, ring the doorbell, and wait for a short while, hoping that the householder would come and make a donation. Only about half of the doors were answered. The children less directly involved with the garland amused themselves by swinging on gates or scaffolding, decapitating garden flowers, fighting and being generally unruly. The women and some of the older girls told the youngsters to 'keep behind the garland'. Otherwise they made little, if any, effort to control the rabble. At the other end of the village, the wildflower garland, decorated with bunches of bluebells, cow parsley, cowslips, early purple orchids, primroses and sea campion, was accompanied by about 20 children, who were mostly older than the children with the other garland, and two women, who maintained control. Usually two or three of the older children took the garland to a door, while the others watched from the other side of the road. Again only about half of the doors were opened.[97]

At Bampton, Oxfordshire, more famous for its morris dancing:

> The making of May Garlands by the children of the village is a custom stretching back centuries. The showing and judging of the garlands takes place on the Monday of the Spring Bank Holiday, at 11 a.m. in the Market Square. To make May Garlands is very easy, but time consuming. All you need are two hoops which you cover with wildflowers. These wildflowers can be dandelions, buttercups, cow parsley – in fact anything which is easy to find. Tie them into small bunches and attach them to the hoops with string. Fix the two hoops together so they form a 'ball' shape. On top fix a bunch of flowers – years ago the top posy had to be made up of red or pink peonies. Sit your favourite doll or teddy in the centre, find a long stick or broom handle to hook it through and two people to carry it and you have yourself a traditional May Garland.[98]

Also on Spring Bank Holiday Monday, Garland Day is held at Lewes in East Sussex. This event was started in the 1870s and has been revived by the Knots of May, a local women's morris dance club.[99] In 2008 70 children took garlands to the Gun Garden of Lewes Castle, where they were judged by the Mayor and Chairman of the District Council.[100]

In many urban areas, typically in southern England, Jack-in-the-Green, a man or youth enclosed in a wooden or wicker frame covered in foliage, danced the streets on May Day. For much of the twentieth century it was thought that Jack was another manifestation of the foliate head motif that ornaments medieval churches,[101] or a rare and curious survival of an ancient rite – 'the annual victim of the vegetation drama'.[102] However, in the 1970s it was shown that Jack-in-the-Green had no connection with the foliate head,[103] and, in fact, evolved towards the end of the eighteenth century as a begging activity practised by chimney-sweeps and others on May Day.[104] In most places the Jack had become extinct by the outbreak of World War I or the 1920s. Thus, what was supposedly an ancient ritual, existed for little more than a century, but from the 1950s onwards revivals have taken place in a number of places, notably at Hastings on the Sussex coast. Here Jack-in-the-Green celebrations, which take place on the May Day Bank Holiday, were revived in 1983, and attract a huge number of morris dancers, giant-carriers, and neopagans (who are either unaware of, or prefer to ignore, Jack's late origin). The highlight of the Hastings festival is a morning procession of morris dancers and others through the town, and in the midst of which is the Jack figure, a conical structure covered in robust leaves of rhododendron, ribbons and a topknot of flowers. During the early afternoon, dance displays take place at Hastings Castle, and at 3.30 p.m., 'after dancing the Bogies [escorts] parade Jack down to the stage where he is symbolically slain and the Spirit of Summer is set free for another year'.[105]

In some coastal areas of south Devon, Sussex and Norfolk, 2 May was known as Sting Nettle Day. In the 1930s and 1940s around Hove and Worthing in Sussex:

The first of May is Pinch-Bum Day,
The second of May is Sting-Nettle Day.

Similarly at Brixham, Devon, on 1 May (Ducking Day) boys squirted people with water pistols, on 2 May they chased the girls with stinging nettles and on 3 May (Petticoat Day) they chased the girls and tried to lift their dresses. It seems that this custom died out just before, or during, World War II.[106]

Between 1903 and 1958 24 May (Queen Victoria's birthday) was celebrated as Empire Day, when the 'non-party, non-sectarian, non-aggressive' Empire Movement encouraged the wearing of daisies: 'Fly the Union Jack and wear daisies, ox-eyed daisies, bachelor's buttons, marigolds, or marguerites annually.'[107]

When we celebrated Empire Day at school [we] were expected to wear some daisies pinned to our chests or buttonholes. My sister and I would rise early to collect out dew-fresh 'buttonhole daisies', feeling proud as we walked to school waving a Union Jack![108]

Children in West Kensington, London, were told that daisies grew in every country of the Empire,[109] while for children in Earlsfield, south London:

The daisy is a symbol of our greatness. Indeed it was. The golden centre was us – Great Britain; the petals were the colonies, absolutely inseparable and dependent on us.[110]

Oak Apple Day, or Royal Oak Apple Day, 29 May, commemorated the restoration of the monarchy and King Charles II's entry to London in 1660. Charles had been associated with oak trees since 1651 when he hid in one at Boscobel, after the Battle of Worcester,[111] and at one time he planned to set up a new order of chivalry, the Knights of the Royal Oak, but abandoned the idea as being 'likely to keep awake animosities which it was part of wisdom to lull to sleep'.[112] For many years, on 29 May, children, at least, wore leafy oak twigs, preferably with an oak apple attached. If oak was not available field maple was an acceptable substitute,[113] but a child who failed to produce either was liable to be punished:

When I was attending Little Gaddeson Village School [Hertfordshire, c. 1945] it was always the custom to carry a piece of oak to school to prevent being caught and stung with nettles on Oak Apple Day.[114]

Writing in 1959, the Opies found that Oak Apple Day celebrations were remembered in a dwindling number of places, 'in parts of the north country, especially in Cumberland, Westmorland, Furness, and the North Riding, and also quite commonly in the north Midlands, in a board belt stretching from Shrewsbury to the Walsh'.[115] These informal celebrations by children seem to have died out soon after, but Oak Apple Day survived in some rather idiosyncratic schools for a further 20 years or so. In the early 1960s at Audley House Prep School, in Chesterton, Oxfordshire, 'run by a deeply traditional eccentric', it was considered 'de rigueur to wear a bunch of oak leaves in the lapel – or risk being labelled a traitorous poltroon', although the punishment of whipping bare legs with stinging nettles had been discontinued.[116] About a decade later, at 'a tiny country voluntary-aided grammar school with an even smaller boarding house attached' in Wem, Shropshire:

> All the boarders would rise at 4 a.m. and head into the country-side: they would gather in trailer loads of nettles and decorate the school stage. It would literally be covered, except for a 'safe route' for the teachers to walk along. On the table behind which the headmaster stood for assembly would be picked out in oak leaves 'Custom demands a holiday' – it may have been 'Custom requests a holiday', I'm not sure. The table would also be decorated with oak apples. I think the headmaster may have been presented with an oak apple by the senior boarder. Assistant masters would know to check whether there was actually a chair beneath the nettles where a chair shape existed, sometimes the chair was not there. Many masters chose to stand, rather than sit in dew-soaked leaves.
>
> It was traditional for first-year boys to wear short trousers as part of their uniform. To get to assembly all day pupils had to run the gauntlet of huge handfuls of nettles being held below waist height (that was a firm rule!) by the boarders. Second-years and above were protected by their long trousers, but for first-years it was quite an ordeal. Wearing an oak apple guaranteed a boy (more or less!) complete immunity from having nettles held against his legs, but mothers would pack their sons off with anti-histamine cream for the after-effects later that morning. I am not aware of any major complaints from parents.[117]

The formal marking of Oak Apple Day continues at Worcester, where the Guildhall gates are decorated with oak branches, and at Northampton, where a wreath of oak leaves is placed around the neck of a statue of Charles II in All Saints' Church.[118] Elsewhere oak branches were hoisted to the top of church towers. At Castleton, Derbyshire, a garland ceremony takes place on 29 May, and for this the church tower is 'decorated with branches of greenery (usually oak)', and 'sometimes the children dance back through the village [from the church] and all the parents who have ever taken part in the ceremony dance behind wearing oak sprays'.[119] St Neot, in Cornwall, celebrates Oak Apple Day by hoisting an oak bough to the top of the parish church's tower.[120]

Charles II founded the Royal Hospital, Chelsea, in 1682 as a home for old soldiers, and its Founder's Day parade, at which a member of the Royal Family or a high-ranking army officer takes the salute, is often said to have been held without break since 1692. However, according to other sources, the Parade was first held in 1817. At the Parade, participants wear sprigs of oak and the Grinling Gibbons statue of Charles in the Hospital's Figure Court is decorated with oak branches. According to the *Sunday Times* of 29 May 1949, the pensioners were provided with 'extra rations, including Christmas pudding, decked [with] sprigs of oak instead of holly'. As the grounds of the Royal Hospital host the annual Chelsea Flower Show in late May each year, the Parade is now usually held on the first Thursday in June.[121]

The strewing of rushes on church floors was formerly widespread and is frequently mentioned in churchwardens' accounts:

S. Mary-at-Hill, London:
1495 For thee burdens of rushes for new pews, 3d.
1504 Paid for 2 berdens rysshes for strewying newe pewes, 3d.

St Margaret's, Westminster:
1544 Paid for rushes against Dedication Day, 1s 5d.

Kirkham, Lancashire:
1604 Rushes to strew the Church cost this year 9s 6d.[122]

Rush-strewing, or rush-bearing, continues in a few parishes, mostly in the north-west of England. In Cumbria, rush-bearings are held at Ambleside, Grasmere, Musgrave, and Warcop. Of these, the Grasmere festival, held on the Saturday nearest St Oswald's Day (5 August), is thought to be the oldest.

Preparations . . . take several days. Apart from sorting out the children who will take part, the 'bearings' have to be made. These are devices which look as if they were made entirely out of rushes but are in fact created by winding the rushes around strong and practical materials like wood, wire, netting and string. They symbolise various biblical and historical themes, as well as things to do with St Oswald. There are nine big bearings each about five feet high and several smaller ones, all of traditional design and used year after year. Many of them have been carried in procession by generations of the same family; the frames are kept in their houses and women carry out the decoration. Miss McAlpine [the event's supervisor] claims the right to make the beautiful cross of golden helenium which is carried at the head of the procession. The work takes the best part of two days as the ladies diligently and lovingly shape the rushes into intricate forms. Most of their preparations are complete by Saturday lunchtime. Meanwhile the church floor has, mysteriously, acquired a layer of rushes. Long before 4 o'clock, the children in their Sunday best begin to arrive in the vicarage garden to be instructed in their duties and to be given a new 5p piece for their trouble. Families appear in the streets at the same time, the children carrying home-made bearings, even the tiny

ones come in pushchairs decorated with rushes and flowers. The
bearings are handed over to their bearers, the larger ones for the
choirboys, the smaller ones for the girls. The most important people in the whole procession are the Rush Maidens.

Originally, when the whole business really was to take rushes to the
church, in Grasmere they used to carry them on cloth or sacking, holding the corners. These girls do the same thing, only six of them, their
load is symbolic, and they use a fine sheet woven very many years ago
in the village . . .

By the time everyone was organized the procession consisted
of about 200 people. The choirboys led with their special rush-
bearings, the golden cross in front. Then came the band, then
the adult choir and the clergy all carrying sprays of rushes. Next
came the Rush Maidens, followed by the bigger girls. There were
few dads to be seen. They started from the church, marched right
round the village and returned for a special service. The official
bearings were placed around the altar, except 'the serpent' which
is traditionally cast out to a special place outside the Sanctuary. All
the other bearings, baskets, posies and rush crosses were left on the
window ledges where they remained over the weekend.
On Monday they all return, collect their bearings and go off on a
shorter tour of the village after which they have sports and tea.[123]

Ambleside celebrates its rush-bearing on a Saturday in July, while Warcop
holds its festival on St Peter's Day, 29 June, or, if this falls on a Sunday,
on the preceding Saturday.
At Sowerby Bridge, in West Yorkshire, rush-bearing was revived in
1977, and is held each year on the first weekend in September:

The focal point of the modern festival is still the rushcart procession which winds its way through the beautiful lanes of the
Ryburn Valley. An unforgettable spectacle, the rushcart, pulled by
60 strong local lads . . . rushes are presented to churches on the
route and the event is accompanied by music from local bands,
visiting morris dancing teams and mummers. The communities
along the procession route take the opportunity to celebrate with
galas, exhibitions, displays, markets, etc.[124]

Further south, Rush Sunday is held at St Mary Redcliffe, Bristol, at
Whitsun, when the church is strewn with rushes and the pews decorated
with nosegays of flowers. This event is said to date back to 1468, and the
flowers are said to have replaced herbs that were used to guard against
infection.[125]

The Bottle Inn at Marshwood, on the Dorset-Devon border, holds the World Nettle Eating Championship on the Saturday before the Summer Solstice each year. The origins of this date back to about 1986 when two farmers were talking about the size of nettles growing on their farms. One of them said to the other, 'I bet mine are bigger than yours; if they're not, I'll eat the buggers'. The landlady suggested that a competition be held to see who had the longest nettle. Three years later a local man, Alex Williams, entered a nettle 15ft 6ins long, and declared that 'If anyone beats that I'll eat it'. A visiting American couple produced a 16ft-long nettle, whereupon Williams promptly ate his nettle. In 1997 the pub's landlord held a musical celebration to mark the Solstice, and discussed suitable sideshows with customers. Williams asked for a corner of the beer garden and challenged anyone to eat more nettles than he could. Since then an annual nettle-eating championship has evolved. The current record is the 76ft nettle eaten in 2002. Although termed the World Nettle Eating Championship, it appears that the event is unique, and apart from the occasional 'celebrity' participant, most of the contestants live within an evening's drive of the venue. Farmers and builders, with their work-hardened hands, are said to do well; celebrities, whose hands tend to be soft, are unlikely to achieve success.[126]

In the autumn, growers of giant vegetables hold competitions to see who has produced champion specimens. It seems as if almost every vegetable has its enthusiasts who compete to grow the heaviest, longest or biggest, but leeks, onions and pumpkins attract the most growers.

Competitive leek-growing has been popular in north-east England since the 1880s. Thus in 1893 the 16-member Pot and Glass Leek Club at Crossgate Moor, County Durham, held its seventh annual show, with the first prize being a pair of blankets and a picture.[127] Two main types of leeks are commonly exhibited: long leeks, which resemble the ones commonly sold by greengrocers, and pot leeks, which are shorter and stouter. Some shows also have classes for intermediate leeks. Each exhibit ('stand') usually consists of a pair of leeks, and it is the pot leeks which create most excitement. Traditionally, judges at leek shows considered the cubic capacity of a leek to be of greatest importance; the Royal Horticultural Society's guidelines concerning condition, solidity and uniformity are also taken into account. From mid September to late October newspapers in leek-growing areas contain numerous accounts of local shows. Thus on 14 September 1974, the *Rugeley Times* reported:

Almost £500 worth of prizes went to this year's 29 entries at Poplars Leek Show held last weekend at the Popular Inn, Handsacre [Staffordshire] . . . Each person submitted three leeks, all of which were grown with the use of 'recipes' formulated by the grower himself, and usually not divulged to others . . . On Monday a 'glutton's supper' was held at the Poplars, where leek soup, leek sandwiches and other food made from leeks were served.

Prizes included a sewing machine, a chest of drawers, a table lamp and an iron. By 1992 the Newcastle Exhibition World Open Leek Show, at the Northern Club, Ashington, boasted a first prize of £1300,[128] while 10 years later at Ashington John Pearson of Hetton-le-Hole 'smashed the existing [world] record by producing three leeks measuring 537.82 cubic inches and won the largest leek in the show with 194.83 cu. in.'[129] However, in 2008 it was reported that Ashington Leek Show

> has been cancelled due to the credit crunch. Rising greenhouse heating bills have hit growers. And the smoking ban was expected to affect beer sales at the event. Dick Atkinson, due to organise the show . . . said: 'People haven't got the money'.[130]

In 1991 at the Dewsbury, West Yorkshire, onion fair, revived after a gap of 101 years, the record-setting 29lb 4oz was grown by Peter Glazebrook, of Newark, Nottinghamshire, who won £50.[131] However, the main annual onion competition takes place at the Harrogate Autumn Show, where in 1995 Mel Ednie produced an onion weighing 15lb 15½oz.[132]

Giant pumpkin competitions are held in scattered villages throughout England. From 1967 the Greyhound Pumpkin Club, named after one of the village pubs at Broughton, Hampshire, held an annual show in October for many years. Here the pumpkin show was the highlight of a season that commenced with a competition for the heaviest stick of rhubarb in June to a competition for the longest blanch leek in December.[133] Other places which hold, or have held, pumpkin competitions include Barrington, Somerset, where in 1994 'more than twenty of the bulging vegetables were on show',[134] and Haydon Bridge, Northumberland, where, at its annual pumpkin and marrow show in 2002, the winning pumpkin weighed 285lb.[135]

In recent years pumpkins have become associated with Hallowe'en (31 October). Until the second half of the twentieth century this festival was virtually unknown in southern England, where children would be busy preparing for Bonfire Night. However, elsewhere swede, turnip or mangold lanterns were made. Thus, at Griffithstown, Monmouthshire, in the early 1950s:

> For this night we take a swede, cut it in half and scoop out the inside of both halves. Then cut two holes in the top half and the bottom half, also two eyes, a hole for the nose and a mouth . . . You then place a candle inside on the lower half and thread strings in the holes and attach it to a pole. On the actual night you light the

candle and go out into the street and if anyone comes along pop out from around a corner and frighten them.[136]

About a decade later Hallowe'en had became more widespread, as in Hertfordshire in the 1960s:

> Every Hallowe'en at school we had to bring in a swede and carve a lantern out of it - difficult enough, more so as the knives were blunt. We then had to put a stub of candle inside and put the lid back on. Nothing like the smell of scorching swede to put you off eating it for life![137]

Soon afterwards pumpkin lanterns, long popular in North America, became ubiquitous. During the 1980s pumpkins began to appear in greengrocers' shops and supermarkets, and there was an explosion of interest in the festival. Not only were pumpkin lanterns carved and displayed in front windows and gardens, but cheap plastic toys, often in the shape of pumpkins began to appear in shops. In 1990 the November issue of the magazine *Family Circle* included a 'Hallowe'en Special', instructing its readers how to make pumpkin cake (a cake decorated to resemble a pumpkin), pumpkin pie and a pumpkin jack o'lantern.

Early in November poppies start appearing to commemorate service-men and -women who lost their lives, or suffered injury, during World War I and more recent conflicts. After the Battle of Waterloo it was said that the poppies that abounded on the ploughed battlefield had grown from the blood of killed soldiers.[138] In 1915 a Canadian doctor, John Macrae, wrote his poem 'In Flanders Fields', in which he established the connection between slain comrades and battlefield poppies, and by 1918 poppies were being made in France and sold to assist people who were returning to war-devastated areas. Thus, when the British Legion organ-ized its first Poppy Day in 1921, it used poppies imported from France. By June 1922 a poppy factory had been established in east London, making lapel poppies, and in 1924 the making of wreaths was added to its activities.[139] Since then millions of poppies have been produced each year. In 2006 the British Legion, which raised £75 million in 2005, hoped to sell a record 37 million poppies.[140] Also on sale at the same time of year are white poppies, which were originally promoted in 1933 by the Co-operative Women's Guild as a 'pledge that wars must never happen again'. These poppies were sporadically produced until 1980, when they were adopted by the Peace Pledge Union, and they are now widely worn by people concerned by the nationalism that they think the red poppy can suggest.[141]

The last great festival of the year, Christmas, involves the decorating of homes and public spaces with greenery and the setting up of Christmas trees. It is often stated that Christmas evergreens are a survival from pre-Christian times,[142] but it seems more probable that they were brought in simply to provide extra colour. In earlier times it seems as if any evergreen plant was brought in at Christmastide, but since the end of the nineteenth century only holly, mistletoe and various conifers have been regularly used. In theory, if not in practice, Christmas greenery should not be brought in before Christmas Eve, and should be taken down before Twelfth Night (6 January),[143] or, more rarely, New Year's Day.[144]

Writing in 1656 William Coles recorded that mistletoe was 'carryed many miles' to decorate houses at Christmas time.[145] In 1875 the owner of Grimsthorpe Park in south Lincolnshire, was so pestered by mistletoe raiders, who came from as far away as Manchester and London, that she found it necessary to employ 14 watchers to protect her park.[146]

Following Pliny the Elder's report of Druids collecting mistletoe,[147] it has been regarded as a pagan plant, and as such was banned from churches.[148]

One of the attractions of hanging up mistletoe indoors is the custom of kissing beneath it, a custom which is said to be unique to, or have originated in, the British Isles. In 1972:

> Covent Garden traders reported that this year's sales of mistletoe are the worst for years. One trader said: 'It's a different sort of age. When they strip off naked in Leicester Square you can see why. They don't need mistletoe today'.[149]

Despite this, in 1996 an alarmed Bournemouth resident wrote to the *Daily Express* urging shopkeepers to stop selling mistletoe:

> It is highly irresponsible for anyone to sell merchandise that encourages people to act in a debauched and immoral fashion. The tradition of kissing beneath the mistletoe is not simply an innocent act and often encourages intoxicated folk to indulge in casual sex. Britain should ban the sale of mistletoe, leading to a return of decent Christian values to society.[150]

The main mistletoe market for many years, local people claim for over a century, is that held at Tenbury Wells, in Worcestershire.[151] In 2004 the cattle market where the mistletoe was sold closed, rousing the local people to organize and promote an annual Mistletoe Festival. The following year it was declared that 1 December or the nearest Saturday should be celebrated in Tenbury as National Mistletoe Day.[152] In 2006 this involved 'a ball, a parade, a mistletoe queen, concerts and a blessing ceremony, performed by Druids from the Mistletoe Foundation'.[153] The 2009 event included 'experts from Debretts' demonstrating how to kiss

under mistletoe, 'including how to kiss safely, without worrying about
. . . flu!'[154]

The origin of the Christmas tree is, literally, lost in legend. According
to some people:

> St Boniface, born in mid-Devon in the seventh century . . . care-
> fully stage-managed a confrontation with the pagan tribes in
> Germany. Having cut down Thor's Oak at Geismar, he pointed
> to a fir tree growing in its roots: 'Let Christ be your light in the
> darkest days', he said. 'Take him into your homes that are built of
> this humble wood. His arms shall embrace you and he point you
> to heaven.'[155]

Alternatively, Martin Luther (1483–1546), 'after wandering one
Christmas Eve under the clear winter sky lit by a thousand stars, he set
up for his children a tree with countless candles, an image of the starry
heaven whence Christ came down'.[156]

The first record of a Christmas tree, such as we would recognize today,
dates from 1605, when at Christmas in Strasburg people set up decorated
fir trees in their parlours.[157] About two hundred years later, Christmas
trees began to appear in British homes, being introduced by Hessian
soldiers serving in the army of King George III, German members of
the Court, and German merchants who had settled in British cities.[158]
In 1800 Queen Charlotte 'celebrated Christmas evening with a German
fashion' by having a tall fir tree, with lighted tapers, decorations and
presents for the children, attached to it.[159] However, the Christmas tree
did not become widely known until 1841, when Queen Victoria and
Prince Albert had a tree at Windsor, which was extensively reported
and illustrated in the press. Thereafter, Christmas trees became popular, although as late as 1912 they were still described as 'a luxury for the
well-to-do'.[160]

Although various coniferous species are almost always selected as
Christmas trees, holly trees or branches were sometimes, and in parts of
Cornwall still are, favoured.[161]

It is said that the first lighted Christmas tree to be set up in a public
place was in 1909 in Pasadena, California.[162] Despite health and safety
concerns most public authorities place decorated trees in major shopping
centres and outside their town halls. In Britain the best known of these
trees is the one placed in Trafalgar Square, London, each year. Since 1947
this tree has been given to the people of London by the citizens of Oslo,
in appreciation of Britain's help to Norway during World War II.

A recent innovation is for churches to hold Christmas Tree Festivals,
to which parish organizations are invited to contribute a decorated
tree for display in the church. St Mary's Church, in Thorncombe, west

Dorset, organized such an event in 2006, and in 2008 Christ Church, Erith, in the London Borough of Bexley, held its third festival, with a display of 75 trees.[163]

The Christmas tree can, perhaps, be regarded as typical of twenty-first-century plant-lore: commercial, traditional but evolving, personal and communal.

Notes

1. A TIME FOR EVERY PURPOSE

1 Lerwick, Shetland, March 1994.
2 Addlestone, Surrey, September 1997.
3 Irish Folklore Commission Schools' Scheme MSS 750, p. 296, Co. Longford.
4 St Albans, Hertfordshire, referring to 'a Lincolnshire village', October 1994.
5 Newton Rigg, Cumbria, September 1988.
6 Lucas, 1960, p. 186.
7 *Notes & Queries*, 2 ser. 3, p. 343, 1857.
8 Wicken, Cambridgeshire, April 1993.
9 Mordiford, Herefordshire, December 1991.
10 Bromfield, 1856, p. 141; Thorncombe, Dorset, April 1974; St Osyth, Essex, February 1989; Letchworth, Hertfordshire, May 2001.
11 Salisbury, Wiltshire, February 1989.
12 Letter from Wickhambrook, Suffolk, in *Farmer's Weekly*, 10 January 1964.
13 Palmer, R., 1976, p. 62.
14 Wharton MSS, 1974, p. 35.
15 de Garis, 1975, p. 121.
16 *Notes & Queries*, 4 ser., 1, p. 361, 1868.
17 Havercroft, West Yorkshire, January 1969; Survey of Folklore and Language (now National Centre for English Cultural Tradition), University of Sheffield, archive.
18 Britten and Holland, 1886, p. 19.
19 Marquand, 1906, p. 39.
20 Thiselton Dyer, 1889, p. 120.
21 Amery, 1907, p. 108.
22 Ballycastle, Co. Antrim, January 1991.
23 Letter from Enmore, Somerset, in *The Times*, 20 March 1990.
24 Thorncombe, Dorset, March 1975; St Osyth, Essex, February 1989; Bexhill-on-sea, East Sussex, February 1991; Goddard, 1942, p. 45.
25 Palmer, R., 1976, p. 61.
26 Leather, 1912, p. 247.
27 *Notes & Queries*, 1 ser., 8, p. 512, 1853.
28 Carre, 1975, p. 12.
29 Linwood Pitts, 1893, p. 276.
30 Copper, 1971, p. 101.
31 Palmer, R., 1976, p. 46.
32 Laycock, 1940, p. 115.
33 Thorncombe, Dorset, March 1975.
34 Palmer, K., 1976, p. 102.
35 Stevens Cox, 1974, p. 51.
36 Great Bedwyn, Wiltshire, 1999.
37 O'Suilleabhain, 1967, p. 63.
38 Lisburn, Co. Antrim, March 1986.

39 Hole, 1961, p. 30.
40 Gloucester, January 2007.
41 October 2000.
42 May 2003.
43 August 2004.
44 November 2004.
45 Udal, 1922, p. 21.
46 Patten, 1974, p. 10.
47 Barnham, West Sussex, March 1997.
48 Simpson, 2002, p. 112.
49 Chester, Cheshire, July 1996.
50 Hamworthy, Dorset, May 1991.
51 Letter from Toynton All Saints, Lincolnshire, in the *Daily Mirror*, 26 May 1962, and Merthyr Tydfil, Mid Glamorgan, October 2000.
52 Craven Arms, Shropshire, October 1996.
53 Merthyr Tydfil, Mid Glamorgan, October 2000.
54 Simpson, 2002, p. 113.
55 Leather, 1912, p. 21.
56 Grosmont, Gwent, November 1994.
57 *Notes & Queries*, 4 ser., 6, p. 211, 1870.
58 St Marys, Isles of Scilly, September 1992; similar beliefs recorded from Sutton, Surrey, August 1993, and Charmouth, Dorset, January 1994.
59 Letter from Barry, Glamorgan, in the *Daily Mirror*, 7 June 1989; similar beliefs recorded from Wimbledon, Surrey, November 1983, and Rushmere St Andrews, February 1989.
60 Friend, 1884, p. 8; Chope, 1935, p. 132.
61 *Notes & Queries*, 5 ser., 11, p. 18, 1879; Jones-Baker, 1977, p. 69.
62 Porter, 1969, p. 47.
63 Radstock, Avon, October 1975.
64 Leather, 1912, p. 15.
65 Evans, 1966, p. 142.
66 Briggs, 1974, p. 119.
67 Thorncombe, Dorset, March 1975.
68 Palmer and Lloyd, 1972, p. 166.
69 'News from the Past' column in *Pulman's Weekly News*, 15 July 1975.
70 In December 1975 neither Mr M. C. Brown of the Somerset County Museum, Taunton, nor Mr J. W. Ansell, Headmaster of Castle County Primary School, Stoke-sub-Hamdon, were able to find any documentary evidence for, or recollections of, the survival of the Feast into the twentieth century.
71 Warkleigh, Devon, April 1975.
72 Palmer and Lloyd, 1972, p. 168.
73 Willis Watson, 1920, p. 276.
74 *Lichfield Mercury*, 4 June 1830.
75 Edgware, Middlesex, March 1977; Great Bedwyn, Wiltshire, January 1991.
76 Thorncombe, Dorset, October 2005.
77 Llandrindod Wells, Powys, November 1991.
78 Nixon, 1977, p. 181.
79 *Gardeners' Chronicle*, 11 August 1870, p. 738.
80 Balham, London, December 2008.
81 Peter, 1915, p. 132.
82 Thorncombe, Dorset, autumn 1974.

83 *Notes & Queries*, 11 ser., 10, p. 87, 1914.
84 *Ibid.*
85 *Ibid.*, 3 ser., 8, p. 146, 1865.
86 *Ibid.*, 8 ser., 10, p. 112, 1896.
87 Brand, 1853, 1, p. 346.
88 *Notes & Queries*, 2 ser., 1, p. 386, 1856.
89 Radford, 1961, p, 16.
90 Leather, 1912, p. 104.
91 Cranbrook, Kent, July 1983; Barnes, London, July 2005.
92 Leather, 1912, p. 21.
93 Kavanagh, 1975, p. 64.
94 Harrow-on-the-Hill, Middlesex, October 2004.
95 Bath, Avon, January 1988.
96 Stoke Bishop, Avon, December 1982.
97 Norton Fitzwarren, Somerset, July 1983.
98 Sampford Brett, Somerset, October 1993.
99 East Tuddenham, Norfolk, October 1984.
100 Whalton, Northumberland, October 1984; Sunderland, Tyne and Wear, August 2001.
101 Lenamore, Co. Longford, April 1991.
102 IFCSS MSS 800, p. 113, Co. Offaly.
103 Rowling, 1976, p. 101.
104 Cowan, 1902, p. 132.
105 Chelsea, London, February, 1986; Wexford, May 1993; St Martin, Guernsey, April 2002.
106 Caistor, Lincolnshire, October 1994.
107 *Plants, People, Places* 5, p. 4, 1994.

2. THE GOLDEN CORN

1 Danaher, 1972, p. 35.
2 Brand, 1877, p. 40.
3 Marwick, 1975, p. 68.
4 Brand, 1877, p. 27.
5 Evans, 1966, p. 140; St Clair, 1971, p. 88.
6 O'Suilleabhain, 1967, p. 20.
7 Leather, 1912, p. 99.
8 van der Zweep, 1984, p. 166.
9 Porter, 1969, p. 119.
10 Barrett, 1967, p. 112.
11 Porter, 1969, p. 120.
12 *Ibid.*
13 Peate, 1971, p. 179.
14 Thorncombe, Dorset, March 1975.
15 Danaher, 1972, p. 190.
16 Peate, 1971, p. 177.
17 Mitchison, 1973, p. 252.
18 Ross, 1976, p. 143.
19 Danaher, 1972, p. 191.
20 *Ibid.*
21 Killip, 1975, p. 174.

22 Danaher, 1972, p. 191.
23 Marwick, 1975, p. 69.
24 *Ibid.*
25 Brand, 1877, p. 302.
26 This name is now commonly used for a wide range of traditional and non-traditional straw ornaments.
27 Brand, 1877, p. 305.
28 Peate, 1971, p. 177.
29 *Ibid.*
30 Deane and Shaw, 1975, p. 183.
31 Whitlock, 1977, p. 150.
32 Danaher, 1972, p. 191.
33 Peate, 1971, p. 183.
34 *Ibid.*
35 Frazer, 1922, chaps. 45–50.
36 Deane and Shaw, 1975, p. 183; Hole, 1976, p. 92.
37 Hone, n.d., p. 586.
38 Miss R. Franklin, Honorary Secretary of the Federation of Old Cornwall Societies, November 1976.
39 http://www.oldcornwall.org/crying_the_neck.htm (accessed November 2008).
40 Ross, 1976, p. 14.
41 Danaher, 1972, p. 191.
42 Ross, 1976, p. 144.
43 Peate, 1971, p. 178.
44 Danaher, 1972, p. 191.
45 Peate, 1971, p. 179.
46 Hole, 1937, p. 31.
47 Thorncombe, Dorset, March 1975.
48 Woodstock, Oxfordshire, January 1983.
49 Whitlock, 1976, p. 60.
50 Copper, 1971, p. 148.
51 Porter, 1974, p. 67.
52 Jones-Baker, 1977, p. 158.
53 Kingston, A., 1893, *Fragments of Two Centuries*; quoted in Jones-Baker, 1977, p. 158.
54 *Notes & Queries*, 4 ser., 12, p. 491, 1873.
55 Porter, 1969, p. 121.
56 *Notes & Queries*, 4 ser., 12, p. 491, 1873.
57 Chamberlain, 1975, p. 29 and 34.
58 Dacombe, 1951, p. 38.
59 Porter, 1969, p. 124.
60 Raven, 1978, p. 86.
61 Evans, 1966, p. 157.
62 Raven, 1978, p. 168.
63 Udal, 1922, p. 257.
64 Peter Oakley, corn-dolly maker, Essex, September 1970.
65 Lambeth, 1977, pp. 23–43; other books that give useful instructions for making dollies include Lambeth's *A Golden Dolly*, London, 1969 and *Corn Dollies and How to Make Them* by Lettice Sandford and Philla Davis, first published by the Herefordshire Federation of Women's Institutes in 1958 and frequently reprinted.

66 Leather, 1912, p. 104; Peate, 1971, p. 178; Danaher, 1972, p. 198.
67 Peate, 1971, p. 178; Danaher, 1972, p. 198.
68 Ross, 1976, p. 143.
69 Mitchison, 1973, p. 253.
70 Danaher, 1972, p. 198.
71 Mt. 26.26-7.

3. NECESSITY THE MOTHER OF INVENTION

1 Letter from Five Ashes, East Sussex, in *The Times*, 1 March 1929.
2 Callington, Cornwall, October 1996.
3 St Martin's, Guernsey, April 2002.
4 Martinstown, Dorset, May 1991.
5 Glynn, Co. Antrim, February 1992.
6 Evelyn, 1664, p. 38.
7 *The Phytologist*, 2 ser., 2, p. 143, 1857.
8 Howkins and Sampson, 2000, p. 33.
9 Bromfield, 1856, p. 23.
10 Laver, 1990, p. 236.
11 Callington, Cornwall, October 1996.
12 Addlestone, Surrey, May 1998; for an overview of the use of nettles for fibre see Edom, 2010.
13 Gullane, East Lothian, February 1997.
14 Ranson, 1949, p. 84.
15 Lightfoot, 1777, p. 86.
16 Lerwick, Shetland, March 1994.
17 IFCS SS MSS 575, p. 382, Co.Tipperary.
18 Milliken and Bridgewater, 2004, p. 177.
19 Evans, 1800, p. 197.
20 Johnston, 1831, p. 85.
21 Milliken and Bridgewater, 2004, p. 181.
22 Miller, 1858, p. 17.
23 McNeill, 1910, p. 118.
24 Nelson and McCracken, 1987, p. 11.
25 Hart, 1898, p. 384.
26 Edlin, 1949, p. 115.
27 Chatfield, 2008.
28 SFL MSS, Walkley, South Yorkshire, October 1969.
29 SFL MSS, Epworth, Humberside, May 1971.
30 Court, 1967, p. 42.
31 IFCSS SS MSS 575, p. 282, Co. Tipperary.
32 Dacombe, 1951, p. 44.
33 Briggs, 1976, p. 75 and 285.
34 Simpson, 2002, p. 62, referring to Sussex in the 1940s.
35 Waltham Abbey, Essex, referring to Newton Ferrers, Northamptonshire, c. 1910; Letchworth, Hertfordshire, referring to mid Oxfordshire, 1940s; London, SW2, referring to Dover, Kent, 1950s, June 2006; Womborne, Staffordshire, February 2007; Ilkley, West Yorkshire, February 2007.
36 Lindegaard, 1978, p. 8.
37 Stevenage, Hertfordshire, January 1993.
38 Maida Hill, London, March 1978.

39 Balham, London, November 2008.
40 Grigson, 1987, p. 147.
41 Pratt, 1857, 1, p. 31.
42 McNeill, 1910, p. 119.
43 Carmichael, 1941, p. 119.
44 Tooting, London, May 2006.
45 Mabey, 1996, p. 186.
46 Phillips, 1983, p. 155.
47 E-mail, July 2002, referring to Sea Mills, Bristol, c. 1980.
48 Tangye, 2008, p. 46.
49 Solihull, West Midlands, March 1991.
50 Farnborough, Kent, January 1993.
51 Fleet, Hampshire, March 1993.
52 Sidmouth, Devon, referring to Dorset, 1930s, October 1991; Old Cleeve, Somerset, referring to Berwickshire, October 1993; Taunton, Somerset, April 1994; Lamplugh, Cumbria, July 1997.
53 Plymstock, Devon, January 1993; Callington, Cornwall, October 1996.
54 Lisburn, Co. Antrim, March 1986.
55 Waddesdon, Buckinghamshire, November 1996.
56 Didcot, Oxfordshire, February 1991; Redruth, Cornwall, January 1994; Holbeach, Lincolnshire, January 2003; Barrow-in-Furness, Cumbria, August 2004.
57 Whitfield, Dundee, November 1988; Edinburgh, referring to Jedburgh, Scottish Borders, 1940s, February 1996.
58 Lamplugh, Cumbria, July 1997; Pickering, 1995, p. 20. See pp. 33–4 of this volume for further plants collected for food by children.
59 Pickering, 1995, p. 20.
60 Gutch, 1901, p. 61.
61 Dixon, 1890, p. 111.
62 SSS MSS SA1969/28/A12.
63 Lerwick, Shetland, March 1994.
64 Bayswater, London, October 1980; letter from Bath, Avon, in the *Independent*, 31 October 1990.
65 Grigson, 1987, p. 120.
66 Quoted in *ibid.*
67 *Ibid.*, p. 119.
68 Wyatt, n.d., p. 81.
69 Letter from Bristol, in the *Sunday Telegraph*, 20 November 1994.
70 St Osyth, Essex, February 1989; Harrogate, North Yorkshire, referring to the Essex/Suffolk border; Dorking, Surrey, February 2007.
71 Peter, 1915, p. 123.
72 *Notes & Queries*, 11 ser. 12, p. 489, 1915, referring to the Midlands.
73 Horseheath, Cambridgeshire, April 1991.
74 *Notes & Queries*, 11 ser. 12, p. 489, 1915; Girton, Cambridge, May 1988.
75 St Saviour, Jersey, May 1993.
76 Larne, Co. Antrim, November 1991; Woodnewton, Northamptonshire, June 1992.
77 Churchdown, Gloucestershire, January 1988; Rushmere St Andrew, Suffolk, February 1989; Barnstaple, Devon, May 1991.
78 Canterbury, Kent, November 1993.
79 Ranson, 1949, p. 55.

80 Lenamore, Co. Longford, April 1991.
81 Anonymous telephone call, February 1998.
82 New Longton, Lancashire, June 1993.
83 Southampton, Hampshire, November 1996.

4. HEALING HEDGEROWS

1 Vickery, 2006, p. 19; see also www.rbgkew.org.uk/ethnomedica/.
2 E.g. Woking, Surrey, 1984; Maynooth, Co. Kildare, February 1991; Ryde, Isle of Wight, November 1998; Sutton Coldfield, West Midlands, February 2007.
3 Botesdale, Suffolk, February 1998.
4 Vickery, 2008, p. 16.
5 Parsons MSS, 1952, referring to Horseheath, Cambridgeshire; SLF MSS, Sheffield, November 1966; Rochester, Kent, referring to sliced onion dipped in vinegar applied to scorpion bites in India, October 1996; Bratton, Wiltshire, January 2007.
6 Streatham, London, September 1994.
7 Parsons MSS, 1952.
8 Pershore, Worcestershire, October 1991.
9 Canterbury, Kent, November 1993.
10 Ifield, Sussex, March 1997.
11 Vickery, 1995, p. 266.
12 Bloom, 1930, p. 245
13 UCL EFS MSS M13, Carshalton Beeches, Surrey, October 1963.
14 Baker, 1996, p. 115, referring to Cheshire; letter from south Devon, read on Radio 4's PM Programme, 23 March 2001.
15 St Andrews, Fife, September 1988.
16 West Wimbledon, London, November 2003.
17 Lerwick, Shetland, March, 1994; Hailsham, East Sussex, referring to Cambridgeshire, c. 1900, October 1996; letter from Lincolnshire, in the News of the World, Sunday magazine, 1 March 1998; Mulchelney, Somerset, January 2007.
18 Cinderford, Gloucestershire, November 1993.
19 Luton, Bedfordshire, January 1997.
20 Ryde, Isle of Wight, November 1988.
21 Lerwick, Shetland, March 1994 (where water was used instead of milk).
22 St Osyth, Essex, February 1989; Suffolk, May 2003, referring to Yorkshire; Streatham, London, September 2006; Pevensey, Sussex, February 2007.
23 West Wickham, Kent, April 2003.
24 IFCSS MSS 175, p. 313, County Sligo; St Osyth, Essex, February 1989; Tulse Hill, London, referring to north Scotland, March 1997.
25 Letter from Richmond, Surrey, in the Daily Telegraph, 22 July 1995; similar practices recorded from Spain (Roehampton, London, June 2001) and Vietnam (South Kensington, London, April 2003).
26 Stockport, Cheshire, April 1991.
27 Llanuwchylln, Gwynedd, April 1991; West Wickham, Kent, March 1997.
28 Smith, 1959, p. 414, referring to Chipping Ongar, Essex.
29 Lisburn, Co. Antrim, March 1986; Altarnum, Cornwall, April 1986; letter from West Sussex, in the News of the World, Sunday magazine, 12 April 1998.
30 IFCSS MSS 812, p. 110, Co. Offaly.
31 Whistler, 1908, p. 89.

32 Rushmere St Andrew, Suffolk, February 1989.
33 *Daily Mirror*, 8 April 1993, referring to Ireland.
34 Streatham, London, October 1991.
35 Kensington, London, October 1979.
36 Kew, Surrey, January 1999.
37 Gomme, 1884, p. 134, referring to Worcestershire, possibly elder was intended.
38 Alvingham, Lincolnshire, October 1994.
39 Steele MSS, 1978, p. 38.
40 IFCSS MSS 50, p. 458, Co. Galway.
41 Vesey-FitzGerald, 1944, p. 23.
42 Metherington, Lincolnshire, April 1994.
43 E-mail, December 2008.
44 Brown, 1972, p. 267; for a survey of the medicinal uses of nettles see Vickery, 2008, pp. 5–8.
45 Lisburn, Co. Antrim, March 1986.
46 Kingsbridge, Devon, April 1999.
47 Great Plumstead, Norfolk, October 1989.
48 Whitlock, 1976, p. 167.
49 Worcester, January 1998.
50 Gosport, Hampshire, March 1997.
51 Dartnell and Goddard, 1894, p. 101.
52 Taylor MSS, Yoxford, Suffolk.
53 Yeovil, Somerset, October 1975.
54 Windermere, Cumbria, November 1988.
55 Glynn, Co. Antrim, February 1992.
56 Davey, 1909, p. 325.
57 Marquand, 1906, p. 45.
58 McNeill, 1910, p. 96, referring to Colonsay; Newcastle-on-Clun, Shropshire, November 2004.
59 Vickery, 1995, p. 109.
60 Hatfield, 1999, p. 90.
61 Palmer, K., 1976, p. 113, referring to Somerset, c. 1970.
62 Vesey-FitzGerald, 1944, p. 23.
63 Horsted Keynes, West Sussex, February 1991.
64 Glynn, Co. Antrim, February 1992.
65 Rudkin, 1936, p. 26.
66 *Ibid.*, p. 28.
67 Latham, 1878, p. 38.
68 Leather, 1912, p. 82.
69 Simpson, 1976, p. 108.
70 Raven, 1978, p. 51.
71 Trevelyan, 1909, p. 320.
72 Udal, 1922, p. 255.
73 Deane and Shaw, 1975, p. 135.
74 Palmer, K., 1976, p. 114.
75 IFCSS MSS 450, p. 163, Co. Kerry; IFC MSS 782, p. 257, Co. Kerry, 1941.
76 Letchworth, Hertfordshire, referring to mid Oxfordshire, 1930s; Merthyr Tydfil, Mid Glamorgan, October 2000; Muchelney, Somerset, January 2007; Sutton Coldfield, West Midlands, February 2007.
77 Langtoft, Humberside, July 1985; Llanbedr, Gwynedd, February 1998; Tooting, London, January 2007; Stow-on-the-Wold, Gloucestershire, March 2007.

78 Whitlock, 1976, p. 164; Hatfield, 1998, p. 10.
79 South Kensington, London, May 2003.
80 Britten and Holland, 1886, p. 548.
81 Macmillan, 1922, p. 280.
82 Britten and Holland, 1886, p. 484.
83 Dittisham, Devon, February 1998; practice also recorded from Bexhill-on-Sea, East Sussex, February 1991; Aldbury, Hertfordshire, February 1998; Llanidloes, Powys, January 2007.
84 Newcastle-on-Clun, Shropshire, November 2004.
85 Davey, 1909, p. 23.
86 Hatfield, 1998, p. 10.
87 Axminster, Devon, April 1985; Much Hadham, Hertfordshire, August 2002; Wormshill, Kent, May 2003, Crewkerne, Somerset, referring to the Cotswolds, January 2007.
88 Ryde, Isle of Wight, November 1988.
89 Hill, Worcestershire, November 1991.
90 Bacon, 1631, p. 258.
91 Opie and Opie, 1959, p. 315.
92 Hatfield, 1998, p. 14.
93 IFCSS MSS 450, p. 55, Co. Kerry; Daingean, Co. Offaly, January 1985.
94 Lenamore, Co. Offaly, April 1991.
95 Lerwick, Shetland, March 1994.
96 Binfield Heath, Oxfordshire, February 1998.
97 Quoted in Grigson, 1987, p. 400.
98 Vesey-FitzGerald, 1944, p. 28.
99 Applethwaite, Cumbria, September 1996.
100 Tooting, London, August 1987.
101 Stockport, Greater Manchester, April 1991.
102 Glynn, Co. Antrim, February 1992; Fleetwood, Lancashire, February 1998; Burton-upon-Trent, Staffordshire, July 2003.
103 Portesham, Dorset, January 2007.
104 Burton-upon-Trent, Staffordshire, February 1998.
105 Barton-under-Needwood, Staffordshire, May 2002.
106 Sedgwick, Cumbria, January 2007.
107 Holbeach, Lincolnshire, January 2003.
108 Omagh, Co. Tyrone, October 1986.
109 IFCSS MSS 515, p. 148, Co. Limerick.
110 Chapelhope, Selkirk, April 2002.
111 Wormshill, Kent, May 2003.
112 Preston et al., 2002, p. 309.
113 See p. 59 of this volume.
114 Allen and Hatfield, 2004, p. 134.
115 Davey, 1909, p. 193.
116 Kiltimagh, Co. Mayo, April 1983.
117 Shingle Street, Suffolk, February 1998.
118 Armathwaite, Cumbria, October 1988; wart cure also recorded from Steeton, West Yorkshire, 'from an old Scottish doctor in the 1950s', February 1998.
119 Bexhill-on-Sea, East Sussex, February 1991.
120 Norton Subcourse, Norfolk, July 2003.
121 E-mail, June 2008.
122 Liversedge, West Yorkshire, April 2004.

123 Sandiway, Cheshire, October 2004.
124 Borrowash, Derbyshire, January 2007.
125 Deptford, London, May 2002; also reported from Staffordshire in *News of the World*, *Sunday* magazine, 22 March 1998, and from Cheshire in the *Independent*, 10 October 2006.
126 Letter from Newtownabbey, Co. Antrim in *Arthritis Today*, Winter 2006, similar cure reported from Cambridge in the same issue, and, for stomach cramp, in *News of the World*, *Sunday* magazine 27 December 1998.
127 *The Times*, 17 August 2007.
128 Streatham, London, September 2006.
129 Limavady, Co. Londonderry, October 1996; letter from the West Midlands in *News of the World*, *Sunday* magazine, 2 August 1998, London, WC2, 'it has to be savoy, not any other cabbage', March 2007.
130 Sandiway, Cheshire, referring to Newcastle-on-Clun, Shropshire, October 2004.
131 South Kensington, London, July 2005.
132 *Sunday Telegraph*, 31 August 2003.

5. MOTHER-DIE AND FRIENDSHIP BUSHES

1 Vickery, 1985.
2 Matlock, Derbyshire, February 2007.
3 Blurton, Staffordshire, March 1983.
4 Newcastle-under-Lyme, Staffordshire, March 1983.
5 Witham, Essex, May 1983.
6 Anonymous telephone call, referring to Redhill, Surrey.
7 Catford, London, September 1984.
8 Mickleover, Derbyshire, March 1983; Exeter, Devon, July 1984; Shingle Street, Suffolk, February 1998; East Sheen, London, February 1998.
9 Maple, 1971, p. 31.
10 Letter from East Grinstead, East Sussex, in the *Sunday Express*, 16 May 1982.
11 Warner, 1978, p. 281; the Guardian of the Franciscan Priory, Portishead, Avon, June 1982.
12 Gomme, 1884, p. 206.
13 http://inthebloodstream.wordpress.com/2009/01/21.whitsun-sylvia-plath/ (accessed June 2010).
14 Allen, 1980, p. 119.
15 Challenger, 1955, p. 266.
16 Wallasey, Merseyside, September 1996.
17 Mac Manus, 1973, p. 52.
18 IFCSS MSS 1020, p. 243, Co. Cavan.
19 Stirling, April 2005.
20 IFCSS MSS 717, p. 103, Co. Meath.
21 IFCSS MSS 919, p. 216, Co. Wicklow.
22 South Stainley, North Yorkshire, March 1992.
23 Queen's University, Belfast, September 1997.
24 South Kensington, London, June 2003; similar beliefs recorded, for example, from Worthing, Surrey, February 1982; Aberdovey, Gwynedd, July 1983; Earlsfield, London, referring to Co. Fermanagh, April 1998; Kingsbridge, Devon, April 1999.
25 Gorleston, Norfolk, April 1991; Addlestone, Surrey, June 2001.

26 Maynooth, Co. Kildare, February 1991; Grantchester, Cambridge, April 1991; Woking, Surrey, December 1991.
27 Llangorse, Powys, November 1983.
28 Norwich, Norfolk, 'from my mother, a Yorkshire woman', July 1983; Chiswick, London, referring to Flixton, Manchester, late 1950s, July 1983; Marple Bridge, Cheshire, March 1998.
29 Paddington, London, referring to Hampshire, 1920s, December 1982.
30 Britten and Holland, 1886, p. 342.
31 *Ibid.*, p. 555.
32 *Flora Facts & Fables*, 1, p. 1, 1996.
33 Gloucester, August 1997, referring to the West Riding of Yorkshire.
34 Driffield, Humberside, March 1985.
35 Fleetwood, Lancashire, February 1998; Bungay, Suffolk, August 1999; Skelton, Cumbria, referring to Wakefield, West Riding of Yorkshire, 1950s, March 2007.
36 Ashley, Shropshire, March 1983; name also known in Manchester, c. 1920 (Kew, Surrey, July 2003).
37 London, E1, December 2003.
38 Britten and Holland, 1886, p. 567.
39 Hackney, London, February 1998.
40 Corbridge, Northumberland, January 1993.
41 Edgware, Middlesex, November 1994.
42 Stowmarket, Suffolk, September 1985.
43 Dublin, 1993.
44 Helensburgh, Dunbartonshire, February 1991.
45 Wicken, Cambridgeshire, March 1993.
46 East Finchley, London, March 1998.
47 Lamplugh, Cumbria, July 1997.
48 Opie and Tatem, 1989, p. 164.
49 Barton-on-Humber, Humberside, February 1992.
50 Bennett, 1992, p. 185.
51 Kensington, London, January 1983; New Longton, Lancashire, June 1993; Crewkerne, Somerset, referring to the Cotswolds, January 2007.
52 Melling, 1981, p. 28.
53 Catford, London, September 1984.
54 Fleet Street, London, August 1983.
55 Dorchester, Dorset, February 1992; Oswestry, Shropshire, February 1993; Newcastle-on-Clun, November 2004.
56 Wiswell, Lancashire, April 1982.
57 Members of Oxfordshire Women's Institute groups, 1950s.
58 Skibbereen, Co, Cork, January 1993.
59 Longford, Shropshire, April 1997.
60 Anon., 1916, p. 425; belief also recorded from Longford, Shropshire, April 1997.
61 Scotton, Lincolnshire, October 1996.
62 Wombourne, Staffordshire, February 2007; similar beliefs recorded from Whitwick, Leicestershire, August 1983; Ponsanooth, Cornwall, November 1993, referring to Staffordshire, 1930s; South Kensington, London, referring to Pembrokeshire, March 2004.
63 Hardy, 1895, p. 325.
64 See p. 34 of this volume.

NOTES

65 Trevelyan, 1909, p. 103.
66 Webster, 1978, p. 342.
67 St Martin, Guernsey, April 2002.
68 Bracknell, Berkshire, August 1984.
69 *Daily News*, 27 January 1926.
70 London, E1, November 1996.
71 Ranson, 1949, p. 55.
72 Quelch, 1941, p. 78.
73 Aubrey, 1847, p. 56.
74 *Phytologist*, ser. 2, 2, p. 480, 1858.
75 Lightfoot, 1777, p. 257.
76 Armstrong, 1976, p. 36.
77 Dromsally, Co. Limerick, October 1984.
78 Ashreigney, Devon, July 1983; Waltham Abbey, Essex, referring to Higham Ferrers, Northamptonshire, March 1991; Hemel Hempstead, Hertfordshire, August 2004.
79 Stewart, 1823, p. 91.
80 Rhys, 1901, p. 85.
81 Worthing, West Sussex, March 1982.
82 Nelson, Lancashire, August 1983.
83 Grigson, 1987, p. 172.
84 Boase, 1976, p. 118.
85 Oxford, 1991.
86 Kiltimagh, Co. Mayo, 1983.
87 See pp. 46-7 of this volume.
88 Ó Danachair, 1970, p. 25.
89 South Collingham, Nottinghamshire, January 1992.
90 Hempstead Holt, Norfolk, January 2003; Norton Subcourse, Norfolk, July 2003.
91 Baker, 1996, p. 109.
92 Deacon, 1930, p. 26.
93 Skipton, North Yorkshire, November 1991.
94 Bratton, Wiltshire, January 2007.
95 Ui Conchubhair, 1995, p. 72.
96 Bessacar, South Yorkshire, April 1984.
97 Johnston, 1853, p. 30.
98 *Notes & Queries*, 3 ser. 8, p. 319, 1865.
99 Driffield, Humberside, March 1985.
100 Histon, Cambridgeshire, January 1989.
101 *Notes & Queries*, 5 ser. 9, p. 488, 1878.
102 Britten and Holland, 1886, p. 50.
103 Davey, 1909, p. 19.
104 Parsons MSS.
105 Edinburgh, December 1991.
106 Wareham, Dorset, August 1982.
107 Borrowash, Derbyshire, January 2007.
108 Five Ashes, East Sussex, April 1983.
109 Leek, Staffordshire, August 1983.
110 Weymouth, Dorset, December 2008.
111 Kensington, London, November 1979.
112 Woolton, Merseyside, December 1980; see also Vickery, 1983.

113 Quoted in Opie and Tatem, 1989, p. 88.
114 Quoted in Roud, 2003, p. 102.
115 Clark, 1882, p. 83; O'Sullivan, 1966, p. 280.
116 SSS MSS SA1976.196.A7.
117 Colwyn Bay, Clwyd, June 1992; Ballymote, Co. Sligo, May 1994; Newcastle-on-Clun, Shropshire, November 2004; Aultvaich, Inverness-shire, March 2007.
118 Stirling, April 2005.
119 Letter from Woore, Cheshire, in *Farmers Weekly*, 25 June 1976.
120 Hardy, 1895, p. 142.
121 Hunt, 1881, p. 107.
122 McNicholas, 1992, p. 210.
123 O'Sullivan, 1966, p. 280.
124 Wenis and Wenis, 1990, p. 24.
125 Nelson, 2006, p. 45.
126 Victoria, 1868, p. 154.
127 Battiscombe, 1969, p. 36.
128 Waring, 1978, p. 118.
129 Nelson, 2005, p. 253.
130 McClintock, 1970, p. 159.
131 http://www.tropicos.org/name890092 (accessed December 2008).
132 Wimbledon, London, November 1983.
133 St Paul's Boys' School, London, February 1986.
134 Personal observation.
135 Holborn, London, April 1983.
136 Stevenage, Hertfordshire, January 1996.
137 See pp. 6 and 136 of this volume.
138 Portland, Dorset, March 1991; also recorded from Hampshire, *Notes & Queries*, 4 ser., 11, p. 341, 1873.
139 Vickery, 1978, p. 158; similar beliefs recorded from L'Ancresse, Guernsey, April 1984; Hemel Hempstead, Hertfordshire, August 2004.
140 Headington, Oxford, August 1997; similar beliefs recorded from Craven Arms, Shropshire, March 1985; Truro, Cornwall, November 1993.
141 Friend, 1884, p. 8; Chope, 1935, p. 132.
142 Knight, 1945, p. 94; *The English Dialect Dictionary* defines 'brandis-wise' as 'forming a triangular figure'.
143 Friend, 1884, p. 8; similar belief recorded from Plymouth, Devon, January 1993.
144 Friend, 1884, p. 8, L'Ancresse, Guernsey, April 1984.
145 Taylor MSS.
146 St Martin, Guernsey, April 2002.
147 Parkstone, Dorset, June 1991.
148 Stowmarket, Suffolk, referring to Halstead, Essex, 1943–59, August 1989.
149 Charmouth, Dorset, January 1994; Streatham, London, referring to Hampshire, April 1993.
150 Streatham, London, July 1992.

6. SIMPLE PASTIMES

1 Worcester, October 1991.
2 Briggs, 1976, p. 87.

3 Little Sandhurst, Surrey, April 1994.
4 Sittingbourne, Kent, August 1991.
5 St Mary's, Isles of Scilly, November 1992.
6 Harrow Weald, Middlesex, October 1996.
7 Leamington Spa, Warwickshire, January 1993; Weobley, Herefordshire, referring to Kent, 1940s, August 1998.
8 Balham, London, December 2008.
9 Merthyr Tydfil, Mid Glamorgan, October 2000.
10 Grigson, 1987, p. 393.
11 Macmillan, 1922, p. 209.
12 *Ibid.*, p. 243.
13 Fowler, 1890, p. 76.
14 Grigson, 1987, p. 393.
15 Llanuwchyllyn, Gwynedd, April 1991.
16 Worcester, October 1991.
17 South Kensington, London, May 1979.
18 Stevenage, Hertfordshire, January 1993.
19 St Albans, Hertfordshire, referring to Brixton, London, 1950s, November 1989;
   Tickhill, South Yorkshire, February 1998; East Finchley, London, referring to
   Monmouthshire, 1950s, March 1998.
20 Grigson, 1987, p. 393.
21 Clappersgate, Cumbria, October 1985.
22 Accrington, Lancashire, March 1982.
23 Daingean, Co. Offaly, January 1985.
24 March 1984.
25 Waltham Abbey, Essex, March 1991; Plymouth, January 1993; Addingham
   Moorside, West Yorkshire, April 1993; Lerwick, Shetland, March 1994.
26 Hewins, 1985, p. 69, referring to Shottery, Warwickshire, 1930s.
27 *Notes & Queries*, 5 ser., 5, p. 364, 1876.
28 Minchinhampton, Gloucestershire, January 1991.
29 Great Bedwyn, Wiltshire, February 1992; Longford, Shropshire, April 1997;
   Harrow on the Hill, Middlesex, October 2004.
30 Tooting, London, July 2003.
31 St Marys, Isles of Scilly, September 1992.
32 Lousley, 1971, p. 276.
33 Larne, Co. Antrim, October 1993.
34 Sidmouth, Devon, December 1992.
35 Macmillan, 1922, p. 17.
36 St Ervan, Cornwall, February 1992.
37 Lee, London, April 1993.
38 Friend, 1882, p. 18.
39 *Ibid.*; also recorded from East Yorkshire, where water figwort was called fiddle-
   wood (Britten and Holland, 1886, p. 181).
40 Parsons MSS, 1952.
41 Jones, 1980, p. 100; similar practices recorded from Thorncombe, Dorset, April
   1990, and St Day, Cornwall, January 1994.
42 Morris, 1869, p. 79.
43 Hart, 1898, p. 374.
44 Cardiff, January 1994.
45 Lerwick, Shetland, March 1994.
46 Hillingdon, Middlesex, March 2001.

47 Farnham, Surrey, December 1985.
48 Driffield, Humberside, July 1985; name also recorded from Exeter, Devon, January 1982; Wheatley, Oxfordshire, June 1993; Capel, Kent, February 1998; Orpington, Kent, referring to north Hampshire, February 2007.
49 Mardu, Shropshire, November 2004.
50 Britten and Holland MSS.
51 Market Drayton, Shropshire, April 1997.
52 East Tuddenham, Norfolk, May 1994.
53 Macmillan, 1922, p. 184.
54 Holland Park, London, May 2004.
55 Nuneaton, Warwickshire, January 1982; Oxshott, Surrey, referring to Aberdeen, November 2002.
56 Marquand, 1906, p. 42.
57 Yafforth, North Yorkshire, January 1990.
58 Longford, Shropshire, April 1997.
59 Lenamore, Co. Longford, April 1991.
60 Opie and Opie, 1969, p. 226.
61 *Ibid.*
62 Felmersham, Bedfordshire, April 1993.
63 Opie and Opie, 1969, p. 226.
64 Limpsfield, Surrey, June 1993.
65 Grigson, 1987, p. 387.
66 *Ibid.*, p. 374.
67 *Ibid.*, p. 134.
68 Hart, 1898, p. 369.
69 Grigson, 1987, p. 425.
70 Tait, 1947, p. 74.
71 Wright, 1905, 1, p. 842.
72 Ringwood, Hampshire, November 1990.
73 Edinburgh, referring to Dumfries-shire, 'many years ago', December 1991.
74 East Finchley, London, March 1998.
75 Capel, Kent, April 1998.
76 Britten and Holland, 1886, p. 292.
77 Macmillan, 1922, p. 139.
78 Llandrindod Wells, Powys, September 1991.
79 Trevelyan, 1909, p. 97.
80 Daingean, Co. Offaly, January 1985; similar practices recorded from Llanuwchylln, Gwynedd, April 1991; Pinner, Middlesex, May 2001.
81 Candlin, 1947, p. 131; similar practices recorded from Herefordshire (Leather, 1912, p. 63) and Lincolnshire (Cottam MSS, 1989, p. 27).
82 Britten and Holland MSS.
83 Grigson, 1959, p. 15.
84 Macmillan, 1922, p. 272, 294.
85 Milliken and Bridgewater, 2004, p. 136.
86 Hart, 1898, p. 373.
87 Udal, 1922, p. 254.
88 Thorncombe, Dorset, June 1976.
89 *Ibid.*; also recorded from Herefordshire (Leather, 1912, p. 63).
90 Trevelyan, 1909, p. 97.
91 Harberton, Devon, October 1992.
92 IFCSS MSS 825, p. 123, Co. Laois.

93 Wicken, Cambridge, March 1993.
94 Wickham, Hampshire, July 1996.
95 Fowler, 1909, p. 296.
96 Sidmouth, Devon, March 1998.
97 Conquer, 1970.
98 St Day, Cornwall, January 1994.
99 Stevenage, Hertfordshire, January 1993.
100 Llandrindod Wells, Powys, September 1991.
101 Winchester, Hampshire, September 1991.
102 Leamington Spa, Warwickshire, and South Kensington, London, referring to Durham, 1980, November 1991.
103 Horley, Surrey, January 1999.
104 Earlsfield, London, April 1998.
105 Longford, Shropshire, April 1997; also recorded from Somerset, late 1940s (Leamington Spa, Warwickshire, January 1993).
106 London, N1, February 1997.
107 Llantysilio, Denbighshire, February 1998.
108 Exeter, Devon, March 1991; practice also recorded from South Collingham, Nottinghamshire, January 1992; West Stow, Suffolk, referring to Norfolk, September 2002; Wandsworth, London, July 2003.
109 Totton, Hampshire, August 1993.
110 *The Norfolk Natterjack*, 78, p. 3, 2002.
111 Gravesend, Kent, February 2007.
112 Mulchelney, Somerset, January 2007.
113 See p. 60 of this volume.
114 St Marys, Isles of Scilly, referring to '50 years ago, probably in Staffordshire', September 1992; practice also recorded from Kent, 1940s (Weobley, Herefordshire, August 1998).
115 Barton-upon-Humber, February 1992.
116 Lerwick, Shetland, March 1994.
117 Gerard, 1597, p. 1188.
118 Alton, Hampshire, June 1993.
119 Britten and Holland, 1886, p. 439.
120 Gepp, 1923, p. 104.
121 Elder, 1997, p. 201.
122 Maulden, Bedfordshire, April 1993.
123 Macmillan, 1922, p. 252.
124 Dallman, 1954, p. 65.
125 Macmillan, 1922, p. 253.
126 Grigson, 1987, p. 24.
127 Hall, 1957, p. 124.
128 Clevedon, Avon, March 1993; also recorded from Caernarvon, Gwynedd, March 1993; Co. Clare, referring to Co. Tipperary, June 2002; Wormshill, Kent, May 2003.
129 Holywood, Co. Down, referring also to Co. Antrim, December 1991.
130 Grigson, 1987, p. 132.
131 *Ibid.*, p. 134.
132 Edinburgh, October 1991.
133 Wright, 1914, p. 333.
134 Britten and Holland, 1886, p. 544.
135 Tait, 1947, p. 79.

136 Lerwick, Shetland, March 1994.
137 Mac Coitir, 2006, p. 247.
138 Hart, 1898, p. 378.
139 Shipston-on-Stour, Warwickshire, September 1993; practice also recorded from Farmoor, Oxfordshire, July 1993.
140 Rugby, Warwickshire, February 1998.
141 St Day, Cornwall, January 1994.
142 McNeill, 1910, p. 137.
143 Winchester, Hampshire, October 1996.
144 Rodmell, East Sussex, January 1995; name and practice also recorded from Clevedon, Avon, March 1993.
145 Britten and Holland, 1886, p. 471; practice also recorded from Bedfordshire, 1930s [Norman, 1969, p. 34].
146 West Stow, Suffolk, November 1991.
147 Gossops Green, West Sussex, October 1994.
148 Preston et al., 2002, p. 437.
149 Britten and Holland, 1886, p. 116, 293.
150 Notes & Queries, 5 ser., 10, 1878, p. 378.
151 Sidmouth, Devon, October 1991.
152 Hadfield, 1957, p. 392.
153 Evans, 1881, p. 126; see also Gomme, 1894, p. 71.
154 Bean, 1914, p. 170.
155 Dickinson MSS, 1974, p. 38.
156 Sharman, 1977, p. 60.
157 Cloves, 1993, p. 76.
158 Letter from Stoke Poges, Buckinghamshire, in The Times, 28 September 1987.
159 Ogden, 1978, p. 71.
160 The Independent, 10 October 1990.
161 http://www.worldconkerchampionships.com/ (accessed December 2008).
162 South Wales Echo, 9 November 1981.
163 East Anglian Daily Times, 26 October 1994.
164 The Times, 18 October 1989 and 15 November 1990.
165 http://www.cityoflondon.gov.uk/Corporation/media_centre/files2008/Go+for+conkers+at+Hampstead+Heath.htm (accessed December 2008).
166 Prague, November 1995, conkers unknown in the Czech Republic; Great Bedwyn, Wiltshire, June 1994, unknown in France; Budapest, October 1984, unknown in Hungary; letter from Luxembourg, in The Times, 27 October 1989, unknown in the Grand Duchy; Balderton, Nottinghamshire, September 1996, unknown in Sweden; Exeter, Devon, October 1984, unknown in the USA.
167 http://www.timesonline.co.uk/tol/news/world/europe/article660517.ece (accessed June 2010).
168 Moore, 1989, p. 21.
169 Letter in the New Scientist, 7 February 1998.
170 Letter from Norwich, Norfolk, in The Times, 27 October 1989.
171 Stoke Newington, London, August 2000.
172 South Kensington, London, November 1991.
173 Members of the Botanical Society of the British Isles, meeting in London, November 1991.

7. HISTORY AND LEGEND

1 O'Sullivan, 1977, p. 113.
2 IFCSS MSS 770, p. 143, Co. Longford.
3 Salisbury, Wiltshire, November 1985.
4 Bratton, Wiltshire, April 1983.
5 Britten and Holland, 1886, p. 481.
6 *Ibid.*, p. 295.
7 Udal, 1922, p. 17.
8 Macmillan, 1922, p. 128.
9 Bromfield, 1856, p. 529.
10 *Quarterly Review*, July 1863, p. 231.
11 Radstock, Avon, March 1982.
12 Cameron, 1883, p. 61.
13 Davey, 1909, p. 389.
14 IFCSS MSS 375, p. 90, Co. Cork.
15 Friend, 1884, p. 6.
16 Bristol, January 1999.
17 Marquand, 1906, p. 42.
18 Islington, London, February 1997.
19 Anon., 1520.
20 Phipps, 2003, p. 16.
21 See Roud, 2006, p. 255.
22 Hole, 1976, p. 26.
23 Batten, 1881, p. 116.
24 Collinson, 1791, vol. 2, p. 265.
25 Rawlinson, 1722, p. 109.
26 Collinson, 1791, vol. 2, p. 265.
27 Taylor, 1649, p. 6.
28 Rawlinson, 1722, p. 301.
29 Hole, 1965, p. 29.
30 Rawlinson, 1722, p. 1.
31 Hole, 1965, p. 35.
32 Rawlinson, 1722, p. 2.
33 Anon., n.d.c, p. 6.
34 Wilks, 1972, p. 98.
35 Christensen, 1992, p. 111.
36 *Gentleman's Magazine*, 1753, p. 578.
37 Vickery, 1979, p. 10.
38 Rawlinson, 1722, p. 112.
39 Palmer, K., 1976, p. 125
40 *Ibid.*, p. 37.
41 Morton, 1998, p. 38.
42 Manaccan, Cornwall, April 1998.
43 Bett, 1952, p. 54.
44 *Kent Messenger*, 28 December 1956.
45 Westwood and Simpson, 2005, p. 353.
46 *Notes & Queries*, 11 ser., 8, p. 425, 1913.
47 Westwood and Simpson, 2005, p. 350.
48 Boase, 1976, p. 115.
49 Anonymous telephone call, April 1991.
50 Aubrey, 1847, p. 50.

51 Sargant, n.d., p. 2.
52 Asberg and Stearn, 1973, p. 40.
53 Parkinson, 1640, p. 210.
54 Grigson, 1953.
55 *Country Life*, 113, p. 290, 1953.
56 *Ibid.*, p. 585.
57 Both Defoe and Baker quoted in Westwood and Simpson, 2005, p. 528.
58 *Ibid.*, p. 531.
59 Hitchman, 1975, p. 22.
60 Simpson, 2002, p. 31.
61 Dunsford, 1981, p. 176.
62 Rev. Louis Coulson, Vicar of Hartland, January 1982.
63 Bergamar, n.d., p. 7.
64 *Gentleman's Magazine* 74, p. 1194, 1804.
65 Westwood, 1985, p. 127.
66 Hythe, Kent, June 1973 and November 1987.
67 Armagh, September 1985.
68 Rushton, Northamptonshire, July 1985.
69 Wilks, 1972, p. 101.
70 http://www.rampantscotland.com/know.blknow_fortingall.htm (accessed January 2009).
71 *The Times*, 3 October 1998.
72 Bevan-Jones, 2002, p. 32.
73 *Ibid.*, p. 30.
74 *Ibid.*, p. 44.
75 Palmer, K., 1976, p. 56.
76 Jeacock, 1982; Chandler, 1992, p. 5.
77 Chandler, 1992, p. 6.
78 Stoke, Devon, April 1993; *Sunday Mirror*, 30 March 1997.
79 Chandler, 1992, p. 6.
80 Smith, 1969, p. 12.
81 *Barnet First*, August–September 2003.
82 Bevan-Jones, 2002, p. 91.
83 http://bromyardhistorysociety.org.uk/newsletter_5.htm (accessed January 2009).
84 Piper, 1896, p. 141.
85 Tim Hills of the Ancient Yews website, January 2009.
86 Harley, 1988, p. 5.
87 Rev. G. Marsden, September 1993; Rev. Michael Tillett, January 2009, both Rectors of Polstead; Wilks (1972, p. 22) claims 'the ceremony has been conducted under the old Polstead Gospel Oak for a thousand years'.
88 Morton, 1986, p. 58.
89 Wilks, 1972, p. 22.
90 *Ibid.*, p. 158.
91 *Ibid.*, p. 30.
92 *Ibid.*, p. 159.
93 *Ibid.*, p. 157.
94 *Ibid.*, p. 158.

8. NOTES ON NAMES

1 Macmillan, 1922.
2 *Flora, Facts and Fables*, 24, p. 6, 2000.
3 Macmillan, 1922, p. 46.
4 *Ibid.*, p. 7.
5 St Marys, Isles of Scilly, May 1993.
6 Britten and Holland, 1886, p. 135.
7 Grigson, 1987, p. 406.
8 Britten and Holland, 1886, p. 36.
9 *Ibid.*, p. 524.
10 *Ibid.*, p. 525.
11 Grigson, 1987, p. 406.
12 Dartnell and Goddard, 1894, p. 102.
13 Hart, 1898, p. 371.
14 Britten and Holland MSS.
15 Hart, 1898, p. 371.
16 Grigson, 1987, p. 58.
17 Pope *et al.*, 2003, p. 133.
18 Macmillan, 1922, p. 7.
19 Grigson, 1987, p. 424.
20 *Ibid.*
21 Britten and Holland MSS.
22 Grigson, 1987, p. 424.
23 Macmillan, 1922, p. 8.
24 Grigson, 1987, p. 425.
25 Britten and Holland MSS.
26 Grigson, 1987, p. 425.
27 *Ibid.*
28 Leather, 1912, p. 21.
29 Grigson, 1987, p. 425.
30 See p. 91 of this volume.
31 Grigson, 1987, p. 424.
32 Rich *et al.*, 1996, p. 231.
33 Histon, Cambridgeshire, January 1989.
34 Dartnell and Goddard, 1894, p. 125.
35 Macmillan, 1922, p. 288,
36 Grigson, 1987, p. 429; Macmillan, 1922, p. 7.
37 Macmillan, 1922, p. 11.
38 Britten and Holland, 1886, p. 74; wheys = heifers.
39 Grigson, 1987, p. 429.
40 *Ibid.*, p. 430.
41 Macmillan, 1922, p. 223.
42 Elder, 1997, p. 172.
43 Grigson, 1987, p. 429.
44 *Ibid.*
45 January 1993.
46 Britten and Holland, 1886, p. 133.
47 Lancaster, January 1991.
48 Britten and Holland, 1886, p. 383.
49 Grigson, 1987, p. 430.
50 Macmillan, 1922, p. 168.

51 Davey, 1909, p. 73; also Herefordshire (Grigson, 1987, p. 90).
52 Orpington, Kent, February 2007.
53 Grigson, 1987, p. 90.
54 Macmillan, 1922, p. 260.
55 Britten and Holland, 1886, p. 34.
56 Abell, 1980, p. 223.
57 Fowler, 1890, p. 77.
58 Britten and Holland, 1886, p. 134.
59 Lees, 1888, p. 783.
60 Grigson, 1987, p. 90.
61 *Ibid.*
62 *Ibid.*
63 Macmillan, 1922, p. 49; Davey, 1909, p. 73.
64 Macmillan, 1922, p. 82.
65 Friend, 1882, p. 162.
66 Grigson, 1987, p. 90.
67 *Ibid.*
68 Wareham, Dorset, January 1991.
69 Laycock, 1909, p. 81.
70 *Plants, People, Places*, 8, p. 1, 1996.
71 Milliken and Bridgewater, 2004, p. 121.
72 Grigson, 1987, p. 136.
73 *Ibid.*
74 *Ibid.*
75 Britten and Holland, 1886, p. 185.
76 Macmillan, 1922, p. 82.
77 Rhymney, Gwent, March 1991.
78 Bexhill-on-Sea, East Sussex, February 1991.
79 Lerwick, Shetland, March 1994.
80 Grigson, 1987, p. 136.
81 *Ibid.*
82 Mabey, 1996, p. 221.
83 St Mary's, Isles of Scilly, September 1997.
84 Grigson, 1987, p. 136.
85 September 2005.
86 Chessington, Surrey, February 1993.
87 Grigson, 1987, p. 136.
88 Worcester, January 1991.
89 Long Melford, Suffolk, November 1993.
90 Macmillan, 1922, p. 164.
91 Grigson, 1987, p. 71.
92 Wright, 1914, p. 339.
93 Grigson, 1987, p. 72.
94 Macmillan, 1922, p. 165.
95 *Ibid.*, p. 156.
96 Wareham, Dorset, January 1991.
97 Britten and Holland, 1886, p. 21.
98 Grigson, 1987, p. 385.
99 Britten and Holland, 1886, p. 21.
100 Macmillan, 1922, p. 16.
101 Britten and Holland, 1886, p. 508.

102 Tooting, London, July 1996.
103 Dartnell and Goddard, 1891, p. 87.
104 McKenna, 2004, p. 226.
105 Anon., n.d.b, p. 100.
106 Grigson, 1987, p. 27.
107 Hammer, 2008, p. 32.
108 Britten and Holland, 1886, p. 21.
109 *Flora of North America*, 19, p. 184, 2006.
110 Britten and Holland, 1886, p. 508.
111 Wormshill, Kent, May 2004.
112 Grigson, 1987, p. 82.
113 Britten and Holland, 1886, p. 21.
114 Hexham, Northumberland, May 1988.
115 Macmillan, 1922, p. 105.
116 Stace, 1991, p. 315.
117 Britten and Holland, 1886, p. 134.
118 Grigson, 1987, p. 84.
119 *Ibid.*, p. 82.
120 Britten and Holland MSS.
121 Britten and Holland, 1886, p. 134.
122 *Ibid.*, p. 43.
123 Macmillan, 1922, p. 23.
124 Britten and Holland, 1886, p. 43.
125 Macmillan, 1922, p. 23.
126 Britten and Holland MSS.
127 Britten and Holland, 1886, p. 43.
128 Macmillan, 1922, p. 23.
129 Britten and Holland, 1886, p. 43.
130 *Ibid.*
131 Macmillan, 1922, p. 23.
132 *Ibid.*
133 Davey, 1909, p. 260.
134 Macmillan, 1922, p. 21.
135 *Ibid.*, p. 22.
136 Grigson, 1987, p. 27.
137 Wheldon and Wilson, 1907, p. 128.
138 Grigson, 1987, p. 379.
139 Britten and Holland, 1886, p. 41.
140 Preston *et al.*, 2002, p. 418.
141 Curtis, 1798, 2, p. [1].
142 Lees, 1867, p. 24.
143 Murray, 1937, p. 179.
144 Grigson, 1987, p. 196.
145 Hart, 1898, p. 375.
146 Grigson, 1987, p. 196.
147 Lytchett Matravers, Dorset, May 1991.
148 Dallman, 1954, p. 322.
149 Frankland, 2001, p. 27.
150 Corbridge, Northumberland, December 1995.
151 Capel, Kent, February 1998.
152 Anonymous telephone call, April 1999.

153 Tivetshall, Norfolk, August 1999.
154 Sisland, Norfolk, May 1999.
155 Harrogate, North Yorkshire, October 1998.
156 East Bridgford, Nottinghamshire, March 1982.
157 Preston *et al.*, 2002, p. 605.
158 Britten and Holland, 1886, p. 506.
159 Grigson, 1987, p. 359.
160 Macmillan, 1922, p. 279.
161 Grigson, 1987, p. 359.
162 Macmillan, 1922, p. 92.
163 Laver, 1996, p. 253.
165 Grigson, 1987, p. 358.
165 *Ibid.*
166 Macmillan, 1922, p. 92.
167 *Ibid.*, p. 128.
168 Grigson, 1987, p. 359.
169 Macmillan, 1922, p. 128.
170 Grigson, 1987, p. 359.
171 Macmillan, 1922, p. 228.
172 Britten and Holland, 1886, p. 515.
173 Macmillan, 1922, p. 64.
174 *Ibid.*, p. 84.
175 Rowe MSS.
176 Fair Oak, Hampshire, January 2007.
177 Preston *et al.*, 2002, p. 451.
178 Elworthy, 1893, p. 203.
179 Britten and Holland MSS.
180 Preston *et al.*, 2002, p. 451.
181 Britten and Holland, 1886, p. 65; 'bride-laces were a kind of riband or small streamer often worn at weddings'.
182 *Ibid.*, p. 199.
183 *Ibid.*, p. 295.
184 Britten and Holland MSS.
185 Britten and Holland, 1886, p. 225.
186 *Ibid.*, p. 257.
187 Wright, 1914, p. 338.
188 Britten and Holland, 1886, p. 30.
189 *Ibid.*, p. 20.
190 Macmillan, 1922, p. 24.
191 Britten and Holland, 1886, p. 133.
192 Britten and Holland MSS.
193 Macmillan, 1922, p. 135.
194 Grigson, 1987, p. 33.
195 Macmillan, 1922, p. 47.
196 *Ibid.*, p. 110.
197 Grigson, 1987, p. 296.
198 Macmillan, 1922, p. 171.
199 Wright, 1914, p. 338.
200 See p. 77-8 of this volume.
201 Letchworth, Hertfordshire, May 2001, referring to mid Oxfordshire, 1930s.

202 Wormshill, Kent, May 2003; Robertsbridge, East Sussex, June 2003, referring to Desborough, Northamptonshire, 1920s.
203 Britten and Holland MSS.
204 Grigson, 1987, p. 267.
205 Britten and Holland, 1886, p. 123.
206 Macmillan, 1922, p. 67.
207 Grigson, 1987, p. 300.
208 Vickery, 2004, p. 59.
209 Friend, 1882, p. 41; for further information on Oak Apple Day see pp. 165–7 of this volume.
210 E., 1884, p. 382.
211 Downley, Buckinghamshire, February 1995.

9. THE CHANGING SCENES OF LIFE

1 Radford, 1961, p. 251.
2 See p. 47 of this volume.
3 Roberts, 1971, p. 100.
4 Helm, 1981, p. 26; 'man-woman' – a man crudely dressed as a woman, a common character in mummers' plays.
5 Shepherdswell, Kent, October 1979.
6 Leeds, October 1991; 'would have worked anyway', e.g. if it was a case of a late period, rather than pregnancy.
7 Menheniot, Cornwall, 1991.
8 Opie and Tatem, 1989, p. 299; similar practices known in the Basque country of Spain (South Kensington, London, July 1991).
9 Porter, 1958, p. 113.
10 Grigson, 1987, p. 24.
11 Child, 1889, p. 387.
12 Porter, 1974, p. 21.
13 Gen. 30.1-24.
14 St Clair, 1971, p. 58.
15 Porter, 1969, p. 12.
16 *Ibid.*
17 *Notes & Queries*, 1 ser., 6, p. 386, 1852.
18 Stevens Cox, 1971, p. 7.
19 *Notes & Queries*, 12 ser., 4, p. 219 and 256, 1918.
20 *Ibid.*, p. 256.
21 *Ibid.*
22 *Notes & Queries* 12, 4, p. 256, 1918.
23 Trevelyan, 1909, p. 266.
24 Porter, 1974, p. 20; Widdowson, 1975, p. 10.
25 McKelvie MSS, 1963, p. 273.
26 Steele MSS, 1978, p. 81.
27 Hemsley, 1892, p. 371.
28 Carmichael, 1928, p. 225.
29 Streatham, London, 1975.
30 Duncan, 1896, p. 163.
31 Harte, 2004, p. 119.
32 Sikes, 1880, p. 57.
33 Hatfield, 1984, p. 90.

34 Limavady, Co. Londonderry, October 1996; similar practices recorded from Stoke Fleming, Devon, October 1996 and Sandiway, Cheshire, October 2004.
35 Allen and Hatfield, 2004, p. 256.
36 See pp. 76–8 of this volume.
37 Opie and Opie, 1959, p. 337.
38 Great Bedwyn, Wiltshire, November 1988.
39 Opie and Opie, 1959, p. 274.
40 Williams, 1987, p. 98; Allantide = Allhallow-eve = Hallowe'en.
41 Deane and Shaw, 1975, p. 53.
42 *Notes & Queries*, 4 ser., 6, p. 340, 1870.
43 Kensington, London, November 1991; for other apple pastimes practised at Hallowe'en see Vickery, 1995, p. 10.
44 Opie and Tatem, 1989, p. 196.
45 Stevens Cox, 1971, p. 10.
46 Parker, 1923, p. 324.
47 Wright, 1940, p. 12.
48 Wright, 1938, p. 152.
49 *Ibid.*, p. 187.
50 Gregor, 1874, p. 103.
51 Danaher, 1972, p. 223.
52 IFCSS MSS 812, p. 155, Co. Offaly.
53 Pollock, 1960, p. 62.
54 Killip, 1975, p. 134.
55 *Notes & Queries*, 4 ser., 4, p. 505: 1869.
56 Marwick, 1975, p. 86.
57 Simpson, 2002, p. 90.
58 Porter, 1974, p. 25.
59 Macmillan, 1922, p. 36.
60 *Ibid.*, p. 122.
61 *Ibid.*, p. 164.
62 Neale MSS, 1975, p. 173.
63 Britten and Holland MSS.
64 Elworthy, 1895, p. 51.
65 Porter, 1974, p. 25.
66 Ingram, 1869, p. 347.
67 *Ibid.*, p. 348.
68 *Ibid.*, p. 349.
69 Elliott, 1984, p. 63.
70 Ingram, 1869, p. 352.
71 Mahood, 2008, p. 164; *erbe della Madonna* = ivy-leaved toadflax, regarded by Ruskin as his personal emblem.
72 Wormwood Scrubs, London, June 2009.
73 Stewart, 1987, p. 96.
74 *Ibid.*, p. 98.
75 Barrett, 1967, p. 97; similar belief recorded from Thetford, Norfolk – 'it had no effect on me, I must say' (West Stow, Suffolk, January 1991).
76 Cartland, 1971, chap. 5.
77 Macmillan, 1922, p. 181.
78 Simpson, 2002, p. 123.
79 Leather, 1912, p. 64.

80 Simpson, 2002, p. 123, where it is said that the practice 'may well be still current'.
81 Aubrey, 1881, p. 25.
82 Grigson, 1987, p. 377.
83 Allen and Hatfield, 2004, p. 301.
84 Britten and Holland, 1886, p. 17.
85 Udal, 1922, p. 251.
86 Latham, 1868, p. 30.
87 Danaher, 1972, p. 219.
88 Marwick, 1975, p. 85.
89 Opie and Opie, 1959, p. 274.
90 *Ibid.*
91 Barnes, London, October 1979.
92 Lovett, 1913, p. 121.
93 Stewart and Corry, 1938, p. 69.
94 Baker, 1974, p. 25.
95 McCulloch, 1903, p. 101.
96 Leather, 1912, p. 115.
97 Killip, 1975, p. 80.
98 Leather, 1912, p. 115.
99 Baker, 1974, p. 25.
100 Birmingham and Birmingham, 1964, p. 110.
101 Baker, 1974, p. 28.
102 *Ibid.*
103 *The Times*, 10 February 1840.
104 *Ibid.*, 29 June 1843.
105 *Ibid.*, 26 January 1858, 6 July 1866, 22 March 1871, 24 January 1874.
106 *Ibid.*, 11 March 1863.
107 Broomborough, Merseyside, November 1990.
108 Baker, 1974, p. 28.
109 Trevelyan, 1909, p. 105.
110 Advertisement for Bramley's Nurseries (South Benfleet, Essex), in the *Telegraph*, 24 June 1995.
111 *The Times*, 28 January 1858.
112 *Ibid.*, 6 July 1866, 22 March 1871, 20 April 1882, 6 July 1893, 10 October 1913.
113 *The Language of Flowers*, Warne's Bijou Books, London, n.d., p. 41.
114 de Cleene and Lejeune, 2003, 1, p. 202.
115 *Ibid.*; Ballard, 1998, p. 91; Humphries, 2004, p. 98.
116 Bennett, 1992, p. 128.
117 Davies, 2000, p. 144.
118 *Ibid.*, p. 124.
119 *Ibid.*, p. 125.
120 Humphries, 2004, p. 90.
121 South Kensington, London, October 1979.
122 Personal observation, South London Crematorium, May 1981; West London Crematorium, August 1981, and elsewhere.
123 Cunnington and Lucas, 1972, p. 70.
124 Humphries, 2004, p. 92.
125 *The World's Fair*, 1 January 1977.
126 Humphries, 2004, p. 90.
127 Bermant, 1974, p. 91.

128 Baker, 1996, p. 36.
129 Wembley, Middlesex, October 1977.
130 Quennell, 1984, p. 111.
131 Baring-Gould, n.d., p. 32.
132 Tongue, 1965, p. 135.
133 Porteous, 1971, p. 32.
134 Hammond MSS, p. 28.
135 Whitlock, 1976, p. 115.
136 Porter, 1969, p. 47.
137 Best and Brightman, 1973, p. 8.
138 Culpeper, 1652, p. 170.
139 See pp. 6 and 67 of this volume.
140 Wherry, 1905, p. 67.
141 Jones-Baker, 1977, p. 69.
142 Friend, 1884, p. 8.
143 Plymouth, January 1993.
144 Great Barr, West Midlands, October 1982.
145 *Notes & Queries*, 5 ser., 6, p. 463, 1876.
146 Simpson, 1976, p. 148.
147 Udal, 1922, p. 191.
148 Vickery, 1985, p. 16, and see pp. 49–51 and 53 of this volume.
149 *Ibid.*, p. 5, and see p. 54 of this volume.
150 See p. 53 of this volume.
151 Burton-on-Trent, Staffordshire, August 2003.
152 Stockport, Greater Manchester, October 1984; Opie and Tatem, 1989, p. 287.
153 Grigson, 1987, p. 84.
154 See pp. 54–5 of this volume; Opie and Tatem, 1989, p. 164; Roud, 2003, p. 199.
155 *Notes & Queries*, 4 ser., 12, p. 469, 1873; also Taylor MSS, probably referring to Norfolk, and Roud, 2003, p. 356, referring to Norfolk.
156 Evershed, 1877, p. 40.
157 Wilks, 1972, p. 133.
158 Whitlock, 1976, p. 163.
159 Leather, 1912, p. 20.
160 Briggs, 1971, p. 541; according to Milliken and Bridgewater, 2004, p. 147, minor criminals were secured to joug trees and then subjected to ridicule or physical abuse; whereas criminals who were condemned to being hung were hanged from dool, or dule, trees.
161 Wilks, 1972, p. 133.
162 Lisdrum, Co. Antrim, April 1978.
163 Daingean, Co. Offaly, January 1985; Udal, 1922, p. 267.
164 *Notes & Queries*, 9 ser., 12, p. 133, 1903.
165 Towcester, Northamptonshire, August 1982.
166 Maida Hill, London, March 1978.
167 Burne, 1883, p. 299.
168 Wherry, 1905, p. 66.
169 Parker, 1923, p. 325.
170 Brontë, 1847, chap. 16.
171 Robinson, 1975, p. 75.
172 Lloyd, 1967, p. 220.
173 Some, rather too clever, writers have suggested that 'white roses' is a corruption

of 'white mercury', formerly used in the treatment of syphilis, from which it is said the sailor died.

174 *The Daily Telegraph*, 1 December 1868; reprinted in *Notes & Queries*, 4 ser., 6, p. 496, 1870.
175 Pigott and Walters, 1953, p. 186.
176 Burne, 1883, p. 305.
177 Hole, 1940, p. 57.
178 Collinson, 1791, 1, p. 12.
179 Deane and Shaw, 1975, p. 135.
180 Corscombe, Dorset, March 1978.
181 Quoted in Radford, 1961 p. 268.
182 Burne, 1883, p. 299.
183 Friend, 1884, p. 8.
184 Fried and Elman, 1969, p. 63.
185 *Ibid.*, p. 247.
186 *The Graphic*, Supplementary Funeral Number, 9 February 1901; quoted in Jones, 1967, p. 122.
187 Stewart, 1987, p. 12.
188 Fraser, 1973, p. 164.
189 *The Times*, 9–13 November 2009.
190 Sanderson, 1969, p. 185.
191 Personal observation, London Road Cemetery, Mitcham, Surrey, 2005-9.
192 Dallas, 1971, p. 51.
193 Personal observation.
194 *The Times*, 30 March 1995.
195 *The Times*, 20 April 2000; see also photograph in *The Sun* of the same date.
196 *The Times*, 12 October 2000.
197 *The Times*, 28 October 1966.
198 *Daily Mirror*, 21 April 1989.
199 *Mail on Sunday*, 7 September 1997.
200 *Western Daily Press*, 1 July 1993.
201 *Ealing Guardian*, 10 January 1990.
202 London *Metro*, 16 July 2003.
203 Personal observation, south London crematoria, 1981-2009.
204 *City of London Cemetery and Crematorium Newsletter*, 7, p. 15, 2002.
205 Vickery, 1995, p. 135.
206 *Ibid.*, p. 3.
207 Brentnall, 1975, p. 176.
208 *Ibid.*, p. 177.
209 Personal observation, December 2009.

10. GARLANDS AND NOSEGAYS

1 Roud, 2006.
2 For example, Hutton, 1996.
3 Poole, 1877, p. 6.
4 Hutton, 1996, p. 39.
5 Legg, 1986, p. 54.
6 Willey, 1983, p. 40.
7 http://squirrelinn.co.uk/history.html (accessed November 2009).
8 *Chard and Ilminster News*, 13 January 1999.

9 Personal observation; it was said that the twelve bonds represented the twelve days of Christmas (not the twelve months of the year).
10 Johns, 1847, p. 303.
11 Roud, 2006, p. 404.
12 Patten, 1974, p. 7.
13 *Western Gazette*, 25 January 1974.
14 Dick Playll, past squire of Chanctonbury Ring Morris Men, January 1978.
15 http://www/crmm.org.uk/ (accessed November 2009).
16 Vickery and Vickery, 1974, p. 43.
17 Anon. [1995], p. 18.
18 Personal observation, 1994 and 1995.
19 Hong Kong Cultural Services, Soho, London, February 1991.
20 Goody, 1993, p. 388.
21 Personal observation, 5 February 1995.
22 Hutton, 1996, p. 150.
23 *Daily Telegraph*, 11 February 1995.
24 For an example of the speculations concerning this matter see Wilkinson, 1858, p. 137.
25 Hutton, 1996, p. 173.
26 *Notes & Queries*, 5 ser., 7, p. 206, 1877.
27 *The Times*, 2 March 1989, 2 March 1991.
28 Colgan, 1896, p. 216; for a thorough and richly illustrated account of shamrock see Nelson, 1991.
29 Gerard, 1597, p. 1017.
30 Frazer, 1894, p. 135.
31 For illustrations see Seaby, 1970 and Nelson, 1991, p. 131.
32 Colgan, 1896, p. 347.
33 According to Danaher, 1972, p. 62, St Patrick's Day crosses were made only by girls and children at the opening of the twentieth century, and the practice has since become completely abandoned.
34 Colgan, 1896, p. 351.
35 Threlkeld, 1727, p. 160.
36 Colgan, 1892, p. 96.
37 See p. 33 of this volume.
38 Bicheno, 1831.
39 Colgan, 1893.
40 Britten and Holland, 1886, p. 425.
41 Nelson, 1990.
42 *The Times*, 18 March 2004.
43 *City Recorder*, 9 April 1987; also *ibid.*, 16 April 1987.
44 *The Times*, 14 April 1989; Meloy undoubtedly exaggerated when he wrote of 'many countrymen and women'.
45 Wimbledon, London, November 1983; Atkins, 1986, p. 37, referring to Cornwall.
46 Pershore, Worcestershire, October 1991, referring to Crowborough, Sussex; St Ervan, Cornwall, referring to Heston, Middlesex, 1930s; Opie and Opie, 1959, p. 240.
47 South Kensington, London, March 2004, probably referring to c. 1950.
48 *Daily Telegraph*, 11 February 1995.
49 Personal recollections, Thorncombe, Dorset, 1950s.
50 *Western Gazette*, 30 March 1979.

51 Letter from the Secretary of the Flowers and Plants Association, New Covent Garden Market, in *The Times*, 27 February 1996.
52 *Irish World*, 24 March 2006; casual observations in south London suggest that this might be an underestimate.
53 Mk 11.7-10 (New English Bible).
54 Britten and Holland, 1886, p. 366; Grigson, 1987, p. 258.
55 Wormshill, Kent, May 2003.
56 Personal observation, Dublin, May 1993 and 1994.
57 Danaher, 1972, p. 68.
58 Daingean, Co. Offaly, January 1985.
59 Owen, 1978, p. 80.
60 *Bye-gones*, 9 September 1896; quoted in Hole, 1976, p. 74.
61 St Fagans, South Glamorgan, April 1983.
62 Brentnall, 1975, p. 67; Roud, 2006, p. 101.
63 Obituary of Valerie Bennett-Levy, nosegay-maker, *The Times*, 14 July 2008.
64 Sadborow, Dorset, December 1982.
65 Purley, Surrey, April 1983.
66 *Parish Magazine of Llandrindod Wells and Cefnellys with Diserth*, March 2003.
67 Edinburgh, October 1991, referring to Burghead, Morayshire, 1920s and 30s.
68 Castlerock, Co. Derry, February 1989; also recorded from Burghead, Morayshire, 1920s and 30s [Edinburgh, October 1991] and north London [Balham, London, July 2004].
69 Hole, 1976, p. 212.
70 Naylor and Porter, 2002, p. 11 and 32.
71 See p. 160 of this volume.
72 Naylor and Porter, 2002, p. 16.
73 *Ibid.*
74 Vickery, 1975, p. 178.
75 Anon., 1974; this list is known to be incomplete, but its brevity demonstrates that the custom was not considered to be of any great importance at that time.
76 http://www.derbyshireuk.net/derbyshire_welldressing2009.html (accessed November 2009).
77 *Christian Aid News*, February–March 1996.
78 Naylor and Porter, 2002, p. 80; St Chad's Parish Office, November 2009.
79 Frome, Somerset, December 1998 (Margaret Gale colln).
80 Hults, 1987.
81 Naylor and Porter, 2002, p. 85.
82 Catford, London, September 1984; also recorded from Purley, Surrey, April 1983; Wimbledon, London, November 1983; Trowbridge, Wiltshire, April 1998.
83 Wright, 1936, p. 157.
84 Burne, 1883, p. 350.
85 Froome, Somerset, March 1994.
86 Anon., n.d.a, p. 23.
87 Stella Smart, 'chief flower-lady', Arundel Cathedral, March 1978 and August 1980; personal observation 1980; *Guardian*, 30 April 1991.
88 Jeremy Fairhead, Vicar of All Saints, September 1987.
89 John Gilling, Parish Priest, St Mary's, October 1987.
90 Robertsbridge, East Sussex, June 2003.
91 Hole, 1975, p. 58.
92 Thompson, 1939, chap. 13.

93 Gloucester, 1983, p. 34.
94 Opie and Opie, 1959, p. 259.
95 Robson, 1993.
96 Personal observation, 13 May 1983.
97 Personal observation, 13 May 1996.
98 http://www.bamptonoxon.co.uk/pages.asp?id=69&pageName=Annual Events (accessed November 2009); although the Bampton garlands are carried by children, it is rumoured that they are made by local women.
99 Simpson, 2002, p. 115.
100 *Sussex Express*, 6 May 2008.
101 Raglan, 1939.
102 James, 1961, p. 288.
103 Basford, 1978.
104 Judge, 2000.
105 *Hastings Traditional Jack in the Green 2008*, programme; see also Leech, 2008.
106 Vickery, 2008, p. 13.
107 Anon., [?1910].
108 North Shields, North Tyneside, September 1996, referring to the 1920s; also Bridport, Dorset, February 1985, referring to the early 1920s, when 'all the girls wore daisy chains'.
109 Letter from Stratford-upon-Avon, Warwickshire, in *This England*, Winter 1988.
110 Chamberlain, 1990, p. 164.
111 Weaver, 1987, p. 12.
112 Yallop, 1984, p. 29.
113 See p. 117 of this volume.
114 Hemel Hempstead, Hertfordshire, August 2004.
115 Opie and Opie, 1959, p. 263.
116 Seven Sisters, London, May 2009.
117 Nottingham, May 2009.
118 Simpson and Roud, 2000, p. 302.
119 Lester, 1972, p. 2.
120 Rev. E. G. Allsop, former vicar of St Neot, November 1989.
121 Vickery, 2004, p. 61.
122 Simpson, 1931, p, 6.
123 Shuel, 1985, p. 86.
124 *Sowerby Bridge Rushbearing Festival*, leaflet published by Calderdale Council Leisure Services Department, 1996; according to Fred Knight, Chairman of the Sowerby Bridge Rushbearing Association, November 1994, although the rushcart is 'thatched' with rushes, bulrushes, rather than rushes, are presented to local clergy, 'as a token of the rushbearings of old and a renewal of the community's spiritual beliefs' (Margaret Gale colln).
125 *St Mary Redcliffe, Bristol: A Short Guide*, purchased November 2002.
126 Vickery, 2008, p. 13; the lengths recorded are the length of stem from which the leaves are devoured, the stems themselves are not eaten.
127 Calderbank, 1984, p. 11.
128 *Hexham Journal*, 12 September 1992.
129 *Garden News*, 10 October 2002.
130 *The Sun*, 15 August 2008.
131 *The Times*, 14 October 1991.
132 *Garden News*, 11–17 October 1995.

133 Jack Orrell, Chairman, Greyhound Pumpkin Club, November 1990; in December 2009 Jim McDonald of The Grey Hound reported that the Club no longer existed.

134 *Chard and Ilminster News*, 19 October 1994; this event came to an end in c. 2001 (Barrington, Somerset, December 2009).

135 *Hexham Courant*, 13 September 2002.

136 Opie and Opie, 1959, p. 269.

137 Loughborough, Leicestershire, September 2009.

138 Dyer, 1889, p. 15.

139 Vickery, 1995, p. 288.

140 *Independent*, 11 November 2006.

141 Seed, 1988; leaflets produced by the Peace Pledge Union, 2007 and 2008.

142 See, for example, Hole, 1976, p. 50.

143 Cambridge, November 1985; St Davids, Dyfed, October 1991; Harrow on the Hill, Middlesex, October 2004.

144 McKelvie MSS, 1963, p. 176, referring to Bradford, 1961 and Castleford, 1962.

145 Coles, 1656, p. 41.

146 *Notes & Queries*, 5 ser., 5, p. 126, 1876.

147 Rackham, 1868, p. 549.

148 *Daily Mirror*, 8 December 1958, referring to St Thomas's church, Derby; Maida Hill, London, December 1982, referring to Basingstoke area, Hampshire.

149 *Guardian*, 20 December 1972.

150 *Daily Express*, 11 November 1996.

151 *The Times*, 9 December 1995; South Kensington, London, January 2005.

152 *Tenbury Wells Mistletoe Festival*, media release, 23 November 2009.

153 *Daily Telegraph*, 25 November 2006.

154 See note 151.

155 Letter from Anthony Geering, Rector, Collegiate Church of the Holy Cross, Crediton, Devon, in *The Times*, 10 October 1998.

156 Miles, 1912, p. 265.

157 *Ibid.*

158 Hole, 1976, p. 53.

159 Combermere and Knollys, 1866, p. 419.

160 Miles, 1912, p. 264.

161 Mordiford, Hereford, December 1991, referring to rural Warwickshire in the 1920s; Alicante, Spain, December 1991, referring to Cornwall; Streatham, London, May 1992, referring to west Dorset, 1950s and '60s; St Wenn, Cornwall, November 2003.

162 Hole, 1976, p. 54.

163 Personal observation.

References

Published Sources

Abell, E. T. (1980), '81st report on dialect', *Report and Transactions of the Devonshire Association for the Advancement of Science*, 112, 223-4.

Allen, D. E. (1980), 'A possible scent difference between *Crataegus* species', *Watsonia* 13, 119-20.

Allen, D. E. and Hatfield, [V.] G. (2004), *Medicinal Plants in Folk Tradition*. Portland, Oregon: Timber Press.

Amery, P. F. S. (1907), 'Twenty-fourth report of the Committee on Devonshire folklore', *Report and Transactions of the Devonshire Association for the Advancement of Science*, 39, 105-9.

Anon. (1520), *Here begynneth the Lyfe of Joseph of Armathia*. London: R. Pynson.

Anon. [?1910], *Empire Day, May 24th*, Empire Movement leaflet 14, London.

Anon. (1916), 'Notes on Irish folklore', *Folk-lore* 27, 418-26.

Anon. (1974), *1974 Events in the Peak District National Park*. Bakewell: Peak National Park Office.

Anon. [1995], *Chinese New Year*. London: Chinese Community Centre.

Anon. (n.d.a), *The Cathedral of Our Lady and St Philip Howard, Arundel*. St Ives: Photo Precision.

Anon. (n.d.b), *Farm Weeds: An Aid to their Recognition*. London: Shell Chemical Co.

Anon. (n.d.c), *A Guide to Glastonbury and its Abbey*. Glastonbury: E. C. Helliker & Sons.

Anon. (n.d.d), *The Language of Flowers*. London: Warne's Bijou Books, p. 41.

Armstrong, S. (1976), *A Croft in Clachan*. London: Hutchinson.

Asberg, M. and Stearn, W. T. (1973), 'Linnaeus's Öland and Gotland journey 1741', *Biological Journal of the Linnean Society*, 5, 1-107.

Atkins, E. A. (1986), *Tales from our Cornish Island*. London: Harrap.

Aubrey, J. (1847), *The Natural History of Wiltshire*, J. Britten (ed.). London: Wiltshire Topographical Society.

Aubrey, J. (1881), *Remaines of Gentilisme and Judaisme*, J. Britten (ed.). London: The Folklore Society.

Bacon, F. (1631), *Sylva Sylvarum* (3rd edn). London: J. H. for William Lee.

Baker, M. (1974), *Discovering the Folklore of Love and Marriage*. Princes Risborough: Shire.

Baker, M. (1977), *Wedding Customs and Folklore*. Newton Abbot: David & Charles.

Baker, M. (1996), *Discovering the Folklore of Plants*. Princes Risborough: Shire.

Ballard, L. M. (1998), *Forgetting Frolic: Marriage Traditions in Ireland*. Belfast: Institute of Irish Studies, Queen's The University of Belfast.

Baring-Gould, S. (n.d.), *A Book of Folklore*. London: Collins Clear Type Press.

Barrett, H. (1967), *Early to Rise*. London: Faber.

Basford, K. (1978), *The Green Man*. Ipswich: Boydell & Brewer.

Batten, E. C. (1881), 'The Holy Thorn of Glastonbury', *Proceedings of the Somerset Archaeological and Natural History Society*, 26, 2, 118-25.

Battiscombe, G. (1969), *Queen Alexandra*. London: Constable.

REFERENCES

Bean, J. W. (1914), *Trees and Shrubs Hardy in the British Isles*, 1. London: John Murray.

Bennett, M. (1992), *Scottish Customs from Cradle to Grave*. Edinburgh: Polygon.

Bergamar, K. (n.d.), *Discovering Hill Figures*. Tring: Shire.

Bermant, C. (1974), *The Walled Garden*. London: Whitefield & Nicolson.

Best, M. R. and Brightman, F. H. (eds) (1973), *The Book of Secrets of Albertus Magnus*. Oxford: Clarendon Press.

Bett, H. (1952), *English Myths and Traditions*. London: B. T. Batsford.

Bevan-Jones, R. (2002), *The Ancient Yew*. Bollington: Windgather Press.

Bicheno, J. E. (1831), 'On the plant intended by the shamrock of Ireland', *Journal of the Royal Institution of Great Britain*, 1, 453–8.

Birmingham, F. and Birmingham, F. (1964), *The Wedding Book*. New York: Harper & Row.

Bloom, J. H. (1930), *Folk Lore, Old Customs and Superstitions in Shakespeare Land*. London: Mitchell Hughes & Clarke.

Boase, W. (1976), *The Folklore of Hampshire and the Isle of Wight*. London: B. T. Batsford.

Brand, J. (1853), *Observations on the Antiquities of Great Britain* (rev. Sir Henry Ellis). London: Henry G. Bohn.

Brand, J. (1877), *Observations on the Antiquities of Great Britain* (rev. Sir Henry Ellis). London: Bell.

Brentnall, M. (1975), *Old Customs and Ceremonies of London*. London: B. T. Batsford.

Briggs, K. M. (1971), *A Dictionary of British Folk-tales*, Part B, 2. London: Routledge & Kegan Paul.

Briggs, K. M. (1974), *The Folklore of the Cotswolds*. London: B. T. Batsford.

Briggs, K. M. (1976), *A Dictionary of Fairies*. London: Allen Lane.

Britten, J. and Holland, R. (1886), *A Dictionary of English Plant-names*. London: Trübner, for the English Dialect Society.

Bromfield, W. A. (1856), *Flora Vectensis*. London: W. Pamplin.

Brontë, E. (1847), *Wuthering Heights*. London: Thomas Cautley Newby.

Brown, T. (1972), '69th report on Devonshire folk-lore', *Report and Transactions of the Devonshire Association for the Advancement of Science*, 104, 263–8.

Burne, C. S. (1883), *Shropshire Folk-lore*. London: Trübner.

Calderbank, D. A. (1984), *Canny Leek Growing*. Wimborne: RightAngle Books.

Cameron, J. (1883), *Gaelic Names of Plants*. Edinburgh: William Blackwood and Sons.

Candlin, L. N. (1947), 'Plant lore of Sussex', *Sussex County Magazine*, 21, 130–1.

Carmichael, A. (1928), *Carmina Gadelica*, 2. Edinburgh: Oliver & Boyd.

Carmichael, A. (1941), *Carmina Gadelica*, 4. Edinburgh: Oliver & Boyd.

Carre, F. (1975), *Folklore of Lytchett Matravers, Dorset*. St Peter Port: Toucan Press.

Cartland, B. (1971), *We Danced all Night*. London: Hutchinson.

Challenger, F. (1955), 'Chemistry – the grand master key', *University of Leeds Review*, 4 (3), 264–72.

Chamberlain, E. (1990), *29 Inman Road*. London: Virago.

Chamberlain, M. (1975), *Fenwomen*. London: Quartet Books.

Chandler, J. (1992), 'Old men's fancies: the case of the churchyard yew', *FLS News*, 15, 3–6.

Chatfield, J. (2008), 'Rush lights', *SLBI Gazette*, ser. 2, 6, 10–11.

Child, F. J. (ed.) (1889), *The English and Scottish Popular Ballads*, 3. Boston, Massachusetts: Little Brown.

Chope, R. P. (1935), 'Thirty-fifth report on Devonshire folk-lore', *Report and Transactions of the Devonshire Association for the Advancement of Science*, 67, 131–44.

REFERENCES

Christensen, K. I. (1992), 'Revision of *Crataegus* sect. *Crataegus* and Nothosection Crataeguineae (Rosaceae – Maloideae) in the Old World', *Systematic Botany Monographs*, 35.

Clark, R. (1882), 'Folk-lore collected in Co. Wexford', *Folk-lore Record*, 5, 81–3.

Cloves, J. (1993), *The Official Conker Book*. London: Jonathan Cape.

Coles, W. (1656), *The Art of Simpling*. London: Nathaniel Brook.

Colgan, N. (1892), 'Shamrock: an attempt to fix its species', *Irish Naturalist*, 1, 95–7.

Colgan, N. (1893), 'The shamrock: a further attempt to fix its species', *Irish Naturalist*, 2, 207–11

Colgan, N. (1896), 'The shamrock in literature: a critical chronology', *Journal of the Royal Society of Antiquaries of Ireland*, 26, 211–26, 349–61.

Collinson, J. (1791), *The History and Antiquities of the County of Somerset*. Bath: R. Cruttwell.

Combermere, Mary, Viscountess, and Knollys, W. W. (1866), *Memories and Correspondence of Field Marshall Viscount Combermere*, 2. London: Hurst & Blackett.

Conquer, L. (1970), 'Corn dollies and "trees"', *Folklore*, 81, 145–7.

Copper, B. (1971), *A Song for Every Season*. London: William Heinemann.

Court, T. (1967), '"Urt" picking on Exmoor', *Exmoor Review*, 1967, 42–3.

Cowan, J. L. (1902), 'Welsh superstitions', *Journal of American Folklore*, 15, 131–2.

Culpeper, N. (1652), *The English Physitian*. London: Peter Cole.

Cunnington, P. and Lucas, C. (1972), *Costume for Births, Marriages and Deaths*. London: A. & C. Black.

Curtis, W. (1798), *Flora Londinensis*. London: the author / B. White & Son.

Dacombe, M. (ed.) (1951), *Dorset Up Along and Down Along* (3rd edn). Dorchester: Dorset Federation of Women's Institutes.

Dallas, D. (1971), *The Travelling People*. London: Macmillan.

Dallman, A. A. (1954), 'Local plant names', *North Western Naturalist*, 10, 65.

Danaher, K. (1972), *The Year in Ireland*. Cork: Mercier Press.

Dartnell, G. E. and Goddard, E. H. (1891), 'Contributions towards a Wiltshire glossary', *Wiltshire Archaeological and Natural History Magazine*, 26, 84–168.

Dartnell, G. E. and Goddard, E. H. (1894), *A Glossary of Words used in the County of Wiltshire*. London: English Dialect Society.

Davey, F. H. (1909), *Flora of Cornwall*. Penryn: F. Chegwidden.

Davies. J. (2000), *Saying it with Flowers: The Story of the Flower Shop*. London: Headline Book Publishing.

de Cleene, M. and Lejeune, M. C. (2003), *Compendium of Symbolic and Ritual Plants in Europe*. Ghent: Mens & Cultuur Uitgevers.

De Garis, M. (1975), *Folklore of Guernsey*. St Pierre du Bois: the author.

Deacon, E. (1930), 'Some quaint customs and superstitions in north Staffordshire and elsewhere', *North Staffordshire Field Club Transactions and Annual Report*, 64, 18–32.

Deane, T. and Shaw, T. (1975), *The Folklore of Cornwall*. London: B. T. Batsford.

Dixon, D. D. (1890), 'Northumbrian plant-names', *Nature Notes*, 1, 110–11.

Duncan, L. L. (1896), 'Fairy beliefs and other folklore notes from County Leitrim', *Folk-lore*, 7, 161–83.

Dunsford, M. E. (1981), '23rd report of the Folklore Section', *Report and Transactions of the Devonshire Association for the Advancement of Science*, 113, 173–6.

Dyer, T. F. T. (1889), *The Folk-lore of Plants*. New York: D. Appleton & Co.

E. (1884), 'Oak and Nettle Day in Nottinghamshire', *Folk-lore Journal*, 2, 381–2.

Edlin, H. L. (1949), *Woodland Crafts in Britain*. London: B. T. Batsford.

REFERENCES

Edom, G. (2010), *From Sting to Spin: A History of Nettle Fibre*, Bognor Regis: the author.

Elder, E. (ed.) (1997), *The Peacock Lincolnshire Word Books 1884–1920*. Barton-on-Humber: Scunthorpe Museum Society.

Elliott, B. (1984), 'The Victorian language of flowers', in [A.] R. Vickery (ed.), *Plant-lore Studies*. London: Folklore Society, pp. 61–5.

Elworthy, F. T. (1893), 'Thirteenth report of the Committee on Devonshire Verbal Provincialisms', *Report and Transactions of the Devonshire Association for the Advancement of Science*, 25, 181–211.

Elworthy, F. T. (1895), 'Fourteenth report of the Committee on Devonshire Verbal Provincialisms', *Report and Transactions of the Devonshire Association for the Advancement of Science*, 27, 40–60.

Evans, A. B. (1881), *Leicestershire Words, Phrases and Proverbs*. London: English Dialect Society.

Evans, G. E. (1966), *The Pattern under the Plough*. London: Faber.

Evans, J. (1800), *A Tour through part of North Wales in the year 1798, and at other times*. London: J. White.

Evelyn, J. (1664), *Sylva, or, a Discourse on Forest-trees*. London: J. Martyn and J. Allestry.

Evershed, H. (1877), 'The Cedars of Lebanon', *Gardeners' Chronicle*, 7, 39–40.

Flora of North America Editorial Committee (2006), *Flora of North America*, 19.

Fowler, W. M. E. (1890), 'Local animal and plant names in north east Hants', *Hampshire Field Club Papers and Proceedings*, 4, 75–7.

Fowler, W. M. E. (1909), 'Yorkshire folklore', in T. M. Fallow (ed.), *Memorials of Old Yorkshire*. London: George Allen, pp. 286–305.

Frankland, J. N. (2001), *A Flora of Craven*. Settle: North Craven Heritage Trust.

Fraser, A. S. (1973), *The Hills of Home*. London: Routledge & Kegan Paul.

Frazer, J. G. (1922), *The Golden Bough* (abridged edition). London: Macmillan.

Frazer, W. (1894), 'The shamrock: its history', *Journal of the Royal Society of Antiquaries of Ireland*, 24, 132–5.

Fried, A. and Elman, R. M. (1969), *Charles Booth's London*. London: Hutchinson.

Friend, H. (1882), *A Glossary of Devonshire Plant-names*. London: English Dialect Society.

Friend, H. (1884), *Flowers and Flower Lore*. London: Sonnerschein & Co.

Gepp, E. (1923), *An Essex Dialect Dictionary*. London: Routledge.

Gerard, J. (1597), *The Herball, or Generall Historie of Plants*. London: John Norton.

[Gloucester, Duchess of] (1983), *The Memoirs of Princess Alice, Duchess of Gloucester*. London: Collins.

Goddard, E. H. (ed.) (1942), 'Wiltshire folk lore jottings', *Wiltshire Archaeological and Natural History Magazine*, 50, 24–46.

Gomme, A. B. (1894), *The Traditional Games of England, Scotland, and Ireland*, 1. London: Nutt.

Gomme, G. L. (ed.) (1884), *The Gentleman's Magazine Library: Popular Superstitions*. London: Elliot Stock.

Goody, J. (1993), *The Culture of Flowers*. Cambridge: Cambridge University Press.

Gregor, W. (1874), *An Echo of Olden Time*. Edinburgh: John Menzies & Co.

Grigson, G. (1953), 'The legend of a plant', *Country Life*, 113, 145.

Grigson, G. (1959), *A Herbal of All Sorts*. London: Phoenix House.

Grigson, G. (1987), *The Englishman's Flora*. London: J. M. Dent & Sons [first published 1955].

Gutch, E. (1901), *County Folk-lore*, 2, *Printed Extracts concerning the North Riding of Yorkshire, York and the Ainsty*. London: David Nutt.

REFERENCES

Hadfield, M. (1957), *British Trees: A Guide for Everyman*. London: J. M. Dent & Son.

Hall, H. (1957), *A Dictionary of Sussex Dialect*. Chichester: the author.

Hammer, J. (2008), *Island of Flowers*. Yarmouth: Ampersand.

Hardy, J. (1895), *The Denham Tracts*, 2. London: Folklore Society.

Harley, L. S. (1988), *Polstead Church and Parish*. Hadleigh: BGA Print.

Hart, H. C. (1898), *Flora of County Donegal*. Dublin: Sealy & Co.

Harte, J. (2004), *Explore Fairy Traditions*. Loughborough: Explore Books.

Hatfield, V. G. (1984), 'Herbs in pregnancy, childbirth and breast-feeding', in [A.] R. Vickery (ed.), *Plant-lore Studies*. London: Folklore Society, pp. 84–93.

Hatfield, [V.] G. (1998), *Warts: Summary of Wart-cure Survey of the Folklore Society*. London: The Folklore Society.

Hatfield, [V.] G. (1999), *Memory, Wisdom and Healing: The History of Domestic Plant Medicine*. Stroud: Sutton Publishing.

Hatton, R. G. (1909), *The Craftman's Plant-book*. London: Chapman & Hall.

Helm, A. (1981), *The English Mummers' Play*. Woodbridge: D. C. Brewer.

Hemsley, W. B. (1892), 'A drift-seed (*Ipomoea tuberosa*)', *Annals of Botany*, 6: 369–72.

Hewins, M. E. (1985), *Mary after the Queen: Memories of a Working Girl*. Oxford: Oxford University Press.

Hitchman, J. (1975), *Such a Strange Lady*. London: New English Library.

Hole, C. (1937), *Traditions and Customs of Cheshire*. London: Williams & Norgate.

Hole, C. (1940), *English Folklore*. London: B. T. Batsford.

Hole, C. (1961), *Easter and its Customs*. London: Richard Bell.

Hole, C. (1965), *Saints in Folklore*. London: G. Bell & Sons.

Hole, C. (1975), *English Traditional Customs*. London: B. T. Batsford.

Hole, C. (1976), *British Folk Customs*. London: Hutchinson & Co.

Hone, W. (n.d.), *The Everyday Book*, 2. London: Thomas Tegg.

Howkins, C. and Sampson, N. (2000), *Searching for Hornbeam: A Social History*, Addlestone: the author.

Hults, D. S. (1987), 'A Derbyshire custom in transition? Well dressing in Perth, Western Australia', *Australian Folklore*, 1, 25–43.

Humphries, C. (2004), *Modern Wedding Etiquette Essentials*. Slough: W. Foulsham & Co.

Hunt, R. (1881), *Popular Romances of the West of England*. London: Chatto & Windus.

Hutton, R. (1996), *The Stations of the Sun: A History of the Ritual Year in Britain*. Oxford: Oxford University Press.

Ingram, J. (1869), *Flora Symbolica or the Language and Sentiment of Flowers*. London: Warne.

James, E. O. (1961), *Seasonal Feasts and Festivals*. London: Thames & Hudson.

Jeacock, R. (1982), *Plants and Trees in Legend, Fact and Fiction*. Chester: Mothers' Union.

Johns, C. A. [1847], *Forest Trees of Britain*. London: Society for Promoting Christian Knowledge.

Johnston, G. (1831), *Flora of Berwick-upon-Tweed*, 2. Edinburgh: Carfrae.

Johnston, G. (1853), *The Botany of the Eastern Borders*. London: Van Voorst.

Jones, B. (1967), *Design for Death*. London: Deutsch.

Jones, L. (1980), *Schoolin's Log*. London: Michael Joseph.

Jones-Baker, D. (1977), *The Folklore of Hertfordshire*. London: B. T. Batsford.

Judge, R. (2000), *The Jack-in-the-Green*. London: Folklore Society.

Kavanagh, P. (1975), *The Green Fool*. London: Penguin.

REFERENCES

Killip, M. (1975), *The Folklore of the Isle of Man*. London: B. T. Batsford.

Knight, W. F. G. (1945), 'Forty-second report on Devonshire folk-lore', *Report and Transactions of the Devonshire Association for the Advancement of Science*, 77, 93-7.

Lambeth, M. (1977), *Discovering Corn Dollies*. Princes Risborough: Shire Publications.

Latham, C. (1878), 'Some west Sussex superstitions lingering in 1868', *Folk-lore Record* 1, 1-67.

Laver, F. J. (1990), '91st report on dialect', *Report and Transactions of the Devonshire Association for the Advancement of Science*, 122, 233-8.

Laver, F. J. (1996), '97th report on dialect', *Report and Transactions of the Devonshire Association for the Advancement of Science*, 128, 253-4.

Laycock, C. H. (1909), 'Twenty-second report of the Committee on Devonshire Verbal Provincialisms', *Report and Transactions of the Devonshire Association for the Advancement of Science*, 41, 64-92.

Laycock, C. H. (1940), 'Thirty-ninth on Devonshire folklore', *Report and Transactions of the Devonshire Association for the Advancement of Science*, 72, 115-16.

Leather, E. M. (1912), *The Folk-lore of Herefordshire*. Hereford: Jakeman & Carver.

Leech, K. (2008), *The Hastings Traditional Jack in the Green*. Hastings: Hastings Borough Council.

Lees, E. (1867), *The Botany of Worcestershire*. Worcester: Worcestershire Naturalists' Club.

Lees, F. A. (1888), *The Flora of West Yorkshire*. London: Lovell Reeve.

Legg, P. (1986), *So Merry Let Us Be – the Living Tradition of Somerset Cider*. Bridgwater: Somerset County Council Library Service.

Lester, G. (1972), *Castleton Garland*, Sheffield: The Survey of Language and Folklore.

Lightfoot, J. (1777), *Flora Scotica*. London: B. White.

Lindegaard, P. (1978), 'The colliers' tale – a Bristol incident of 1753', *Journal of the Bath and Avon Family History Society*, Spring 1978, 8.

Linwood Pitts, J. (1893), 'Report of the Folklore Section', *Report and Transactions of the Guernsey Society for Natural Science*, 2, 270-9.

Lloyd, A. L. (1967), *Folk Song in England*. London: Lawrence & Wishart.

Lousley, J. E. (1971), *Flora of the Isles of Scilly*. Newton Abbot: David & Charles.

Lovett, E. (1913), 'Folk-medicine in London', *Folk-lore*, 24, 120-1.

Lucas, A. T. (1960), *Furze – A Survey and History of its Uses in Ireland*. Dublin: National Museum of Ireland.

Mabey, R. (1996), *Flora Britannica*. London: Sinclair-Stevenson.

McClintock, D. (1970), 'Why is white heather lucky?', *Country Life*, 15 January, 159.

Mac Coitir, N. (2006), *Irish Wild Plants: Myths, Legends & Folklore*. Wilton, Cork: The Collins Press.

MacCulloch, E. (1903), *Guernsey Folk Lore*. London: Elliot Stock.

McKenna, N. (2004), *The Secret Life of Oscar Wilde*. London: Arrow.

Mac Manus, D. (1973), *The Middle Kingdom: The Faerie World of Ireland*. Gerrards Cross: Colin Smythe.

Macmillan, A. S. (1922), *Popular Names of Flowers, Fruits, etc*. Yeovil: Western Gazette.

McNeill, M. (1910), *Colonsay*. Edinburgh: David Douglas.

McNicholas, E. (1992), 'The four-leaved shamrock and the cock', *ARV*, 47, 209-16.

Mahood, M. M. (2008), *The Poet as Botanist*. Cambridge: Cambridge University Press.

REFERENCES

Maple, E. (1971), *Superstition and the Superstitious*. London: W. H. Allen.

Marquand, E. D. (1906), 'The Guernsey dialect and its plant names', *Transactions of the Guernsey Society of Natural Science and Local Studies*, 5, 31–47.

Marwick, E. (1975), *The Folklore of Orkney and Shetland*. London: B. T. Batsford.

Melling, J. K. (1981), *Discovering London's Guilds and Liveries*. Princes Risborough: Shire Publications.

Miles, C. A. (1912), *Christmas in Ritual and Tradition, Christian and Pagan*. London: Unwin.

Miller, H. (1858), *The Cruise of the Betsey*. London: Hamilton, Allen.

Milliken, W. and Bridgewater, S. (2004), *Flora Celtica*. Edinburgh: Birlinn.

Mitchison, N. (1973), 'A harvest experience', *Folklore*, 84, 252–3.

Moore, A, (1989), *Where is Brown Hill?* Victoria Park: Hesperian Press.

Morris, J. P. (1869), *A Glossary of the Words and Phrases of Furness (North Lancashire)*. London: George Coward.

Morton, A. (1986), *The Trees of Shropshire*. Shrewsbury: Airlife.

Morton, A. (1998), *Tree Heritage of Britain and Ireland*. Shrewsbury: Swan Hill Press.

Murray, J. (1937), 'Cumbrian plant names', *North Western Naturalist*, 12, 178–82.

Naylor, P. and Porter, L. (2002), *Well Dressing*. Ashbourne: Landmark Publishing.

Nelson, E. C. (1990), 'Shamrock 1988', *Ulster Folklife*, 36, 32–42.

Nelson, E. C. (1991), *Shamrock: Botany and History of an Irish Myth*. Aberystwyth: Boethius Press.

Nelson, [E.] C. (2005), 'For luck and love', *Scots Magazine*, 163, (3), 250–3.

Nelson, E. C. (2006), 'Lucky white heather: a sesquicentennial review of a Scottish Victorian conceit', *Heathers*, 3, 38–46.

Nelson, E. C. and McCracken, E. M. (1987), *The Brightest Jewel: A History of the National Botanic Gardens, Glasnevin*. Kilkenny: Boethius Press.

Nixon, D. B. (1977), *Walk Soft in the Fold*. London: Chatto & Windus.

Norman, F. (1969), *Banana Boy*. London: Secker & Warburg.

Ó Danachair, C. (1970), 'The luck of the house', *Ulster Folklife*, 15/16, 20–7.

Ogden, J. (1978), 'Marbles and Conkers', *Lore and Language*, 2, (9), 71–2.

Opie, I. and Opie, P. (1959), *The Lore and Language of Schoolchildren*. Oxford: Oxford University Press.

Opie, I. and Opie, P. (1969), *Children's Games in Street and Playground*. Oxford: Oxford University Press.

Opie, I. and Tatem, M. (1989), *A Dictionary of Superstitions*. Oxford: Oxford University Press.

O'Suilleabhain, S. (1967), *Irish Folk Custom and Belief*. Dublin: Cultural Relations Committee of Ireland.

O'Sullivan, S. (1966), *Folktales of Ireland*. Chicago: University of Chicago Press.

O'Sullivan, S. (1977), *Legends from Ireland*. London: B. T. Batsford.

Owen, T. M. (1978), *Welsh Folk Customs*. Cardiff: National Museum of Wales.

Palmer, G. and Lloyd, N. (1972), *A Year of Festivals*. London: Frederick Warne & Co.

Palmer, K. (1976), *The Folklore of Somerset*. London: B. T. Batsford.

Palmer, R. (1976), *The Folklore of Warwickshire*. London: B. T. Batsford.

Parker, A. (1923), 'Oxfordshire village folklore, II', *Folk-lore*, 34, 323–33.

Parkinson, J. (1640), *Theatrum Botanicum*. London: T. Cotes.

Patten, R. W. (1974), *Exmoor Custom and Song*. Dulverton: Exmoor Press.

Peate, I. C. (1971), 'Corn ornaments', *Folklore*, 82, 177–84.

Peter, T. (1915), 'Cornish folklore notes', *Journal of the Royal Cornwall Institution*, 20, 117–33.

REFERENCES

Phillips, R. (1983), *Wild Food*. London: Pan.

Phipps, J. B. (2003), *Hawthorns and Medlars*. Portland, Oregon: Timber Press.

Pickering, I. (1995), *Some Goings On!: A Selection of Newspaper Articles about Fowey, Polruan and Lanteglos Districts from 1800–1899*. Fowey: the author.

Pigott, C. D. and Walters, S. M. (1953), 'Is the box tree a native of England?', in J. E. Lousley (ed.), *The Changing Flora of Britain*. Oxford: Botanical Society of the British Isles, pp. 184–7.

Piper, G. (1896), 'The gospel yew', *Transactions of the Woolhope Naturalists' Field Club*, 1896, 141.

Pollock, A. J. (1960), 'Hallowe'en customs in Lecale, Co. Down', *Ulster Folklife*, 6, 62–4.

Poole, C. H. (1877), *The Customs, Superstitions and Legends of the County of Somerset*. London: Sampson Low.

Pope, C., Snow, L. and Allen, D. (2003), *The Isle of Wight Flora*. Wimborne: Dovecot Press.

Porteous, C. (1971), *The Ancient Customs of Derbyshire*. Derby: Derbyshire Countryside.

Porter, E. M. (1958), 'Some folk beliefs of the Fens', *Folklore*, 69, 112–22.

Porter, E. [M.] (1969), *Cambridgeshire Customs and Folklore*. London: Routledge & Kegan Paul.

Porter, E. [M.]. (1974), *The Folklore of East Anglia*. London: B. T. Batsford.

Pratt, A. (1857), *Wild Flowers*. London: Society for Promoting Christian Knowledge.

Preston, C. D., Pearman, D. A. and Dines, T. D. (2002), *New Atlas of the British and Irish Flora*. Oxford: Oxford University Press.

Quelch, M. T. (1941), *Herbs for Daily Use*. London: Faber.

Quennell, P. (ed.) (1984), *Mayhew's London*. London: Bracken Books.

Rackham, H. (trans.) (1968), *Pliny the Elder, Natural History, IV, Books XII–XVI*. London: William Heinemann.

Radford, E. and Radford, M. A. (1961), *Encyclopaedia of Superstitions*, C. Hole (ed. and rev.). London: Hutchinson & Co.

Raglan, Lady (1939), 'The Green Man in church architecture', *Folk-lore*, 50, 45–57.

Ranson, F. (1949), *British Herbs*. Harmondsworth: Penguin Books.

Raven, J. (1978), *The Folklore of Staffordshire*. London: B. T. Batsford.

Rawlinson, R. (1722), *The History and Antiquities of Glastonbury*. Oxford: printed at the Theater.

Ray, J. (1670), *Catalogus Plantarum Angliae*. London: John Martyn.

Rhys, J. (1901), *Celtic Folklore*. Oxford: Oxford University Press.

Rich, T. *et al*. (1996), *Flora of Ashdown Forest*. East Grinstead: Sussex Botanical Recording Society.

Roberts, R. (1971), *The Classic Slum*. Manchester: Manchester University Press.

Robinson, J. (1975), *The Life and Times of Francie Nichol of South Shields*. London: Allen & Unwin.

Robson, P. (1993), 'Dorset Garland Days on the Chesil coast', in T. Buckland and J. Wood (eds), *Aspects of British Calendar Customs*. Sheffield: Sheffield Academic Press, pp. 155–66.

Ross, A. (1976), *The Folklore of the Scottish Highlands*. London: B. T. Batsford.

Roud, S. (2003), *The Penguin Guide to the Superstitions of Britain and Ireland*. London: Penguin Books.

Roud, S. (2006), *The English Year*. London: Penguin Books.

Rowling, M. (1976), *The Folklore of the Lake District*. London: B. T. Batsford.

REFERENCES

Rudkin, E. H. (1936), *Lincolnshire Folklore*. Gainsborough: Beltons.
St Clair, S. (1971), *Folklore of the Ulster People*. Cork: Mercier Press.
Sanderson, S. F. (1969), 'Gypsy funeral customs', *Folklore*, 80, 181–7.
Sargant, W. L. (n.d.), *Daneweed & the Danish Vikings in Rutland & Kesteven*. Stamford: The Central Press.
Seaby, P. J. (1970), *Coins and Tokens of Ireland*. London: B.A. Seaby.
Seed, P. (1988), 'Quakers and the white poppy', *Quaker Monthly*, 67, 219–20.
Sharman, N. (1977), *Nothing to Steal*. London: Kaye & Ward.
Shuel, B. (1985), *The National Trust Guide to Traditional Customs of Britain*. Exeter: Webb & Bower.
Sikes, W. (1880), *British Goblins*. London: Sampson Low.
Simpson, G. M. (1931), *The Rushbearing in Grasmere and Ambleside*. Manchester: John Heywood.
Simpson, J. (1976), *The Folklore of the Welsh Border*. London: B. T. Batsford.
Simpson, J. (2002), *Folklore of Sussex*. Stroud: Tempus Publishing.
Simpson, J. and Roud, S. (2000), *A Dictionary of English Folklore*. Oxford: Oxford University Press.
Smith, A. W. (1959), 'Some local lore collected in Essex', *Folklore*, 70, 414–15.
Smith, A. [W.] (1969), *Discovering Folklore in Industry*. Tring: Shire Publications.
Stace, C. (1991), *New Flora of the British Isles*. Cambridge: Cambridge University Press.
Stevens Cox, J. (1971), *Guernsey Folklore recorded in the Summer of 1882*. St Peter Port: Toucan Press.
Stevens Cox, J. (1974), *An Ilchester Word List and some Folklore Notes*. St Peter Port: Toucan Press.
Stewart, S. (1987), *Lifting the Latch*. Oxford: Oxford University Press.
Stewart, S. A. and Corry, T. H. (1938), *A Flora of the North-east of Ireland* (2nd edn). Belfast: Quota Press.
Stewart, W. G. (1823), *The Popular Superstitions and Festive Amusements of the Highlanders of Scotland*. Edinburgh: Archibald Constable & Co.
Tait, R. W. (1947), 'Some Shetland plant names', *Shetland Folk Book*, 1, 74–88.
Tangye, M. (2008), 'Traditional uses of Japanese knotweed', *Old Cornwall*, 13, (10), 46–7.
Taylor, J. (1649), *John Taylor's Wandering to see the Wonders of the West*. London: John Martyn.
Thiselton Dyer, T. F. (1889), *The Folk-lore of Plants*. New York: D. Appleton & Co.
Thompson, F. (1939), *Lark Rise*. London: Oxford University Press.
Threlkeld, C. (1727), *Synopsis stirpium Hibernicarum*. Dublin: S. Powell for F. Davys. [The pages are unnumbered in the original edition; the page numbers cited are those given in the Boethius Press, 1988, facsimile.]
Thurston, E. (1930), *British and Foreign Trees and Shrubs in Cornwall*. Cambridge: Cambridge University Press, for the Royal Institution of Cornwall.
Tongue, R. L. (1965), *Somerset Folklore*. London: The Folklore Society.
Trevelyan, M. (1909), *Folk-lore and Folk-stories of Wales*. London: Elliot Stock.
Turner, W. (1548), *The Names of Herbes*. London: John Day & Wyllyam Seres.
Udal, J. S. (1922), *Dorsetshire Folk-lore*. Hertford: Stephen Austin & Sons.
Ui Chonchubhair, M. (1995), *Flóra Chorca Dhuibhne*. Baile an Fheirtéaraigh: Oidhreacht Chorca Dhuibhne.
van der Zweep, W. (1984), 'Linguistic, artistic and folklore aspects of tares in the biblical parable', in [A.] R. Vickery (ed.), *Plant-lore Studies*. London: The Folklore Society, pp. 162–79.

REFERENCES

Vesey-FitzGerald, B. (1944), 'Gypsy medicine', *Journal of the Gypsy Lore Society*, 23, 21–33.

Vickery, A. R. (1975), 'The use of lichens in well-dressing', *Lichenologist* 7, 178–9.

Vickery, A. R. (1978), 'West Dorset folklore notes', *Folklore*, 89, 154–9.

Vickery, A. R. (1979), *Holy Thorn of Glastonbury*. St Peter Port: Toucan Press.

Vickery, A. R. (1983), '*Lemna minor* and Jenny Greenteeth', *Folklore*, 94, 247–50.

Vickery, [A.] R. (1985), *Unlucky Plants*. London: The Folklore Society.

Vickery, [A.] R. (1995), *A Dictionary of Plant-lore*. Oxford: Oxford University Press.

Vickery, A. R. (2004), 'Oaks in British and Irish Folklore', *International Oaks*, 15, 50–67.

Vickery, [A.] R. (2006), 'Remembered remedies', *Herbs*, 31, (4), 18–19.

Vickery, [A.] R. (2008), *Naughty Man's Plaything – Folklore and Uses of Stinging Nettles in the British Isles*. London: the author.

Vickery, A. R. and Vickery, M. E. (1974), 'Chinese New Year celebrations in London 1971–1973', *Folklore*, 85, 43–5.

Victoria, Queen (1868), *Leaves from the Journal of a Life in the Highlands*. London: Smith, Elder.

Waring, P. (1978), *A Dictionary of Omens and Superstitions*. London: Souvenir Press.

Warner, M. (1978), *Alone of all her sex*. London: Quartet Books.

Weaver, O. J. (1987), *Boscobel House and White Ladies Priory*. London: English Heritage.

Webster, M. M. (1978), *Flora of Moray, Nairn and East Inverness*. Aberdeen: Aberdeen University Press.

Wenis, E. and Wenis, H. (1990), 'Multi-leaved clovers – again', *BSBI News*, 56, 24.

Westwood, J. (1985), *Albion: A Guide to Legendary Britain*. London: Granada Publishing.

Westwood, J. and Simpson, J. (2005), *The Lore of the Land*. London: Penguin.

Wheldon, J. A. and Wilson, A. (1907), *The Flora of West Lancashire*. Eastbourne: V. T. Sumfield.

Wherry, B. A. (1905), 'Miscellaneous notes from Monmouthshire', *Folk-lore*, 16, 63–7.

Whistler, C. W. (1908), 'Sundry notes from west Somerset and Devon', *Folk-lore*, 19, 88–91.

Whitlock, R. (1976), *The Folklore of Wiltshire*. London: B. T. Batsford.

Widdowson, J. D. A. (1975), 'The things they say about food: a survey of traditional English foodways', *Folklife*, 13, 1–12.

Wilkinson, Lady (1858), *Weeds and Wild Flowers: Their Uses, Legends, and Literature*. London: John Van Voorst.

Wilks, J. H. (1972), *Trees of the British Isles in History and Legend*. London: Frederick Muller.

Willey, G. R. (1983), 'Burning the ashen faggot: a surviving Somerset custom', *Folklore*, 94, 40–3.

Williams, D. (1987), *Festivals of Cornwall*. Bodmin: Bossiney.

Willis Watson, W. G. (1920), *Calendar of Customs, Superstitions, Weather-lore, Popular Sayings and important Events connected with the County of Somerset*. Taunton: County Herald.

Wright, A. R. (1936), *British Calendar Customs: England*, 1. London: The Folklore Society.

Wright, A. R. (1938), *British Calendar Customs: England*, 2. London: The Folklore Society.

REFERENCES

Wright, A. R. (1940), *British Calendar Customs: England*, 3. London: The Folklore
Society.
Wright, E. M. (1914), *Rustic Speech and Folk-lore*. Oxford: Oxford University Press.
Wright, J. ([1898-] 1905), *The English Dialect Dictionary*. London: Henry Frowde.
Wyatt, I. (n.d.), *Book of Huish*. Yeovil: Western Gazette.
Yallop, H. J. (1984), 'An example of 17th century Honiton lace', *Devon Historian*,
28, 27-13.

Unpublished Sources

Britten and Holland MSS - slips accumulated by James Britten (1846-1924) and
Robert Holland (1829-93), intended for a supplement to their *Dictionary of
English Plant-names* (1878-86), now in the Botany Library, Natural History
Museum, London.
Cottam MSS, 1989 - 'A survey of the farming traditions and role of animals in
Retford and the surrounding district', student project by T. Cottam, the
Centre for English Cultural Tradition and Language, University of Sheffield,
1989.
Dickinson MSS, 1974 - 'Ayton past and present', thesis for the examination of
English Special Studies BA supervised by Mr Sanderson of the Folk Life Studies
Department [University of Leeds], by M. E. Dickinson.
Hammond, P. R. MSS, 1970 - 'The folk lore of wild flowers in the parish of
Leckhampton, Cheltenham in Gloucestershire', thesis submitted in partial
requirement for the degree of BA, Institute of Dialect and Folk Life Studies,
University of Leeds.
IFCSS MSS - material contributed to the Irish Folklore Commission's Schools'
Scheme, 1937-8, in which children in Irish primary schools collected and
recorded local folkore; now in the Department of Irish Folklore, University
College, Dublin.
McKelvie MSS, 1963 - 'Some aspects of oral, social and material tradition in an
industrial urban area', a thesis presented for the degree of PhD, University of
Leeds, by D. McKelvie.
Neale MSS, 1975 - 'A new look at old Manuscript and its author', University of
Leeds.
Parsons MSS, 1952 - 'Horseheath: some recollections of a Cambridgeshire parish',
1952, in the Cambridge Record Office.
Rowe MSS - list of plant names supplied by Mrs H. K. Rowe, of Minehead, Somerset,
November 1993.
SLF MSS - items contributed to the Survey of Folklore and Language, University
of Sheffield.
SSS MSS - transcriptions or summaries of tape-recordings in the School of Scottish
Studies, Edinburgh.
Steele MSS, 1978 - 'The medicinal value and usage of plants', by Margaret Ann Steele,
student project, the Centre for English Cultural Tradition and Language,
University of Sheffield, 1978.
Taylor MSS - notes on East Anglian herbal remedies and folklore compiled in the
1920s by Dr Mark Taylor; in the Norfolk Record Office, Norwich.
UCL EFS MSS - material accumulated in the 1960s as a result of a Survey of English
Folklore conducted by staff of the Department of English, University College
London.

REFERENCES

Wharton, C., 1974. 'The folklore of south Warwickshire: a field collection with comparative annotations and commentary', thesis presented for the degree of PhD in the Institute of Dialect and Folk Life Studies, School of English, University of Leeds.

Index

INDEX

INDEX

INDEX